AF580891

Insights for Managers from Confucius to Gandhi

Insights for Managers from Confucius to Gandhi

Confucius
Laozi
Aristotle
Murasaki Shikibu
Bernier
Niccolo Machiavelli
Francis Bacon
William Shakespeare
Thomas Hobbes
René Descartes
Jean-Jacques Rousseau
Adam Smith
George Washington
John Adams
Patrick Henry
Thomas Jefferson
Thomas Paine
Ralph Waldo Emerson
Abraham Lincoln
Karl Heinrich Marx
Andrew Carnegie
Alfred Marshall
Russell Conwell
Elbert Hubbard
Louis Brandeis
Thorstein Veblen
Alfred North Whitehead
O. Henry
George Santayana
Irving Fisher
W.E.B. DuBois
Mohandas Karamchand Gandhi
Calvin Coolidge
Alfred E. Smith
Owen D. Young
William O. Douglas
Arthur E. Nilsson
Fred Schwed, Jr.

Harold Bierman, Jr
Donald Schnedeker
Cornell University, USA

NEW JERSEY • LONDON • SINGAPORE • BEIJING • SHANGHAI • HONG KONG • TAIPEI • CHENNAI

Published by

World Scientific Publishing Co. Pte. Ltd.
5 Toh Tuck Link, Singapore 596224
USA office: 27 Warren Street, Suite 401-402, Hackensack, NJ 07601
UK office: 57 Shelton Street, Covent Garden, London WC2H 9HE

British Library Cataloguing-in-Publication Data
A catalogue record for this book is available from the British Library.

INSIGHTS FOR MANAGERS FROM CONFUCIUS TO GANDHI

ISBN-13 978-981-4365-08-6
ISBN-10 981-4365-08-4

Typeset by Stallion Press
Email: enquiries@stallionpress.com

Printed in Singapore by World Scientific Printers.

Preface

It is difficult to define the most meaningful type of readings for managers. While current topical literature is fun and useful, we have decided that sampling the classics is fruitful.

The authors and subjects range from Aristotle to Carnegie to Young. The writings are not always easy, but we think you will find them thought provoking.

Most of the writings are short extractions. The basic objective was to give more than quotations, but less than the complete writings of any of the authors. Even the great authors did not write consistently at one high level of relevance for a manager.

Several thoughtful people have asked about the theme of this book. The included papers have several reasons for being chosen. First are the papers with an important message for the business reader. The pieces written by Andrew Carnegie and Owen D. Young are good examples. Second are the papers that are not directly written for business people but are highly relevant. Aristotle and Whitehead's papers are examples. The third type of papers included are those that offer a lesson useful for all readers. O'Henry and Fred Schwed qualify on this dimension. The fourth type of extract is included because they are classic examples of applying the English language to make a point. Lincoln's Gettysburg Address and Calvin

Coolidge's speeches are examples. Should they be left out because they do not apply to a firm's capital structure or capital budgeting decisions? No, they deserve to be read by people interested in business and life.

The readings are for managers and other interested persons. The thoughts are too universal to be restricted to one subset of humanity, but if we have been successful in selection and in editing, the choices are particularly relevant for managers. We offer two suggestions. Do not try speed reading this book. It is a difficult voyage but the passage is likely to be worthwhile. Secondly, if you find an author to be interesting, we suggest you expand your exposure and read a larger sample.

For biographical facts, the internet source Wikipedia, the free encyclopedia was invaluable, though we claim the right to all errors of fact.

Harold Bierman, Jr.
The Nicholas H. Noyes Professor of Business Administration
Cornell University
and
Donald Schnedeker
Librarian
Cornell University

Acknowledgments

Many people contributed to the creation of this book. A sampling follows. Hal's wife, Florence, read the entire manuscript and made numerous very useful suggestions. His assistant, Barb Drake, was invaluable and his two sons, Bruce and Jon, made several good suggestions that made the cut. Tai Wei Lim was a very patient and helpful editor. Jerry Hass, a long-time friend and colleague, was always available to offer assistance.

Joel Silbey, the President White Professor of History, Cornell University, made two great suggestions for inclusions. Can you guess which items he suggested?

Susan Kendrick helped us navigate through the library stacks.

Thank you all.

Contents

Chapter 1

Confucius

Confucius (c. 551 B.C. to 479 B.C.) was a great Chinese thinker and philosopher. His influence was (and is) widespread throughout Asia. His goal was to build a humanistic and harmonious society.

Confucius' teachings have evolved into a set of rules and practices to live one's life by. For example, "What one does not wish for oneself, one ought not to do to anyone else." The system of philosophy is known as "Confucianism."

Confucius is also known as Kong Qiu and Zhong Ni. He put great stress on study (or learning), and wanted his students to think for themselves and study the world and their relationship to the world. He sought peace and prosperity for all people.

The ruler of a country would not inherit the position but rather would earn it by good deeds and thoughts. Human excellence was the goal. Empathy and understanding were the guidelines for relationships of people. Ethical behavior was essential.

Since 1990 China has held memorial ceremonies in honor of Confucius. For twenty years prior to 1990 the Communist Party took the position that Confucianism was reactionary and any homage to Confucius was banned. A naïve reading of his writings by this author leads to a conclusion that he was apolitical and humanitarian.

I looked at the following extract to find statements I do not accept. Consider "Only the highest and lowest characters don't change." At best, I give that a "maybe". Also "You can kill the general of an army but you cannot kill the ambition in a common man." I accept the first thought but the second thought is not obviously correct. Well, no one is perfect. On the average, Confucius does very well. Even the above two weakest quotations are not objectionable.

Confucius, "Wit and Wisdom" (Aphorisms of Confucius) in *The Wisdom of Confucius*, edited and translated with notes by Lin Yutang. New York, Modern Library, 1938, pp. 179–184.

1. Wit and Wisdom

Confucius said, "To know what you know and know what you don't know is the characteristic of one who knows."

Confucius said, "A man who does not say to himself, 'What to do? What to do?'— indeed I do not know what to do with such a person!"

Confucius said, "A man who has committed a mistake and doesn't correct it is committing another mistake."

Confucius said, "A melon-cup that no longer resembles a melon-cup and people still say, 'A melon-cup! A melon-cup!' "

Confucius said: "It is said, 'It is difficult to be a king, but it is not easy to be a minister, either.' "

Baron Wen Chi said that he always thought three times before he acted. When Confucius heard this, he remarked, "To think twice is quite enough."

Confucius said, "I do not expect to find a saint today. But if I can find a gentleman, I shall be quite satisfied."

Confucius said, "A man who has a beautiful soul always has some beautiful things to say, but a man who says beautiful things does not necessarily have a beautiful soul. A true man (or truly great man) will always be found to have courage, but a courageous man will not always be found to have true manhood."

Confucius said, "A man who brags without shame will find great difficulty in living up to his bragging."

Confucius said, "The man who loves truth (or learning) is better than the man who knows it, and the man who finds happiness in it is better than the man who loves it."[1]

Confucius said, "In speaking to a sovereign, one must look out for three things: To talk before you are asked is called 'impulsiveness.' To fail to talk when you are asked is called 'lack of candor.' And to talk without noticing the sovereign's mood is called 'blindness.'"

Confucius said, "When you find a person worthy to talk to and fail to talk to him, you have lost your man. When you find a man unworthy to talk to and you talk to him, you have lost (i.e. wasted) your words. A wise man neither loses his man, nor loses his words."

Confucius said, "A gentleman does not praise a man (or put him in office) on the basis of what he says, nor does he deny the truth of what one says because he dislikes the person who says it (if it is good)."

Tsekung asked Confucius, "What would you say if all the people of the village like a person?" "That is not enough," replied Confucius. "What would you say if all the people of the village dislike a person?" "That is not

[1] There is no indication in the text as to whether the reference is to loving truth or loving learning. It uses only the word "it."

enough," said Confucius. "It is better when the good people of the village like him, and the bad people of the village dislike him." (When you are disliked by the bad persons, you are a good person.)

Confucius said, "The common man often gets in trouble because of his love for the water (literally "gets drowned" in it); the gentleman often gets into trouble because of his love for talking; and the great man often gets into trouble because of his love for the people. All of them get submerged in what they come close to or are familiar with. Water seems so familiar to the people, but easily drowns them because it is a thing that seems so easy to approach and yet is dangerous to get too near to. Talking easily leads one into trouble because when you talk, you use so many words, and it is easy to let them out of your mouth, but difficult to take them back. The people often get one into trouble because they are mean and not open-minded; you can respect them, but you must not insult or offend them. Therefore the gentleman must be very careful."

Confucius said, "The people who live extravagantly are apt to be snobbish (or conceited), and the people who live simply are apt to be vulgar. I prefer the vulgar people to the snobs."

Confucius said, "It is easy to be rich and not haughty; it is difficult to be poor and not grumble."

Confucius said, "When a country is in order, it is a shame to be a poor and common man. When a country is in chaos, it is a shame to be rich and an official."

Confucius said, "Can you ever imagine a petty soul serving as a minister of the state? Before he gets his post, he is anxious to get it, and after he has got it, he is anxious about losing it, and if he begins to be anxious about losing it, then there is nothing that he will not do."

Confucius said, "Do not worry about people not knowing your ability, but worry that you have not got it."

Confucius said, "A gentleman blames himself, while a common man blames others."

Confucius said, "If a man would be severe toward himself and generous toward others, he would never arouse resentment."

Confucius said, "A man who does not think and plan long ahead will find trouble right by his door."

Confucius said, "Polished speech often confuses our notion of who is good and who is bad. A man who cannot put up with small losses or disadvantages will often spoil a big plan."

Confucius said, "In talking about a thoroughbred, you do not admire his strength, but admire his temper."

Someone said, "What do you think of repaying evil with kindness?" Confucius replied, "Then what are you going to repay kindness with?" "Repay kindness with kindness, but repay evil with justice (or severity)."

Confucius said, "When you repay kindness with kindness, then the people are encouraged to do good. When you repay evil with evil, then people are warned from doing bad."

Confucius said, "To repay evil with kindness is the sign of a generous character. To repay kindness with evil is the sign of a criminal."[2]

Confucius said, "Men are born pretty much alike, but through their habits they gradually grow further and further apart from each other."

---

[2] *Liki*, Chapter XXXII.

Confucius said, "Only the highest and the lowest characters don't change."

Confucius said, "I have seen rice plants that sprout, but don't blossom, and I have seen rice plants that blossom, but don't bear grains."

Confucius said, "Even though a man had the beautiful talent of Duke Chou, but if he were proud and egoistic, he would not be worth looking at."

Confucius said, "If the superior man is not deliberate in his appearance (or conduct), then he is not dignified. Learning prevents one from being narrow-minded. Try to be loyal and faithful as your main principle. Have no friends who are not as good as yourself. When you have mistakes, don't be afraid to correct them."

Confucius said, "When you see a good man, try to emulate his example, and when you see a bad man, search yourself for his faults."

Confucius said, "Well, well! I have never yet seen a person who knows his own faults and accuses himself before himself!"

Confucius said, "Don't criticize other people's faults, criticize your own."

Tsekung said, "What do you think of a person who is not snobbish (or subservient to the great) when he is poor, and not conceited when he is rich?" Confucius replied, "That's fairly good. It would be better if he were happy when he was poor, and had self-discipline when he was rich."

Confucius said, "You can kill the general of an army, but you cannot kill the ambition in a common man."

Chapter 2

Laozi (also Lao Tse, Lao Tu, Lao-Tzu, Laotze)

Laozi was an ancient Chinese philosopher who lived in the 4th century B.C. The philosophy of Taoism originated with the writings of Laozi. It is possible that Laozi is a combination of multiple historical authors and Laozi is a mythical figure. But Laozi is a major figure in Chinese culture. Laozi can be written as Lao Laizi, which translates to "Old Master." One version of the tale has him teaching Buddha.

The story of Laozi has taken on strong religious significance. Laozi advocated humility by leaders and restrained approach to government (an anti-authoritarianism approach). In a sense, this viewpoint has been adopted from earlier Confucian writers.

There follows a sample from *The Simple Way* by Laotze (or Laozi) titled "*The Evidence of Simplicity.*" It suggests the advantage of simple sincere words over grand words. It suggests that one avoids disputes. It recommends against hoarding. This is not arguing against savings (hoarding is harmful to someone) but savings is consistent with advancing the well-being of all. Charity is advocated. This is said to lead to the "Tao of Heaven."

I cannot claim to understand all of the Laotze I have read, but in the thoughts that I have difficulty with, are little gems that I am pleased to take away.

Laotze, *The Simple Way*, [by] Laotze, a new translation of the Tao-teh-king; with introduction and commentary, by Walter Gorn Old. London, William Rider, 1913, p. 179.

Two other books I enjoyed are

Lao Tsze, *The Simple Way of Lao Tsze*, London, The Shrine of Wisdom, 1924

and

C. Spurgeon Medhurst, *The Tao The King*, Chicago, Theosophical Book Concern, 1905.

1. The Evidence of Simplicity

Sincere words are not grand.
Grand words are not faithful.
The man of Tao does not dispute.
They who dispute are not skilled in Tao.
Those who know it are not learned.
The learned do not know it.
The wise man does not lay up treasure.
The more he expends on others, the more he gains for himself.
The more he gives to others, the more he has for his own.
This is the Tao of Heaven, which penetrates but does not injure.
This is the Tao of the wise man, who acts but does not strive.

CHAPTER 3

Aristotle

Aristotle (384 B.C.–322 B.C.) was a great Greek philosopher and author. He was a student of Plato (who was a student of Socrates) and a teacher of Alexander the Great.

He was an important founder of Western (European) philosophy and he helped establish the sciences on which our civilization is built.

Most of his writings have been lost. Also today, there is a question as to whether or not Aristotelian writings as we know them were written by Aristotle or by authors trying to improve on Aristotle's legacy.

Whether Aristotle is the author or not, you should judge the following piece on its own merits. Consider: "Every action and pursuit, is thought to aim at some good" and "Shall we not, like archers who have a mark to aim at, be more likely to hit upon what is right?" These thoughts seem obvious but think. How often have we seen people or corporations act without adequate thought about the objective? Did the CEO of Lehman Brothers in 2008 have a well defined target?

Aristotle, "The Subject of Ethics is the Good for Man," [*Nicomachean Ethics 1094a1-b11*] in *Aristotle Selections*, edited by W. D. Ross. Charles Scribner's Sons, New York, 1938, pp. 218–220.

1. The Subject of Ethics is the Good for Man

Every art and every inquiry, and similarly every action and pursuit, is thought to aim at some good; and for this reason the good has rightly been declared to be that at which all things aim. But a certain difference is found among ends; some are activities, others are products apart from the activities that produce them. Where there are ends apart from the actions, it is the nature of the products to be better than the activities. Now, as there are many actions, arts, and sciences, their ends also are many; the end of the medical art is health, that of shipbuilding a vessel, that of strategy victory, that of economics wealth. But where such arts fall under a single capacity — as bridle-making and the other arts concerned with the equipment of horses fall under the art of riding, and this and every military action under strategy, in the same way other arts fall under yet others — in all of these the ends of the master arts are to be preferred to all the subordinate ends; for it is for the sake of the former that the latter are pursued. It makes no difference whether the activities themselves are the ends of the actions, or something else apart from the activities, as in the case of the sciences just mentioned. If, then, there is some end of the things we do, which we desire for its own sake (everything else being desired for the sake of this), and if we do not choose everything for the sake of something else (for at that rate the process would go on to infinity, so that our desire would be empty and vain), clearly this must be the good and the chief good. Will not the knowledge of it, then, have a great influence on life? Shall we not, like archers who have a mark to aim at, be more likely to hit upon what is right? If so, we must try, in outline at least, to determine what it is, and of which of the sciences or capacities it is the object. It would seem to belong to the most authoritative art and that which is most truly the master art. And politics appears to be of this nature; for it is this that ordains which of the sciences should be studied in a state, and which each class of citizens should learn and up to what point they should learn them; and we see even the most highly esteemed of capacities to fall under this, e.g. strategy, economics, rhetoric; now, since politics uses the rest of the sciences, and since, again, it legislates as to what we are to do and what we are to abstain from, the end of this science must include those of the others, so that this end must be the good for man. For even if the end is the same for a single man and for a state, that of the state seems at all events something greater and more complete whether to attain or to preserve; though it is worthwhile to attain the end merely for one man, it is finer and more godlike to attain it for a nation or for city-states. These, then, are the ends at which our inquiry aims, since it is political science, in one sense of that term.

Chapter 4

Murasaki Shikibu (Lady Murasaki)

Lady Murasaki was born circa 973 and died circa 1014. She was a great Japanese novelist and poet. *The Tale of Genji,* written about 1008, is likely to be the world's first novel.

The Tale of Genji consists of fifty-four chapters. The first forty deal with the life of Prince Genji. The first chapter of the saga follows. The fact that the world's first novel was written by a Japanese woman is very interesting and surprising. It is likely to be a fact known by few readers of this book. Lady Murasaki also wrote *The Murasaki Shikibu Collection*, a compilation of 128 poems.

The first chapter of *The Tale of Genji* introduces the reader to Genji, his mother, and his father, the Emperor. The great love of the Emperor for Genji's mother leads to her cruel harsh treatment by the jealous palace retinue and ultimately to her early death. As might be expected of a story that has survived for 1,000 years, the tale holds the reader's interest.

The reproduced chapter contains a large amount of information about the Emperor's court life in Japan before the year 1000. Human emotions and motivations have not changed much in one thousand years.

Shikibu, Murasaki, *The Tale of Genji*, translated by Arthur Waley, London, George Allen & Unwin Ltd., 1929, pp. 2–38.

1. The Tale of Genji — Chapter I — Kiritsubo[3]

At the Court of an Emperor (it matters not when he lived) there was among the many gentlewomen of the Wardrobe and Chamber one, who though she was not of very high rank, was favored far beyond the rest; so that the great ladies of the Palace, each whom had secretly hoped that she herself would be chosen, looked with scorn and hatred upon the upstart who had dispelled their dreams. Still less were her former companions, the minor ladies of the Wardrobe, content to see her raised so far above them. Thus her position at Court, preponderant though it was, exposed her to constant jealousy and ill will; and soon, worn out with petty vexations, she fell into a decline, growing very melancholy and retiring frequently to her home. But the Emperor, far from wearying of her now that she was no longer well or gay, grew every day more tender, and paid not the smallest heed to those who reproved him, till his conduct became the talk of all the land; and even his own barons and courtiers began to look askance at an attachment ill-advised. They whispered among themselves that in the Land Beyond the Sea such happenings had led to riot and disaster. The people of the country did indeed soon have many grievances to show: and some likened her to Yang Kuei-fei, the mistress of Ming Huang.[4] Yet, for all this discontent, so great was the sheltering power of her master's love that none dared openly molest her.

---

[3] This chapter should be read with indulgence. In it Murasaki, still under the influence of her somewhat childish predecessors, writes in a manner which is a blend of the Court chronicle with the conventional fairy-tale.

[4] Famous Emperor of the T'ang dynasty in China; lived A.D. 685–762.

Her father, who had been a Councillor, was dead. Her mother, who never forgot that the father was in his day a man of some consequence, managed despite all difficulties to give her as good an upbringing as generally falls to the lot of young ladies whose parents are alive and at the height of fortune. It would have helped matters greatly if there had been some influential guardian to busy himself on the child's behalf. Unfortunately, the mother was entirely alone in the world and sometimes, when troubles came, she felt very bitterly the lack of anyone to whom she could turn for comfort and advice. But to return to the daughter. In due time she bore him a little Prince who, perhaps, because in some previous life a close bond had joined them, turned out as fine and likely a man-child as well might be in all the land. The Emperor could hardly contain himself during the days of waiting.[5] But when, at the earliest possible moment, the child was presented at Court, he saw that rumor had not exaggerated its beauty. His eldest born prince was the son of Lady Kōkiden, the daughter of the Minister of the Right, and this child was treated by all with the respect due to an undoubted Heir Apparent. But he was not so fine a child as the new prince; moreover the Emperor's great affection for the new child's mother made him feel the boy to be in a peculiar sense his own possession. Unfortunately she was not of the same rank as the courtiers who waited upon him in the Upper Palace, so that despite his love for her, and though she wore all the airs of a great lady, it was not without considerable qualms that he now made

[5] The child of an Emperor could not be shown to him for several weeks after its birth.

it his practice to have her by him not only when there was to be some entertainment, but even when any business of importance was a foot. Sometimes indeed he would keep her when he woke in the morning, not letting her go back to her lodging, so that willy-nilly she acted the part of a Lady-in-Perpetual-Attendance.

Seeing all this, Lady Kökiden began to fear that the new prince, for whom the Emperor seemed to have so marked a preference, would if she did not take care soon be promoted to the Eastern Palace.[6] But she had, after all, priority over her rival; the Emperor had loved her devotedly and she had born him princes. It was even now chiefly the fear of her reproaches that made him uneasy about his new way of life. Thus, though his mistress could be sure of his protection, there were many who sought to humiliate her, and she felt so weak in herself that it seemed to her at last as though all the honors heaped upon her had brought with them terror rather than joy.

Her lodging was in the wing called Kiritsubo. It was but natural that the many ladies whose doors she had to pass on her repeated journeys to the Emperor's room should have grown exasperated; and sometimes, when these comings and goings became frequent beyond measure, it would happen that on bridges and in corridors, here or there along the way that she must go, strange tricks were played to frighten her or unpleasant things were left lying about which spoiled the dresses of the ladies who accompanied her.[7] Once indeed some one locked the door of a portico, so that the poor thing wandered this way and that for a great while in sore distress.

---

[6] i.e. be made Heir Apparent.

[7] She herself was of course carried in a litter.

So many were the miseries into which this state of affairs now daily brought her that the Emperor could no longer endure to witness her vexations and moved her to the Köröden. In order to make room for her he was obliged to shift the Chief Lady of the Wardrobe to lodgings outside. So far from improving matters he had merely procured her a new and most embittered enemy!

The young prince was now three years old. The Putting on of the Trousers was performed with as much ceremony as in the case of the Heir Apparent. Marvellous gifts flowed from the Imperial Treasury and Tribute House. This too incurred the censure of many, but brought no enmity to the child himself; for his growing beauty and the charm of his disposition were a wonder and delight to all who met him. Indeed many persons of ripe experience confessed themselves astounded that such a creature should actually have been born in these latter and degenerate days.

In the summer of that year the lady became very downcast. She repeatedly asked for leave to go to her home, but it was not granted. For a year she continued in the same state. The Emperor to all her entreaties answered only: "Try for a little while longer." But she was getting worse every day, and when for five or six days she had been growing steadily weaker her mother sent to the Palace a tearful plea for her release. Fearing even now that her enemies might contrive to put some unimaginable shame upon her, the sick lady left her son behind and prepared to quit the Palace in secret. The Emperor knew that the time had come when, little as he liked it he must let her go. But that she should slip away without a word of farewell was more than he could bear, and he hastened to her side. He found her still charming and beautiful, but her face very thin and wan. She looked at him tenderly, saying nothing. Was she alive? So faint was the dwindling spark that she scarcely seemed so. Suddenly forgetting all that had happened and all that was to come, he called her by a hundred pretty names and weeping showered upon her a thousand caresses; but she made no answer. For sounds and sights reached her but faintly, and she seemed dazed, as one that scarcely remembered she lay upon a bed. Seeing her thus he knew not what to do. In great trouble and perplexity he sent for a hand litter. But when they would have laid her in it, he forbade them, saying "There was an oath between us that neither should go alone upon the road that all at last must tread. How can I now let her go from me?" The lady heard him and 'At last!' she said: "Though that desired *at last* be come, because I go alone how gladly would I live!"

Thus with faint voice and failing breath she whispered. But though she had found strength to speak, each word was uttered with great toil and pain. Come what might, the Emperor would have watched by her till the end, but that the priests who were to read the Intercession had already been dispatched to her home. She must be brought there before nightfall, and at last he forced himself to let the bearers carry her away. He tried to sleep but felt stifled and could not close his eyes. All night long messengers were coming and going between her home and the palace. From the first they brought no good news, and soon after midnight announced that this time on arriving at the house they had heard a noise of wailing and lamentation, and learned from those within that the lady had just breathed her last. The Emperor lay motionless as though he had not understood.

Though his father was so fond of his company, it was thought better after this event that the Prince should go away from the Palace. He did not understand what had happened, but seeing the servants all wringing their hands and the Emperor himself continually weeping, he felt that it must have been something very terrible. He knew that even quite ordinary separations made people unhappy; but here was such a dismal wailing and lamenting as he had never seen before, and he concluded that this must be some very extraordinary kind of parting.

When the time came for the funeral to begin, the girl's mother cried out that the smoke of her own body would be seen rising beside the smoke of her child's bier. She rode in the same coach with the Court ladies who had come to the funeral. The ceremony took place at Atago and was celebrated with great splendor. So overpowering was the mother's affection that so long as she looked on the body she still thought of her child as alive. It was only when they lighted the pyre she suddenly realized that what lay upon it was a corpse. Then, though she tried to speak sensibly, she reeled and almost fell from the coach, and those with her turned to one another and said: "At last she knows."

A herald came from the palace and read a proclamation which promoted the dead lady to the Third Rank. The reading of this long proclamation by the bier was a sad business. The Emperor repented bitterly that he had not long ago made her a Lady-in-Waiting, and that was why he now raised her rank by one degree. There were many who grudged her even this honor; but some less stubborn began now to recall that she had indeed been a lady of uncommon beauty; and others, that she had very gentle and pleasing manners; while some went so far as to say it was a shame that anybody should have disliked so sweet a lady, and that if she had not been singled out unfairly from the rest, no one would have said a word against her.

The seven weeks of mourning were, by the Emperor's order, minutely observed. Time passed, but he still lived in rigid seclusion from the ladies of the Court. The servants who waited upon him had a sad life, for he wept almost without ceasing both day and night.

Kökiden and the other great ladies were still relentless, and went about saying: "it looked as though the Emperor would be no less foolishly obsessed by her memory than he had been by her person." He did indeed sometimes see Kökiden's son, the first-born prince. But this only made him long even more to see the dead lady's child, and he was always sending trusted servants, such as his own old nurse, to report to him upon the boy's progress. The time of the autumn equinox had come. Already the touch of the evening air was cold upon the skin. So many memories crowded upon him that he sent a girl, the daughter of his quiver-bearer, with a letter to the dead lady's house. It was beautiful moonlit weather, and after he had dispatched the messenger he lingered for a while gazing out into the night. It was at such times as this that he had been wont to call for music. He remembered how her words, lightly whispered, had blended with those strangely fashioned harmonies, remembered how all was strange, her face, her air, her form. He thought of the poem which says that "*real things in the darkness seem no realer than dreams*," and he longed for even so dim a substance as the dreamlife of those nights.

The messenger had reached the gates of the house. She pushed them back and a strange sight met her eyes. The old lady had for long been a widow and the whole charge of keeping the domain in repair had fallen upon her daughter. But since her death the mother, sunk in age and despair, had done nothing to the place, and everywhere the weeds grew high; and to all this desolation was added the wildness of the autumn gale. Great clumps of mugwort grew so thick that only the moonlight could penetrate them. The messenger alighted at the entrance of the house. At first the mother could find no words with which to greet her, but soon she said: "Alas, I have lingered too long in the world! I cannot bear to think that so fine a messenger as you have pressed your way through the dewy thickets that bar the road to my house," and she burst into uncontrollable weeping. Then the quiver-bearer's daughter said: "One of the Palace maids who came here, told his Majesty that her heart had been torn with pity at what she saw. And I, Madam, am in like case." Then after a little hesitation she repeated the Emperor's message: "'For while I searched in the darkness of my mind, groping for an exit from my dream; but after long pondering I can find no way to wake. There is none here to counsel me. Will you not come to me secretly? It is not well that the young prince should spend his days in so desolate and sad a place. Let him come too!' This he said and much else, but confusedly and with many sighs; and I, seeing that the struggle to hide his grief from me was costing him dear, hurried away from the Palace without hearing all. But here is a letter that he sent."

"My sight is dim," said the mother. "Let me hold His letter to the light." The letter said: "I had thought that after a while there might be some blurring, some slight effacement. But no. As days and months go by, the more senseless, the more unendurable becomes my life. I am continually thinking of the child, wondering how he fares. I had hoped that his mother and I together would watch over his upbringing. Will you not take her place in this, and bring him to me as a memory of the past?" Such was the letter, and many instructions were added to it together with a poem which said "*At the sound of the wind that binds the cold dew on Takagi moor, my heart goes out to the tender lilac stems.*"

It was of the young prince that he spoke in symbol; but she did not read the letter to the end. At last the mother said: "Though I know that long life means only bitterness, I have stayed so long in the world that even before the Pine Tree of Takasago I should hide my head in shame. How then should I find courage to go hither and thither in the great Palace of a Hundred Towers? Though the august summons should call me time and again, myself I could not obey. But the young prince (whether he may have heard the august wish I know not) is impatient to return, and, what is small wonder, seems very downcast in this place. Tell his Majesty this, and whatever else of my thoughts you have here learnt from me. For a little child this house is indeed a sorry place...' They say that the child is asleep the quiver-bearer's daughter answered. 'I should like to have seen him and told the Emperor how he looks; but I am awaited at the Palace and it must be late.'

She was hastening away, but the mother: "Since even those who wander in the darkness of their own black thoughts can gain by converse a momentary beam to guide their steps, I pray you sometimes to visit me of your own accord and when you are at leisure. In years past it was at times of joy and triumph that you came to this house, and now this is the news you bring! Foolish are they indeed who trust to fortune! From the time she was born until his death, her father, who knew his own mind, would have it that she must go to Court and charged me again and again not to disappoint his wishes if he were to die. And so, though I thought that the lack of a guardian would bring her into many difficulties, I was determined to carry out his desire. At Court she found that favors only too great were to be hers, and all the while must need endure in secrecy the tokens of inhuman malice; till hatred had heaped upon her so heavy a load of cares that she died as if were murdered. Indeed, the love that in His wisdom He deigned to show her (or so sometimes it seems to me in the uncomprehending darkness of my heart) was crueller than indifference."

So she spoke, till tears would let her speak no more; and now the night had come.

"All this," the girl answered, "He himself has said; and further: 'That thus against My will and judgment I yielded helplessly to a passion so reckless that it caused men's eyes to blink was perhaps decreed for the very reason that our time was fated to be so short; it was the wild and vehement passion of those who are marked down for instant separation. And though I had vowed that none should suffer because of my love, yet in the end she bore upon her shoulders the heavy hatred of many who thought that for her sake they had been wronged.'

"So again and again have I heard the Emperor speak with tears. But now the night is far spent and I must carry my message to the Palace before day comes."

So she, weeping too, spoke as she hurried away. But the sinking moon was shining in a cloudless sky, and in the grass-clumps that shivered in the cold wind, bell-cricket, tinkled their compelling cry. It was hard to leave these grass-clumps, and the quiver-bearer's daughter, loth to ride away, recited the poem which says: "*Ceaseless as the interminable voices of the bell-cricket, all night till dawn my tears flow.*" *The mother answered, "Upon the thickets that teem with myriad insect voices falls the dew of Cloud Dweller's tears*"; for the people of the Court are called *dwellers above the clouds.* Then she gave the messenger a sash, a comb and other things that the dead lady had left in her keeping — gifts from the Emperor which now, since their use was gone, she sent back to him as mementoes of the past. The nurse-maids who had come with the boy were depressed not so much at their mistress's death as at being suddenly deprived of the daily sights and sensations of the Palace. They begged to go back at once. But the mother was determined not to go herself, knowing that she would cut too forlorn a figure. On the other hand if she parted with the boy, she would be daily in great anxiety about him. That was why she did not immediately either go with him herself or send him to the Palace.

The quiver-bearer's daughter found the Emperor still awake. He was, upon pretext of visiting the flower-pots in front of the Palace which were then in full bloom, waiting for her out of doors, while four or five trusted ladies conversed with him.

At this time it was his wont to examine morning and evening a picture of The Everlasting Wrong,[8] the text written by Teiji no In,[9] with poems by Ise[10] and Tsurayuki,[11] both in Yamato speech, and in that of the

---

[8] A poem by the Chinese writer Po Chu-i about the death of Yang Kuei-fei, favorite of the Emperor Ming Huang. *See* Giles, *Chinese Literature,* p. 169.

[9] Name of the Emperor Uda after his retirement in A.D. 897.

[10] Poetess, 9th century.

[11] Famous poet, 883–946 A.D.

men beyond the sea, and the story of this poem was the common matter of his talk.

Now he turned to the messenger and asked eagerly for all her news. And when she had given him a secret and faithful account of the sad place whence she had come, she handed him the mother's letter: "His Majesty's gracious commands I read with reverence deeper than I can express, but their purport has brought great darkness and confusion to my mind." All this, together with a poem in which she compared her grandchild to a flower which has lost the tree that sheltered it from the great winds, was so wild and so ill-writ as only to be suffered from the hand of one whose sorrow was as yet unhealed.

Again the Emperor strove for self-possession in the presence of his messenger. But as he pictured to himself the time when the dead lady first came to him, a thousand memories pressed thick about him, and recollection linked to recollection carried him onward, till he shuddered to think how utterly unmarked, unheeded all these hours and days had fled.

At last he said: "I too thought much and with delight how with most profit might be fulfilled the wish that her father the Councillor left behind him; but of that no more. If the young Prince lives occasion may yet be found… It is for his long life that we must pray."

He looked at the presents she had brought back. 'Would that like the wizard you had brought a kingfisher-hairpin as token of your visit to the place where her spirit dwells?' he cried, and recited the poem: "*Oh for a master of magic who might go and seek her, and by a message teach me where her spirit dwells.*"

For the picture of Kuei-fei, skilful though the painter might be, was but the work of a brush, and had no living fragrance. And though the poet tells us that Kuei-fei's grace was as that of "the hibiscus of the Royal Lake or the willows of the Wei-yang Palace," the lady in the picture was all paint and powder and had a simpering Chinesified air.

But when he thought of the lost lady's voice and form he could find neither in the beauty of flowers nor in the song of birds any fit comparison. Continually he pined that fate should not have allowed them to fulfill the vow which morning and evening was ever talked of between them — the vow that their lives should be as the twin birds that share a wing, the twin trees that share a bough. The rustling of the wind, the chirping of an insect would cast him into the deepest melancholy; and now Kökiden, who for a long while had not been admitted to his chamber, must need sit in the moonlight making music far on into the night! This evidently distressed him in the highest degree and those ladies and courtiers who were with him were equally shocked and distressed on his behalf. But the offending lady was one who stood much upon her dignity and she was determined to behave as though nothing of any consequence had taken place in the Palace.

And now the moon had set. The Emperor thought of the girl's mother in the house amid the thickets and wondered, making a poem of the thought, with what feelings she had watched the sinking of the autumn moon: "For even we Men above the Clouds were weeping when it sank." He raised the torches high in their sockets and still sat up. But at last he heard voices coming from the Watch House of the Right and knew that the hour of the Bull[12] had struck. Then, lest he should

[12] 1 a.m.

be seen, he went into his chamber. He found he could not sleep and was up before daybreak. But, as though he remembered the words "*he knew not the dawn was at his window*" of Ise's poem,[13] he showed little attention to the affairs of his Morning Audience, scarcely touched his dried rice and seemed but dimly aware of the viands on the great Table, so that the carvers and waiting-men groaned to see their Master's plight; and all his servants, both men and women kept on whispering to one another: "What a senseless occupation has ours become!" and supposed that he was obeying some extravagant vow.

Regardless of his subjects' murmurings, he continually allowed his mind to wander from their affairs to his own, so that the scandal of his negligence was now as dangerous to the State as it had been before, and again there began to be whispered references to a certain Emperor of another land. Thus the months and days passed, and in the end, the young prince arrived at Court. He had grown up to be a child of unrivalled beauty and the Emperor was delighted with him. In the spring an heir to the Throne was to be proclaimed and the Emperor was sorely tempted to pass over the first-born prince in favor of the young child. But there was no one at Court to support such a choice and it was unlikely that it would be tolerated by the people; it would indeed bring danger rather than glory to the child. So he carefully concealed from the world that he had any such design, and gained great credit, men, saying: "Though he dotes on the boy, there is at least, some limit to his folly." And even the

[13] A poem by Lady Ise written on a picture illustrating Po Chiu-i's *Everlasting Wrong*.

great ladies of the Palace became a little easier in their minds.

The grandmother remained inconsolable, and impatient to set out upon her search for the place where the dead lady's spirit dwelt, she soon expired. Again the Emperor was in great distress; and this time the boy, being now six years old, understood what had happened and wept bitterly. And often he spoke sadly of what he had seen when he was brought to visit the poor dead lady who had for many years been so kind to him. Henceforward he lived always at the Palace. When he became seven he began to learn his letters, and his quickness was so unusual that his father was amazed. Thinking that now no one would have the heart to be unkind to the child, the Emperor began to take him to the apartments of Kökiden and the rest, saying to them: "Now that his mother is dead I know that you will be nice to him." Thus the boy began to penetrate the Royal Curtain. The roughest soldier, the bitterest foeman could not have looked on such a child without a smile, and Kökiden did not send him away. She had two daughters who were indeed not such fine children as the little prince. He also played with the Court Ladies, who, because he was now very pretty and bashful in his ways, found endless amusement, as indeed did everyone else, in sharing his games. As for his serious studies, he soon learnt to send the sounds of zithern and flute flying gaily to the clouds. But if I were to tell you of all his accomplishments, you would think that he was soon going to become a bore.

At this time some Koreans came to Court and among them a fortune-teller. Hearing this, the Emperor did not send for them to come to the Palace, because of the law against the admission of foreigners which was made by the Emperor Uda.[14] But in strict secrecy he sent the Prince to the Strangers' quarters. He went under the escort of the Secretary of the Right, who was to introduce him as his own son. The fortune teller was astonished by the boy's lineaments and expressed his surprise by continually nodding his head: "He has the marks of one who might become a Father of the State, and if this were his fate, he would not stop short at any lesser degree than that of Mighty King and Emperor of all the land. But when I look again I see that confusion and sorrow would attend his reign. But should he become a great Officer of State and Counsellor of the Realm I see no happy issue, for he would be defying those kingly signs of which I spoke before."

The Secretary was a most talented, wise and learned scholar, and now began to conduct an interesting conversation with the fortune teller. They exchanged essays and poems, and the fortune-teller made a little speech, saying "It has been a great pleasure to me on the eve of my departure to meet with a man of capacities so unusual; and though I regret my departure I shall now take away most agreeable impressions of my visit." The little prince presented him with a very nice verse of poetry, at which he expressed boundless admiration and offered the boy a number of handsome presents. In return the Emperor sent him a large reward from the Imperial Treasury. This was all kept strictly secret. But somehow or other the Heir Apparent's grandfather, the Minister of the Right, and others of his party got wind of it and became very suspicious. The Emperor then sent for native fortune-tellers and made trial of them, explaining that because of

[14] Reigned 889–897. The law in question was made in 894.

certain signs which he had himself observed he had hitherto refrained from making the boy a prince. With one accord, they agreed that he had acted with great prudence and the Emperor determined not to set the child adrift upon the world as a prince without royal standing or influence upon the mother's side. For he thought: "My own power is very insecure. I had best set him to watch on my behalf over the great Officers of State." Thinking that he had thus agreeably settled the child's future, he set seriously to work upon his education, and saw to it that he should be made perfect in every branch of art and knowledge. He showed such aptitude in all his studies that it seemed a pity he should remain a commoner and as it had been decided that it would arouse suspicion if he were made a prince, the Emperor consulted with certain doctors wise in the lore of the planets and phases of the moon. And they with one accord recommended that he should be made a Member of the Minamoto (or Gen) Clan. So this was done. As the years went by the Emperor did not forget his lost lady; and though many women were brought to the Palace in the hope that he might take pleasure in them, he turned from them all, believing that there was not in the world any one like her whom he had lost. There was at that time a lady whose beauty was of great repute. She was the fourth daughter of the previous Emperor, and it was said that her mother, the Dowager Empress, had brought her up with unrivalled care. A certain Dame of the Household, who had served the former Emperor, was intimately acquainted with the young Princess, having known her since childhood and still having occasion to observe her from without: "I have served in three courts," said the Dame, "and in all that time have seen none who could be likened to the departed lady, save the daughter of the Empress Mother. She indeed is a lady of rare beauty." She spoke to the Emperor, and he, much wondering what truth there was in it, listened with great attention. Empress Mother heard of this with great alarm, for she remembered with what open cruelty the sinister Lady had treated her former rival, and though she did not dare speak openly of her fears, she was managing to delay the girl's presentation, when suddenly she died.

The Emperor, hearing that the bereaved Princess was in a very desolate condition, sent word gently telling her he should henceforward look upon her as though she were one of the Lady Princesses, his daughters. Her servants and guardians and her brother, Prince Hyobukyo, thought that life in the Palace might distract her and would at least be better than the gloomy desolation of her home, so they sent her to the Court. She lived in apartments called Fujitsubo (Wisteria Tub) and was known by this name. The Emperor could not deny that she bore an astonishing resemblance to his beloved. She was however of much higher rank, so that everyone was anxious to please her, and, whatever happened, they were prepared to grant her the utmost license: whereas the dead lady had been imperiled by the Emperor's favor only because the Court was not willing to accept her.

His old love did not now grow dimmer, and though he sometimes found solace and distraction in shifting his thoughts from the lady who had died to the lady who was so much like her, yet life remained for him a sad business.

Genji ("he of the Minamoto clan"), as he was now called was constantly at the Emperor's side. He was soon quite at his ease with the common run of Ladies in Waiting and Ladies of the Wardrobe, so it was not likely he would be shy with one who was daily summoned to the Emperors apartments. It was but natural that all these ladies should vie eagerly with one another for the first place in Genji's affections, and there were many whom in various ways he admired very much. But most of them behaved in too grown-up a fashion; only one, the new princess, was pretty and quite young as well, and though she tried to hide from him, it was inevitable that they should often meet. He could not remember his mother, but the Dame of the Household had told him how very like to her the girl was, and this interested his childish fancy, and he would like to have been her great friend and lived with her always. One day the Emperor said to her: "Do not be unkind to him. He is interested because he has heard that you are so like his mother. Do not think him impertinent, but behave nicely to him. You are indeed so like him in look and features that you might well be his mother."

And so, young though he was, fleeting beauty took its hold upon his thoughts; he felt his first clear predilection.

Kökiden had never loved this lady too well, and now her old enmity to Genji sprang up again; her own children were reckoned to be of quite uncommon beauty, but in this they were no match for Genji, who was so lovely a boy that people called him Hikaru Genji or Genji the Shining One; and Princess Fujitsubo, who also had many admirers, was called Princess Glittering Sunshine.

Though it seemed a shame to put so lovely a child into man's dress, he was now twelve years old and the time for his Initiation was come. The Emperor directed the preparations with tireless zeal and insisted upon a magnificence beyond what was prescribed in The Initiation of the Heir Apparent, which had last year been celebrated in the

Southern Hall, was not a whit more splendid in its preparations. The ordering of the banquets that were to be given in various quarters, and the work of the Treasurer and Grain Intendant he supervised in person, fearing lest the officials should be remiss; and in the end all was perfection. The ceremony took place in the eastern wing of the Emperor's own apartments, and the Throne was placed facing towards the east, with the seats of the Initiate to-be and his Sponsor (the Minister of the Left) in front.

Genji arrived at the hour of the Monkey.[15] He looked very handsome with his long childish locks, and the Sponsor, whose duty it had just been to bind them with the purple filet, was sorry to think that all this would soon be changed and even the Clerk of the Treasury seemed loath to sever those lovely tresses with the ritual knife. The Emperor, as he watched, remembered for a moment what pride the would have taken in the ceremony, but soon drove the weak thought from his mind.

Duly crowned, Genji went to his chamber and changing into man's dress went down into the courtyard and performed the Dance of Homage, which he did with such grace tears stood in every eye. And now the Emperor whose grief had of late grown somewhat less insistent, was again overwhelmed by memories of the past.

It had been feared that his delicate features would show to less advantage when he had put aside his childish dress; but on the contrary he looked handsomer than ever.

His sponsor, the Minister of the Left, had an only daughter, whose beauty the Heir Apparent had noticed.

---

[15] 3 p.m.

But now, the father began to think he would not encourage that match, but would offer her to Genji. He sounded the Emperor upon this, and found that he would be very glad to obtain for the boy the advantage of so powerful a connection.

When the courtiers assembled to drink the Love Cup, Genji came and took his place among the other princes. The Minister of the Left came up and whispered something in his ear; but the boy blushed and could think of no reply. A chamberlain now came over to the Minister and brought him a summons to wait upon His Majesty immediately. When he arrived before the Throne, a Lady of the Wardrobe handed to him the Great White Inner Garment and the Maid's Skirt,[16] which were his ritual due as Sponsor to Prince. Then, when he had made him drink out of the Royal Cup, the Emperor recited a poem in which he prayed that the binding of the purple filet might symbolize the union of their two houses; and the Minister answered him that nothing should sever this union save the fading of the purple band. Then he descended the long stairs and from the courtyard performed the Grand Obeisance.[17] Here to were shown the horses from the Royal Stables and the hawks from the Royal Falconry, that had been decreed as presents for Genji. At the foot of the stairs the Princes and Courtiers were lined up to receive their bounties, gifts of every kind were showered upon them. That day the hampers and fruit baskets were distributed in accordance with the Emperor's directions by the learned Secretary of the

[16] These symbolized the unmanly life of childhood which Genji now put behind him.

[17] The *butö,* a form of kowtow so elaborate as to be practically a dance.

Right, and boxes of cake and presents lay about so thick that one could scarcely move. Such profusion had not been seen even at the Heir Apparent's Initiation.

That night Genji went to the Minister's house, where his betrothal was celebrated with great splendor. It was thought that the little Prince looked somewhat childish and delicate, but his beauty astonished everyone. Only the bride, who was four years older, regarded him as a mere baby and was rather ashamed of him.

The Emperor still demanded Genji's attendance at the Palace, so he did not set up a house of his own. In his inmost heart he was always thinking how much nicer *she*[18] was than anyone else, and only wanted to be with people who were like her, but alas no one was the least like her. Everyone seemed to make a great deal of fuss about Princess Aoi, his betrothed; but he could see nothing nice about her. The girl at the Palace now filled all his childish thoughts and this obsession became a misery to him.

Now that he was a "man" he could no longer frequent the women's quarters as he had been wont to do. But sometimes when an entertainment was a-foot he found comfort in hearing her voice dimly blending with the sound of zithern or flute and felt his grown-up existence to be unendurable. After an absence of five or six days he occasionally spent two or three at his betrothed's house. His father-in-law attributing this negligence to his extreme youth was not at all perturbed and always received him warmly. Whenever he came the most agreeable of the young people of the day asked to meet him and endless trouble was taken in arranging games to amuse him.

---

[18] Fujitsubo.

The Shigeisa, one of the rooms which had belonged to his mother, was allotted to him as his official quarters in the Palace, and the servants who had waited on her were now gathered together again and formed his suite. His grandmother's house was falling into decay. The Imperial Office of Works was ordered to repair it. The grouping of the trees and disposition of the surrounding hills had always made the place delightful. Now the basin of the lake was widened and many other improvements were carried out. "If only I were going to live here with some-one whom I liked," thought Genji sadly.

Some say that the name of Hikaru the Shining One was given to him in admiration by the Korean fortune-teller.[19]

[19] This touch is reminiscent of early chronicles such as the *Nihongi* which delight in alternative explanations. In the subsequent chapter such archaisms entirely disappear.

Chapter 5

Bernier

Bernier (12th or 13th century, A.D.). Nothing is known of this author except he wrote the "*Divided Horsecloth.*" Several other authors (e.g. Montaigne and Browning) have made use of the story. Enjoy "*The Divided Horsecloth.*" We did (many years ago). The lesson is clear. Treat others as you would want them to treat you.

Bernier, "The Divided Horsecloth," in *Aucassin and Nicolette and Other Medieval Romances and Legends*, translated from the French by Eugene Mason. E.P. Dutton & Co., Inc., New York, 1937, pp. 75–83.

1. The Divided Horsecloth

Each owes it to his fellows to tell as best he may, or, better still, to write with fair enticing words, such deeds and adventures as are good and profitable for us to know. For as men come and go about their business in the world, many things are told them which it is seemly to keep in remembrance. Therefore, it becomes those who say and relate, diligently and with fair intent to keep such matters in thought and study, even as did our fathers before us. Theirs is the school to which we all should pass, and he who would prove an apt scholar, and live beyond his day, must not be idle at his task. But the world dims our fine gold: the minstrel is slothful, and singers forget to sing, because of the pain and travail which go to the finding of their songs. So without waiting for any to-morrow, I will bring before you a certain adventure which chanced, even as it was told to me.

Some seven years ago it befell that a rich burgess of Abbeville departed from the town, together with his wife, his only son, and all his wealth, his goods and plenishing. This he did like a prudent man, since he found himself at enmity with men who were stronger and of more substance than he. So, fearing lest a worse thing should bechance him, from Abbeville he went up to Paris. There he sought a shop and dwelling, and paying his service, made himself vassal and burgess of the King. The merchant was diligent and courteous, his wife smiling and gracious, and their son was not given over to folly, but went soberly, even as his parents taught him. Much were they praised of their neighbors, and those who lived in the same street often set foot in their dwelling. For very greatly are those loved and esteemed by their fellows who are courteous in speech and address. He who has fair words in his mouth receives again sweet words in his ear, and foul words and foul deeds bring naught but bitterness and railing. Thus was it with this prudent merchant. For more than seven years he went about his business, buying and selling, concerning himself with matters of which he had full knowledge, putting by of his earnings a little every day, like a wise and worthy citizen. So this wealthy merchant lived a happy blameless life, till, by the will of God, his wife was taken from him, who had been his companion for some thirty years. Now these parents had but one only child, a son, even as I have told you before. Very grievously did he mourn the death of her who had cherished him so softly, and lamented his mother with many tears, till he came nigh to swoon. Then, to put a little comfort in his heart, his father said to him:

"Fair son, thy mother is dead, and we will pray to God that He grant her mercy in that day. But dry now thine eyes and thy face, for tears can profit thee nothing. By that road we all must go, neither can any man pass Death upon the way, nor return to bring us any word. Fair son, for thee there is goodly comfort. Thou art a young bachelor, and it is time to take thee a wife. I am full of years, and so I may find thee a fair marriage in an honorable house I will endow thee with my substance. I will now seek a bride for thee of birth and breeding — one of family and descent, one come of ancient race, with relations and friends a gracious company, a wife from honest folk and from an honest home. There, where it is good and profitable to be, I will set thee gladly, nor of wealth and moneys shalt thou find a lack."

Now in that place were three brethren, knights of high lineage, cousins to mighty lords of peerage, bearing rich and honorable blazons on their shields. But these knights had no heritage, since they had pawned all that they owned of woods and houses and lands, the better to take their pleasure at the tourney. Passing heavy and tormented were these brethren because in no wise might they redeem their pledge. The eldest of these brothers had a daughter, but the mother of the maid was dead. Now this damsel owned in Paris a certain fair house, over against the mansion of the wealthy merchant. The house was not of her father's heritage, but came to her from her mother, who had put the maid in ward to guardians, so that the house was free from pledge. She received in rent therefrom the sum of twenty Paris pounds every year, and her dues were paid her right willingly. So the merchant, esteeming her a lady of family and estate, demanded her hand in marriage of her father and of all her friends. The knight inquired in his turn of the means and substance of the merchant, who answered very frankly:

"In merchandise and in moneys I have near upon fifteen hundred pounds. Should I tell you that I had more, I should lie, and speak not the truth. I have besides one hundred Paris pounds, which I have gained in honest dealings. Of all this I will give my son the half."

"Fair sir," made answer the knight, "in no wise can this be agreed to. Had you become a Templar, or a White or a Black monk you would have granted the whole of your wealth either to the Temple or your Abbey. By my faith, we cannot consent to so grudging an offer, certes, sir merchant, no."

"Tell me then what you would have me do."

"Very willingly, fair, dear sir. We would that you grant to your son the sum and total of your substance, so that he be seised of all your wealth, and this in such fashion that neither you, nor any in your name, may claim return of any part thereof. If you consent to this the marriage can be made, but otherwise he shall never wed our child and niece."

The merchant turned this over for a while, now looking upon his son, now deep in thought. But very badly he was served of all his thought and pondering. For at the last he made reply to him and said: "Lord, it shall even be done according to your will. This is our covenant and bargain, that so your daughter is given to my son I will grant him all that I have of worth. I take this company as witness that here I strip myself of everything I own, so that naught is mine, but all is his, of what I once was seised and possessed."

Thus before the witnesses he divested himself utterly of all his wealth, and became naked as a peeled wand in the eyes of the world, for this merchant now had neither purse nor penny, nor wherewithal to break his fast, save it were given him by his son. So when the words were spoken and the merchant altogether spoiled, then the knight took his daughter by the hand and handfasted her with the bachelor, and she became his wife.

For two years after this marriage the husband and the dame lived a quiet and peaceful life. Then a fair son was born to the bachelor, and the lady cherished and guarded him fondly. With them dwelt the merchant in the same lodging, but very soon he perceived that he had given himself a mortal blow in despoiling himself of his substance to live on the charity of others. But perforce he remained of their household for more than twelve years, until the lad had grown up tall, and began to take notice, and to remember that which often he heard of the making of his father's marriage. And well he promised himself that it should never go from mind.

The merchant was full of years. He leaned upon his staff, and went bent with age, as one who searches for his lost youth. His son was weary of his presence, and would gladly have paid for the spinning of his shroud. The dame, who was proud and disdainful, held him in utter despite, for greatly he was against her heart. Never was she silent, but always was she saying to her lord:

"Husband, for love of me, send your father upon his business. I lose all appetite just for the sight of him about the house."

"Wife," answered he, "this shall be done according to your wish."

So because of his wife's anger and importunity, he sought out his father straightway, and said:

"Father, father, get you gone from here. I tell you that you must do the best you can, for we may no longer concern ourselves with you and your lodging. For twelve years and more we have given you food and raiment in our house. Now all is done, so rise and depart forthwith, and fend for yourself, as fend you must."

When the father heard these words he wept bitterly, and often he cursed the day and the hour in which he found he had lived too long.

"Ah, fair, sweet son, what is this thou sayest to me! For the love of God turn me not from thy door. I lie so close that thou canst not want my room. I require of thee neither seat in the chimney corner, nor soft bed of feathers, no, nor carpet on the floor; but only the attic, where I may bide on a little straw. Throw me not from thy house because I eat of thy bread, but feed me without grudging for the short while I have to live. In the eyes of God this charity will cover all thy sins better than if thou went in haircloth next the flesh."

"Fair father," replied the bachelor, "preach me no preachings, but get you forth at once, for reason that my wife would have you gone."

"Fair son, where then shall I go, who am esteemed of nothing worth?"

"Get you gone to the town, for amongst ten thousand others very easily you may light on good fortune. Very unlucky you will be if there you cannot find a way to live. Seek your fortune bravely. Perchance some of your friends and acquaintance will receive you into their houses."

"Son, how then shall men take me to their lodging, when you turn me from the house which I have given you? Why should the stranger welcome that guest whom the son chases from his door? Why should I be received gladly by him to whom I have given naught, when I am evilly entreated of the rich man for whose sake I go naked?"

"Father," said he, "right or wrong, I take the blame upon my own head; but go you must because it is according to my will."

Then the father grieved so bitterly that for a little his very heart would have broken. Weak as he was, he raised himself to his feet and went forth from the house, weeping.

"Son," said he, "I commend thee to God; but since thou wilt that I go, for the love of Him give me at least a portion of packing cloth to shelter me against the wind. I am asking no great matter; nothing but a little cloth to wrap about me, because I am but lightly clad, and fear to die for reason of the cold."

Then he who shrank from any grace of charity made reply:

"Father, I have no cloth, so neither can I bestow, nor have it taken from me."

"Fair, sweet son, my heart trembles within me, so greatly do I dread the cold. Give me, then, the cloth you spread upon your horse, so that I come to no evil."

So he, seeing that he might not rid himself of his father save by the granting of a gift, and being desirous above all that he should part, bade his son to fetch this horsecloth. When the lad heard his father's call he sprang to him, saying:

"Father, what is your pleasure?"

"Fair son," said he, "get you to the stable, and if you find it open give my father the covering that is upon my horse. Give him the best cloth in the stable, so that he may make himself a mantle or a habit, or any other sort of cloak that pleases him."

Then the lad, who was thoughtful beyond his years, made answer:

"Grandsire, come now with me."

So the merchant went with him to the stable, exceedingly heavy and wrathful. The lad chose the best horsecloth he might find in the stable, the newest, the largest, and the most fair; this he folded in two, and drawing forth his knife, divided the cloth in two portions. Then he bestowed on his grandfather one half of the sundered horsecloth.

"Fair child," said the old man, "what have you done? Why have you cut the cloth that your father has given me? Very cruelly have you treated me, for you were bidden to give me the horsecloth whole. I shall return and complain to my son thereof."

"Go where you will," replied the boy, "for certainly you shall have nothing more from me."

The merchant went forth from the stable.

"Son," said he, "chastise now thy child, since he counts thy word as nothing but an idle tale, and fears not to disobey thy commandment. Dost thou not see that he keeps one half of the horsecloth?"

"Plague take thee!" cried the father, "give him all the cloth."

"Certes," replied the boy, "that will I never do, for how then shall you be paid? Rather will I keep the half until I am grown a man, and then give it to you. For just as you have chased him from your house, so I will put you from my door. Even as he has bestowed on you all his wealth, so, in my turn, will I require of you all your substance. Naught from me shall you carry away, save that only which you have granted to him. If you leave him to die in his misery, I wait my day, and surely will leave you to perish in yours."

The father listened to these words, and at the end sighed heavily. He repented him of the evil that he purposed, and from the parable that his child had spoken took heed and warning. Turning himself about towards the merchant, he said:

"Father, return to my house. Sin and the Enemy thought to have caught me in the snare, but, please God, I have escaped from the fowler. You are master and lord, and I render all that I have received into your hands. If my wife cannot live with you in quiet, then you shall be served and cherished elsewhere. Chimney corner, and carpet, pillow and bed of feathers, at your ease you shall have pleasure in them all. I take St. Martin to witness that never will I drink stoup of wine, never carve morsel from dish, but that yours shall be the richer portion. Henceforth you shall live softly in the ceiled chamber, near by a blazing fire, clad warmly in your furred robe, even as I. And all this is not of charity, but of your right, for, fair sweet father, if I am rich it is because of your substance."

Thus the brave witness and the open remonstrance of a child freed his father from the bad thoughts that he harbored. And deeply should this adventure be considered of those who are about to marry their children. Let them not strip themselves so bare as to have nothing left. For he who gives all, and depends upon the charity of others, prepares a rod for his own back.

Chapter 6

Niccolo Machiavelli

Niccolo di Bernardo dei Machiavelli (1469–1527) was an Italian philosopher and writer. He never published *The Prince* but he did circulate the short manuscript among his friends. The term Machiavellian sprang from this text which was published in 1532, five years after his death.

"Machiavellian, ... relating to his political theories, especially to the doctrine that any means, however unscrupulous, may be justifiably employed by a ruler in order to maintain a strong central government. Hence characterized by political cunning or bad faith."[20]

Would Machiavelli challenge this interpretation of his great work, *The Prince*? Was he advocating bad faith or merely defining and exposing the system as it existed?

Whatever the answers to the above questions, there is no doubt that Machiavelli's writings and thoughts are worthy of reading.

Consider:

> "In the capacities of mankind there are three degrees: one man understands things by means of his own natural endowments; another understands things when they are explained to him; and a third can neither

[20] Webster's New Collegiate Dictionary, G. & C. Merriam Co., Springfield, MA, 1956, p. 503.

> understand them of himself nor when they are explained by others. The first are rare and excellent, and the second have their merit, but the last are wholly worthless."

The Prince can be interpreted in several different ways. One is to take its words literally to be advice to a ruthless ruler whose primary objective is to retain and apply power at any cost. At the other extreme is an interpretation that Machiavelli was a republican and that *The Prince* was an exposé of the methods used by evil princes; Machiavelli was not advocating the evil practices described in *The Prince,* but rather revealing them so they can be combated.

Machiavelli, Niccolo, *The Prince,* New York, National Alumni, 1907, pp. 96–97, 102–105.

1. Chapter XXII — Ministers

A proper choice of ministers is of no small importance to a prince, for the first opinion of his capacity arises from the persons by whom he is surrounded. When they are men of ability, he is deemed a wise prince for having discovered their worth and found means to attach them to him. But when they prove otherwise, a mean opinion is entertained of his judgment from the unfit selection he has made. All those that knew Antonio de Venafro rendered justice to the judgment and wisdom of Pandolfo Petrucci, who chose so able a man for the administration of his affairs.

In the capacities of mankind there are three degrees: one man understands things by means of his own natural endowments; another understands things when they are explained to him; and a third can neither understand them of himself nor when they are explained by others. The first are rare and excellent, and the second have their merit, but the last are wholly worthless.

Pandolfo belonged at least to the second class; for when a prince can distinguish what is useful from what is injurious, he may, without being a man of genius, judge of the conduct of his ministers, and praise or blame it with such discretion that they, from a conviction that they cannot deceive him, serve him with zeal and fidelity.

But how are princes to know a minister? There is one infallible rule, viz. to observe whether he attends more to his own interest than to that of the state. A minister should be entirely devoted to the public service, and never should address the prince on his private affairs. It is the part of the prince to attend to the interests of the minister, and to heap honors, riches, fortune, and other favors upon him, that so he may be satisfied in his station, and have no reason to desire a change; in fine, that he may dread, and endeavor with all his power to prevent, any fatal reverse that may threaten his master. And this is the only method of establishing between a prince and his ministers a confidence equally useful and honorable to both.

2. Chapter XXV — How Far Fortune Influences the Things of this World, and How Far She May Be Resisted

I know that several have thought, and many still are of opinion, that all sublunary events are governed either by Divine Providence or by chance, in such a manner that human wisdom has no share in their direction; and hence they infer that man should abstain from interfering with their course, and leave everything to its natural tendency.

The revolutions that in our times are of such frequent recurrence, seem to support this doctrine, and I own that I myself am almost inclined to favor such opinions, particularly when I consider how far those events surpass all human conjecture; yet, as we confessedly possess a free will, it must, I think, be admitted that chance does not so far govern the world as to leave no province for the exercise of human prudence.

For my own part, I cannot help comparing the blind power of chance to a rapid river, which, having overflowed its banks, inundates the plain, uproots trees, carries away houses and lands, and sweeps all before it in its destructive progress; everybody flies, possessing neither resolution nor power to oppose its fury. But this should not discourage us, when the river has returned within its natural limits, from constructing dykes and banks to prevent a recurrence of similar disasters. It is the same with fortune; she exercises her power when we oppose no barrier to her progress.

If we cast our eyes on Italy, which has been the theater of revolutions, and consider the causes by which they have been provoked, we shall find it to be a defenseless country. If she had been properly fortified, like Germany, Spain, or France, such inundations of foreigners never would have happened, or at least their irruptions would have been attended with less devastation.

Let this suffice in general concerning the necessity of opposing fortune. But to descend to particulars. It is no uncommon thing to see a prince fall from prosperity to adversity, without our being able to attribute his fate to any change in conduct or character; for, as I have already shown at large, he who relies solely on Fortune must be ruined inevitably whenever she abandons him.

Those princes who adapt their conduct to circumstances are rarely unfortunate. Fortune is only changeable to those who cannot conform themselves to the varying exigencies of the times; for we see different men take different courses to obtain the end they have in view; for instance, in pursuit of riches or glory, one prosecutes his object at random, the other with caution and prudence: one employs art, the other force; one is impetuosity itself, the other all patience — means by which each may severally succeed. It also happens that of two who follow the same route, one may arrive at his destination, and the other fail; and that if two other persons whose dispositions are diametrically opposite, pursue the same object by wholly different means, yet both shall equally prosper; which is owing entirely to the temper the times, which always prove favorable or adverse, according as men conform to them.

From all these circumstances we may conclude that those who cannot change their system when occasion requires it, will no doubt continue prosperous as long as glide with the stream of fortune but when that turns against them they are ruined from not being able to follow that blind goddess through all her variations.

Besides, I think that it is better to be bold than too circumspect; because Fortune is of a sex that likes not a tardy wooer, and repels all that are not ardent; she declares also, more frequently, in favor of those that are young, because they are bold and enterprising.

Chapter 7

Francis Bacon

Francis Bacon (1561–1629) was an English author and philosopher. In his effort to make a living, he was a statesman, lawyer and scientist.

He developed a methodology for conducting scientific investigations that is still used today.

Bacon was a public servant until 1621 when he pleaded guilty to a charge of corruption and was declared incapable of holding governmental office. He subsequently devoted his life to writing and scientific inquiry.

He was a leading thinker of his time period. He advocated greater rights for women and doing away with slavery. Freedom of religion and separation of church and state were important intellectual contributions of Bacon. Thomas Jefferson, primary author of the Declaration of Independence, cited Bacon as one of the three greatest men who ever lived (Locke and Newton were the other two).

One of Bacon's most widely quoted passages is:

> "Reading maketh a full man, conference a ready man, and writing an exact man; and, therefore, if a man write little, he had need have a great memory; if he confer little, he had need have a present wit; and if he read little, he had need have much cunning, to seem to know that he doth not."

Equally insightful is:

> "Crafty men condemn studies, simple men admire them, and wise men use them, for they teach not their own use; but that is a wisdom without them, and above them, won by observation. Read not to contradict and confute, nor to believe and take for granted, nor to find talk and discourse, but to weight and consider."

Bacon is the source of many great citations.

Bacon, Francis. "Of Studies," and "Icarus and Scylla and Charybdis, or the Middle Way" in *Essays*, [by] Francis Bacon, New York, Hurst & Company Publishers, 1883, pp. 210–211, 355–356.

1. Of Studies

Studies serve for delight, for ornament, and for ability. Their chief use for delight is in privateness and retiring; for ornament, is in discourse; and for ability, is in the judgment and disposition of business. For expert men can execute, and perhaps judge of particulars, one by one, but the general counsels, and the plots and marshalling of affairs come best from those that are learned. To spend too much time in studies is sloth; to use them too much for ornament is affectation; to make judgment wholly by their rules is the humor of a scholar. They perfect nature, and are perfected by experience; for natural abilities are like natural plants, that need pruning by study; and studies themselves do give forth directions too much at large, except they be bounded in by experience. Crafty men contemn studies, simple men admire them, and wise men use them, for they teach not their own use, but that is a wisdom without them, and above them, won by observation. Read not to contradict and confute, nor to believe and take for granted, nor to find talk and discourse, but to weigh and consider. Some books are to be tasted, others to be swallowed, and some few to be chewed and digested; that is, some books are to be read only in parts, others to be read, but not curiously, and some few to be read wholly, and with diligence and attention. Some books also may be read by deputy and extracts made of them by others, but that would be only in the less important arguments and the meaner sort of books, else distilled books are like common distilled waters, flashy things. Reading maketh a full man, conference a ready man, and writing an exact man. And therefore, if a man write little, he had need have a great memory; if he confer little, he had need have a present wit; and if be read little, he had need have much cunning to seem to know that he doth not. Histories make men wise, poets witty, the mathematics subtle, natural philosophy deep, moral grave, logic and rhetoric able to contend. *Abeunt studia in mores.* Nay, there is no stond or impediment in the wit but may be wrought out by fit studies, like as diseases of the body may have appropriate exercises. Bowling is good for the stone and reins, shooting for the lungs and breast, gentle walking for the stomach, riding for the head, and the like. So if a man's wit be wandering, let him study the mathematics; for in demonstrations, if his wit be called away never so little, he must begin again; if his wit be not apt to distinguish or find differences, let him study the school-men, for they are *Cymini sectores.* If he be not apt to beat over matters and to call up one thing to prove and illustrate another, let him study the lawyers' cases; so every defect of the mind may have a special receipt.

2. Icarus and Scylla and Charybdis, or the Middle Way. Explained of Mediocrity in Natural and Moral Philosophy

Mediocrity or the holding a middle course, has been highly extolled in morality, but little in matters of science, though no less useful and proper here; while in politics it is held suspected, and ought to be employed with judgement. The ancients described mediocrity in manners by the course prescribed to Icarus; and in matters of the understanding by the steering between Scylla and Charybdis, on account of the great difficulty and danger in passing those straits.

Icarus, being to fly across the sea, was ordered by his father neither to soar too high nor fly too low, for, as his wings were fastened together with wax, there was danger of its melting by the sun's heat in too high a flight, and of its becoming less tenacious by the moisture if he kept too near the vapor of the sea. But he, with a juvenile confidence, soared aloft, and fell down headlong.

Explanation: The fable is vulgar, and easily interpreted for the path of virtue lies straight between excess on the one side, and defect on the other. And no wonder that excess should prove the bane of Icarus exulting in juvenile strength and vigor; for excess is the natural vice of youth, as defect is that of old age; and if a man must perish by either, Icarus chose the better of the two; for all defects are justly esteemed more depraved than excesses. There is some magnanimity in excess, that, like a bird claims kindred with the heavens; but defect is a reptile, that basely crawls up on the earth. It was excellently said by Heraclitus, "A dry light makes the best soul"; for if the soul contracts moisture from the earth, it perfectly degenerates and sinks. On the other hand, moderation must be observed, to prevent this fine light from burning, by its too great subtility and dryness. But these observations are common.

In matters of the understanding, it requires great skill and a particular felicity to steer clear of Scylla and Charybdis. If the ship strikes upon Scylla it is dashed in pieces against the rocks; if upon Charybdis, it is swallowed outright. This allegory is pregnant with matter; but we shall only observe the force of it lies here, that a mean be observed in every doctrine and science, and in the rules and axioms thereof, between the rocks of distinctions and the whirlpools of universalities; for these two are the bane and shipwreck of fine geniuses and arts.

Chapter 8

William Shakespeare

William Shakespeare (1564–1616) was an English writer (plays, poems, and sonnets). He is probably the world's leading dramatist of all time.

This entire book could have consisted of extracts of Shakespeare's writings. I have rationed the inclusion of his writings to Polonius' advice to his son, Laertes.

Note that the advice for Laertes not to borrow is wise, but that advice has to do with an individual person's actions not those of a corporate enterprise (my advice would be different for a corporation).

"To thine own self be true" is subject to different interpretations, but is also solid advice for a business manager.

Unfortunately, Polonius is soon struck down (killed) by Hamlet. I would have liked more of his wisdom revealed.

Shakespeare, William, "Hamlet, Prince of Denmark," in *Shakespeare, A Historical and Critical Study with Annotated Texts of Twenty-one Plays*, by Hardin Craig, Chicago, Scott, Foresman and Company, 1931, p. 743.

1. Hamlet, Act I. Sc. III

Enter POLONIUS.
A double blessing is a double grace;
Occasion smiles upon a second leave.
POL. Yet here, Laertes! aboard, aboard, for shame!
The wind sits in the shoulder of your sail,
And you are stay'd for. There; my blessing with thee!
And these few precepts in thy memory
See thou character. Give thy thoughts no tongue,
Nor any unproportion'd thought his act.
Be thou familiar, but by no means vulgar.
Those friends thou hast, and their adoption tried,
Grapple them to thy soul with hoops of steel;
But do not dull thy palm with entertainment
Of each new-hatch'd, unfledged comrade. Beware
Of entrance to a quarrel, but being in,
Bear 't that the opposed may beware of thee.
Give every man thy ear, but few thy voice;
Take each man's censure, but reserve thy judgment.
Costly thy habit as thy purse can buy,
But not express'd in fancy; rich, not gaudy;
For the apparel oft proclaims the man,
And they in France of the best rank and station
Are of a most select and generous chief in that.
Neither a borrower nor a lender be;
For loan oft loses both itself and friend,
And borrowing dulls the edge of husbandry.
This above all: to thine own self be true,
And it must follow, as the night the day,
Thou canst not then be false to any man.

Chapter 9

Thomas Hobbes

Thomas Hobbes (1588–1679) was an English philosopher and writer best known for his 1651 book *Leviathan.* A "Leviathan" is a state which, according to Hobbes, is an artificial man. This book was a major basis of Western political philosophy. It established the social foundations of an effective government. Some scholars link the work of Hobbes to the subsequent work in economics by Adam Smith.

In the extracts to follow, Hobbes first defines a "State" to be an artificial man and then defines each governmental function in terms of a person's body.

Later he defines two kinds of knowledge in the section titled "Of the Several Subjects of Knowledge." One is the "knowledge of fact" and the second is the "knowledge of the consequences of one affirmation to another." This second knowledge is called "science."

The section titled "Of Power, Worth, Dignity, Honour, and Worthiness" explores the sources and types of power and value. This is one of the foundations of economic theory and commerce.

> "The 'value' or 'worth' of a man is, as of all other things, his price; that is to say, so much as would be given for the use of his power; and therefore is not absolute, but a thing dependent on the need and judgment of another."

Most of us would describe this as the "market price." Thus the birth of economics.

Hobbes, Thomas, "Of Man, Being the First Part of Leviathan," in *French and English Philosophers: Descartes, Rousseau, Voltaire, Hobbes*, New York, P. F. Collier & Son, 1910, p. 319, 373, pp. 374–375.

1. Introduction

Nature, the art whereby God hath made and governs the world, is by the 'art' of man, as in many other things, so in this also imitated, that it can make an artificial animal. For seeing life is but a motion of limbs, the beginning whereof is in some principal part within; why may we not say, that all 'automata' (engines that move themselves by springs and wheels as doth a watch) have an artificial life? For what is the 'heart' but a 'spring'; and the 'nerves' but so many 'strings'; and the 'joints' but so many 'wheels,' giving motion to the whole body, such as was intended by the artificer? 'Art' goes yet further, imitating that rational and most excellent work of nature, 'man.' For by art is created that great 'Leviathan' called a 'Commonwealth' or 'State,' in Latin *civitas,* which is but an artificial man, though of greater stature and strength than the natural, for whose protection and defence it was intended; and in which the 'sovereignty' is an artificial 'soul,' as giving life and motion to the whole body; the 'magistrates' and other 'officers' of judicature and execution, artificial 'joints'; 'reward' and 'punishment,' by which fastened to the seat of the sovereignty every joint and member is moved to perform his duty, are the 'nerves,' that do the same in the body natural; the 'wealth' and 'riches' of all the particular members are the 'strength'; *salus populi,* the 'people's safety,' its 'business'; 'counsellors,' by whom all things needful for it to know are suggested unto it, are the 'memory'; 'equity' and 'laws,' an artificial 'reason' and 'will'; 'concord,' 'health'; 'sedition,' 'sickness'; and 'civil war,' 'death.' Lastly, the 'pacts' and 'covenants,' by which the parts of this body politic were at first made, set together, and united, resemble that 'fiat,' or the 'let us make man,' pronounced by God in the creation.

2. Chapter IX — Of the Several Subjects of Knowledge

There are of 'knowledge' two kinds, whereof one is 'knowledge of fact,' the other 'knowledge of the consequence of one affirmation to another.' The former is nothing else but sense and memory, and is 'absolute knowledge,' as when we see a fact doing or remember it done; and this is the knowledge required in a witness. The latter is called 'science,' and is 'conditional,' as when we know that 'if the figure shown be a circle, then any straight line through the centre shall divide it into two equal parts.' And this is the knowledge required in a philosopher, that is to say of him that pretends to reasoning.

The register of 'knowledge of fact' is called 'history,' whereof there be two sorts: one called 'natural history,' which is the history of such facts or effects of Nature as have no dependence on man's 'will,' such as are the histories of 'metals,' 'plants,' 'animals,' 'regions,' and the like. The other is 'civil history,' which is the history of the voluntary actions of men in commonwealths.

The registers of science are such 'books,' as contain the 'demonstrations' of consequences of one affirmation to another, and are commonly called 'books of philosophy'.

3. Chapter X — On Power, Worth, Dignity, Honour, and Worthiness

The 'power of a man,' to take it universally, is his present means, to obtain some future apparent good; and is either 'original' or 'instrumental.'

'Natural power' is the eminence of the faculties of body or mind, as extraordinary strength, form, prudence, arts, eloquence, liberality, nobility. 'Instrumental' are those powers which, acquired by these or by fortune are means and instruments to acquire more, as riches, reputation, friends, and the secret working of God, which men call good luck. For the nature of power is in this point like to fame, increasing as it proceeds; or like the motion of heavy bodies, which the further they go make still the more haste.

The greatest of human powers is that which is compounded of the powers of most men, united by consent, in one person, natural or civil, that has the use of all their powers depending on his will such as is the power of a commonwealth. Or depending on the wills of each particular, such as is the power of a faction or of divers factions leagued. Therefore to have servants is power; to have friends is power; for they are strengths united.

Also riches joined with liberality is power, because it procureth friends and servants; without liberality, not so; because in this case they defend not, but expose men to envy, as a prey.

Reputation of power is power, because it draweth with it the adherence of those that need protection.

So is reputation of love of a man's country, called popularity, for the same reason.

Also, what quality soever maketh a man beloved or feared of many, or the reputation of such quality, is power, because it is a means to have the assistance and service of many.

Good success is power, because it maketh reputation of wisdom or good fortune, which makes men either fear him or rely on him.

Affability of men already in power is increase of power, because it gaineth love.

Reputation of prudence in the conduct of peace or war is power, because to prudent men we commit the government of ourselves more willingly than to others.

Nobility is power, not in all places but only in those commonwealths where it has privileges, for in such privileges consisteth their power.

Eloquence is power, because it is seeming prudence.

Form is power, because, being a promise of good, it recommendeth men to the favor of women and strangers.

The sciences are small power, because not eminent and therefore not acknowledged in any man; nor are at all, but in a few, and in them but of a few things. For science is of that nature as none can understand it to be but such as in a good measure have attained it.

Arts of public use, as fortification, making of engines, and other instruments of war, because they confer to defence and victory, are power; and though the true mother of them be science; namely the mathematics, yet, because they are brought into the light by the hand of the artificer, they be esteemed, thc midwife passing with the vulgar for the mother, as his issue.

The 'value,' or 'worth,' of a man is, as of all other things, his price; that is to say, so much as would be given for the use of his power; and therefore is not absolute, but a thing dependent on the need and judgment of another. An able conductor of soldiers is of great price in time of war present, or imminent; but in peace not so. A learned and uncorrupt judge is much worth in time of peace, but not so much in war. And, as in other things so in men, not the seller but the buyer determines the price. For let a man, as most men do, rate themselves (himself) at the highest value they (he) can, yet their (his) true value is no more than it is esteemed by others.

Chapter 10

René Descartes

René Descartes (1596–1650) was born in France, spent most of his life in the Dutch Republic and died in Sweden (he was hired to teach Queen Christina). He was a philosopher, mathematician, physicist and writer but most importantly he was one of the greatest thinkers of all time. He created new disciplines using his mind. "*Cogito ergo sum*" is his most famous quote, usually translated as "I think therefore I am." His mathematical writings in analytic geometry led to the development of calculus.

It is difficult to choose one thought or sentence to capture Descartes' thought, but the following is close. This is the first of four rules of logic:

> "The *first* was never to accept anything for true which I did not clearly know to be such; that is to say, carefully to avoid precipitancy and prejudice, and to comprise nothing more in my judgment than what was presented to my mind so clearly and distinctly as to exclude all ground of doubt."

Descartes, René. "Discourse on the Method of Rightly conducting the Reason and Seeking of Truth in the Sciences," *in French* and English Philosophers*: Descartes, Rousseau, Voltaire, Hobbes*, New York, P. F. Collier & Son, 1910, pp. 5–11.

1. Discourse on the Method of Rightly Conducting the Reason and Seeking the Truth in the Sciences

1.1. *Part I*

Good sense is, of all things among men, the most equally distributed; for everyone thinks himself so abundantly provided with it, that those even who are the most difficult to satisfy in everything else, do not usually desire a larger measure of this quality than they already possess. And in this it is not likely that all are mistaken: the conviction is rather to be held as testifying that the power of judging aright and of distinguishing Truth from Error, which is properly what is called Good Sense or Reason, is by nature equal in all men; and that the diversity of our opinions, consequently, does not arise from some being endowed with a larger share of Reason than others, but solely from this, that we conduct our thoughts along different ways, and do not fix our attention on the same objects. For to be possessed of a vigorous mind is not enough; the prime requisite is rightly to apply it. The greatest minds, as they are capable of the highest excellencies, are open likewise to the greatest aberrations; and those who travel very slowly may yet make far greater progress, provided they keep always to the straight road, than those who, while they run, forsake it.

For myself, I have never fancied my mind to be in any respect more perfect than those of the generality; on the contrary, I have often wished that I were equal to some others in promptitude of thought, or in clearness and distinctness of imagination, or in fullness and readiness of memory. And besides these, I know of no other qualities that contribute to the perfection of the mind; for as to the Reason or Sense, inasmuch as it is that alone which constitutes us men, and distinguishes us from the brutes, I am disposed to believe that it is to be found complete in each individual; and on this point to adopt the common opinion of philosophers, who say that the difference of greater and less holds only among the *accidents*, and not among the *forms* or *natures* of *individuals* of the same *species*.

I will not hesitate, however, to avow my belief that it has been my singular good fortune to have very early in life fallen in with certain tracks which have conducted me to considerations and maxims, of which I have formed a Method that gives me the means, as I think, of gradually augmenting my knowledge, and of raising it by little and little to the highest point which the mediocrity of my talents and the brief duration of my life will permit me to reach. For I have already reaped from it such fruits that, although I have been accustomed to think lowly enough of myself, and although when I look with the eye of a philosopher at the varied courses and pursuits of mankind at large, I find scarcely one which does not appear vain and useless, I nevertheless derive the highest satisfaction from the progress I conceive myself to have already made in the search after truth, and cannot help entertaining such expectations of the future as to believe that if, among the occupations of men as men, there is any one really excellent and important, it is that which I have chosen.

After all, it is possible I may be mistaken; and it is but a little copper and glass, perhaps, that I take for gold and diamonds. I know how very liable we are to delusion in what relates to ourselves, and also how much the judgments of our friends are to be suspected when given in our favor. But I shall endeavor in this Discourse to describe the paths I have followed, and to delineate my life as in a picture, in order that each one may be able to judge of them for himself, and that in the general opinion entertained of them, as gathered from current report, I myself may have a new help towards instruction to be added to those I have been in the habit of employing.

My present design, then, is not to teach the Method which each ought to follow for the right conduct of his Reason, but solely to describe the way in which I have endeavored to conduct my own. They who set themselves to give precepts must of course regard themselves as possessed of greater skill than those to whom they prescribe; and if they err in the slightest particular, they subject themselves to censure. But as this Tract is put forth merely as a history, or, if you will, as a tale, in which, amid some examples worthy of imitation, there will be found, perhaps, as many more which it were advisable not to follow, I hope it will prove useful to some without being hurtful to any, and that my openness will find some favor with all.

From my childhood, I have been familiar with letters; and as I was given to believe that by their help a clear and certain knowledge of all that is useful in life might be acquired, I was ardently desirous of instruction. But as soon as I had finished the entire course of study, at the close of which it is customary to be admitted into the order of the learned, I completely changed my opinion. For I found myself involved in so many doubts and errors, that I was convinced I had advanced no farther in all my attempts at learning, than the discovery at every turn of thy own ignorance. And yet I was studying in one of the most celebrated Schools in Europe, in which I thought there must be learned men, if such were anywhere to be found. I had been taught all that others learned there; and not contented with the sciences actually taught us, I had, in addition, read all the books that had fallen into my hands, treating of such branches as are esteemed the most curious and rare. I knew the judgment which others had formed of me; and I did not find that I was considered inferior to my fellows, although there were among them some who were already marked out to fill the places of our instructors. And, in fine, our age appears to me as flourishing, and as fertile in powerful minds as any preceding one. I was thus led to take the liberty of judging of all other men by myself, and of concluding that there was no science in existence that was of such a nature as I had previously been given to believe.

I still continued, however, to hold in esteem the studies of the Schools. I was aware that the Languages taught in them are necessary to the understanding of the writings of the ancients; that the grace of Fable stirs the mind; that the memorable deeds of History elevate it; and, if read with discretion, aid in forming the judgment; that the perusal of all excellent books is, as it were, to interview with the noblest men of past ages, who have written them, and even a studied interview, in which are discovered to us only their choicest thoughts; that Eloquence has incomparable force and beauty; that Poesy has its ravishing graces and delights; that in the Mathematics there are many refined discoveries eminently suited to gratify the inquisitive, as well as further all the arts and lessen the labor of man; that numerous highly useful precepts and exhortations to virtue are contained in treatises on Morals; that Theology points out the path to heaven; that Philosophy affords the means of discoursing with an appearance of truth on all matters, and commands the admiration of the more simple; that Jurisprudence, Medicine, and the other Sciences, secure for their cultivators honors and riches; and in fine, that it is useful to bestow some attention upon all, even upon those abounding the most in superstition and error, that we may be in a position to determine their real value, and guard against being deceived.

But I believed that I had already given sufficient time to Languages, and likewise to the reading of the writings of the ancients, to their Histories and Fables. For to hold converse with those of other ages and to travel, are almost the same thing. It is useful to know something of the manners of different nations, that we may be enabled to form a more correct judgment regarding our own, and be prevented from thinking that everything contrary to our customs is ridiculous and irrational, — a conclusion usually come to by those whose experience has been limited to their own country. On the other hand, when too much time is occupied in travelling, we become strangers to our native country; and the over curious in the customs of the past are generally ignorant of those of the present. Besides, fictitious narratives lead us to imagine the possibility of many events that are impossible; and even the most faithful histories, if they do not wholly misrepresent matters, or exaggerate their importance to render the account of them more worthy of perusal, omit, at least, almost always the meanest and least striking of the attendant circumstances; hence it happens that the remainder does not represent the truth, and that such as regulate their conduct by examples drawn from this source, are apt to fall into the extravagances of the knight-errants of Romance, and to entertain projects that exceed their powers.

I esteemed Eloquence highly, and was in raptures with Poesy; but I thought that both were gifts of nature rather than fruits of study. Those in whom the faculty of Reason is predominant, and who most skilfully dispose their thoughts with a view to render them clear and intelligible, are always the best able to persuade others of the truth of what they lay down, though they should speak only in the language of Lower Brittany, and be wholly ignorant of the rules of Rhetoric; and those whose minds are stored with the most agreeable fancies, and who can give expression to them with the greatest embellishment and harmony, are still the best poets, though unacquainted with the Art of Poetry.

I was especially delighted with the Mathematics, on account of the certitude and evidence of their reasonings: but I had not as yet a precise knowledge of their true use; and thinking that they but contributed to the advancement of the mechanical arts, I was astonished that foundations, so strong and solid, should have had no loftier superstructure reared on them. On the other hand, I compared the disquisitions of the ancient Moralists to very towering and magnificent palaces with no better foundation than sand and mud: they laud the virtues very highly, and exhibit them as estimable far above anything on earth; but they give us no adequate criterion of virtue, and frequently that which they designate with so fine a name is but apathy, or pride, or despair, or parricide.

I revered our Theology, and aspired as much as anyone to reach heaven: but being given assuredly to understand that the way is not less open to the most ignorant than to the most learned, and that the revealed truths which lead to heaven are above our comprehension, I did not presume to subject them to the impotency of my

Reason; and I thought that in order competently to undertake their examination, there was need of some special help front heaven, and of being more than man.

Of philosophy I will say nothing, except that when I saw that it had been cultivated for many ages by the most distinguished men, and that yet there is not a single matter within its sphere which is not still in dispute, and nothing, therefore, which is above doubt, I did not presume to anticipate that my success would be greater in it than that of others; and further, when I considered the number of conflicting opinions touching a single matter that may be upheld by learned men, while there can be but one true, I reckoned as well-nigh false all that was only probable.

As to the other Sciences, inasmuch as these borrow their principles from Philosophy, I judged that no solid superstructures could be reared on foundations so infirm; and neither the honour nor the gain held out by them was sufficient to determine me to their cultivation: for I was not, thank Heaven, in a condition which compelled me to make merchandise of Science for the bettering of my fortune; and though I might not profess to scorn glory as a Cynic, I yet made very slight account of that honour which I hoped to acquire only through fictitious titles. And, in fine, of false Sciences I thought I knew the worth sufficiently to escape being deceived by the professions of an alchemist, the predictions of an astrologer, the impostures of a magician, or by the artifices and boasting of any of those who profess to know things of which they are ignorant.

For these reasons, as soon as my age permitted me to pass from under the control of my instructors, I entirely abandoned the study of letters, and resolved no longer to seek any other science than the knowledge of myself, or of the great book of the world, I spent the remainder of my youth in travelling, in visiting courts and armies, in holding intercourse with men of different dispositions and ranks, in collecting varied experience, in proving myself in the different situations into which fortune threw me, and, above all, in making such reflection on the matter of my experience as to secure my improvement. For it occurred to me that I should find much more truth in the reasonings of each individual with reference to the affairs in which he is personally interested, and the issue of which must presently punish him if he has judged amiss, than in those conducted by a man of letters in his study, regarding speculative matters that are of no practical moment, and followed by no consequences to himself, farther, perhaps, than that they foster his vanity the better the more remote they are from common sense; requiring, as they must in this case, the exercise of greater ingenuity and art to render them probable. In addition, I had always a most earnest desire to know how to distinguish the true from the false, in order that I might be able clearly to discriminate the right path in life, and proceed in it with confidence.

It is true that, while busied only in considering the manners of other men, I found here, too, scarce any ground for settled conviction, and remarked hardly less contradiction among them than in the opinions of the philosophers. So that the greatest advantage I derived from the study consisted in this, that, observing many things which, however extravagant and ridiculous to our apprehension, are yet by common consent received and approved by other great nations, I learned to entertain too decided a belief in regard to nothing of the truth of which

I had been persuaded merely by example and custom: and thus I gradually extricated myself from many errors powerful enough to darken our Natural Intelligence, and incapacitate us in great measure from listening to Reason. But after I had been occupied several years in thus studying the book of the world, and in essaying to gather some experience, I at length resolved to make myself an object of study, and to employ all the powers of my mind in choosing the paths I ought to follow; an undertaking which was accompanied with greater success than it would have been had I never quitted my country or my books.

Chapter 11

Jean-Jacques Rousseau

Jean-Jacques Rousseau (1712–1778) was born in Switzerland but was of French heritage. He lived most of his life in France and he was buried as a French hero in the Pantheon in Paris 16 years after his death.

He was a philosopher, writer of two novels and many essays, a composer of two operas and author of one play. Though a religious man, his writings succeeded in alienating both the Catholic and Protestant churches. His political philosophy greatly influenced the French Revolution. He thought all religions had merit if they influenced people to be good.

He has been accused of laying the intellectual foundation for fascism but he also influenced Thomas Jefferson and other founding fathers of the United States. The writings of Rousseau touched all bases. They are complex and profound. Any person of any political belief can find justification in the writings of Rousseau.

The extract to follow attempts to explain the nature of inequality in mankind. Rousseau defines two types of inequality. One is the natural inequality (we have different capabilities) and the second arises because of different privileges (e.g. being richer or ranking higher in society). The issues are worthy of thought and discussion.

> "I conceive two species of inequality among men; one which I call natural, or physical inequality, because it

> is established by nature, and consists in the difference of age, health, bodily strength, and the qualities of the mind, or of the soul; the other which may be termed moral, or political inequality, because it depends on a kind of convention, and is established, or at least authorized, by the common consent of mankind. This species of inequality consists in the different privileges, which some men enjoy, to the prejudice of others, such as that of being richer, more honored, more powerful, and even that of exacting obedience from them."

Rousseau, Jean-Jacques, "A Discourse upon the origin and the Foundation of the Inequality Among Mankind," in *French and English Philosophers: Descartes, Rousseau, Voltaire, Hobbes,* New York, P. F. Collier & Son, 1910, pp. 167–170.

1. A Discourse Upon the Origin and the Foundation of the Inequality Among Mankind

Tis of man I am to speak; and the very question, in answer to which I am to speak of him, sufficiently informs me that I am going to speak to men; for to those alone, who are not afraid of honoring truth, it belongs to propose discussions of this kind. I shall therefore maintain with confidence the cause of mankind before the sages, who invite me to stand up in its defence; and I shall think myself happy, if I can but behave in a manner not unworthy of my subject and of my judges.

I conceive two species of inequality among men; one which I call natural, or physical inequality, because it is established by nature, and consists in the difference of age, health, bodily strength, and the qualities of the mind, or of the soul; the other which may be termed moral, or political inequality, because it depends on a kind of convention, and is established, or at least authorized, by the common consent of mankind. This species of inequality consists in the different privileges, which some men enjoy, to the prejudice of others, such as that of being richer, more honored, more powerful, and even that of exacting obedience from them.

It were absurd to ask, what is the cause of natural inequality, seeing the bare definition of natural inequality answers the question: it would be more absurd still to enquire, if there might not be some essential connection between the two species of inequality, as it would be asking, in other words, if those who command are necessarily better men than those who obey; and if strength of body or of mind, wisdom or virtue are always to be found in individuals, in the same proportion with power, or riches: a question, fit perhaps to be discussed by slaves in the hearing of their masters, but unbecoming free and reasonable beings in quest of truth.

What therefore is precisely the subject of this discourse? It is to point out, in the progress of things, that moment, when, right taking place of violence, nature became subject to law; to display that chain of surprising events, in consequence of which the strong submitted to serve the weak, and the people to purchase imaginary ease, at the expense of real happiness.

The philosophers, who have examined the foundations of society, have, every one of them, perceived the necessity of tracing it back to a state of nature, but not one of them has ever arrived there. Some of them have not scrupled to attribute to man in that state the ideas of justice and injustice, without troubling their heads to prove, that he really must have had such ideas, or even that such ideas were useful to him: others have spoken of the natural right of every man to keep what belongs to him, without letting us know what they meant by the word belong; others, without further ceremony ascribing to the strongest an authority over the weakest, have immediately struck out government, without thinking of the time requisite for men to form any notion of the things signified by the words authority and government. All of them, in fine, constantly harping on wants, avidity, oppression, desires and pride, have transferred to the state of nature ideas picked up in the bosom of society. In speaking of savages they described citizens. Nay, few of our own writers seem to have so much as doubted, that a state of nature did once actually exit; though it plainly appears by Sacred History, that even the first man, immediately furnished as he was by God himself with both instructions and precepts, never lived in that state, and that, if we give to the books of Moses that credit which every Christian philosopher ought to give to them, we must deny that, even before the deluge, such a state ever existed among men, unless they fell into it by some extraordinary event: a paradox very difficult to maintain, and altogether impossible to prove.

Let us begin therefore, by laying aside facts, for they do not affect the question. The researches, in which we may engage on this occasion, are not to be taken for historical truths, but merely as hypothetical and conditional reasonings, fitter to illustrate the nature of things, than to show their true origin, like those systems, which our naturalists daily make of the formation of the world. Religion commands us to believe, that men, having been drawn by God himself out of a state of nature, are unequal, because it is his pleasure they should be so; but religion does not forbid us to draw conjectures solely from the nature of man, considered in itself, and from that of the beings which surround him, concerning the fate of mankind, had they been left to themselves. This is then the question I am to answer, the question I propose to examine in the present discourse. As mankind in general have an interest in my subject, I shall endeavor to use a language suitable to all nations; or rather, forgetting the circumstances of time and place in order to think of nothing but the men I speak to, I shall suppose myself in the Lyceum of Athens, repeating the lessons of my masters before the Platos and the Xenocrates of that famous seat of philosophy as my judges, and in presence of the whole human species as my audience.

O man, whatever country you may belong to, whatever your opinions may be, attend to my words; you shall hear your history such as I think I have read it, not in books composed by those like you, for they are liars, but in the book of nature which never lies. All that I shall repeat after her, must be true, without any intermixture of falsehood, but where I may happen, without intending it, to introduce my own conceits. The times I am going to speak of are very remote. How much you are changed from what you once were! Tis in a manner the life of your species that I am going to write, from the qualities which you have received, and which your education and your habits could deprave, but could not destroy. There is, I am sensible, an age at which every individual of you would choose to stop; and you will look out for the age at which, had you your wish, your species had stopped. Uneasy at your present condition for reasons which threaten your unhappy posterity with still greater uneasiness, you will perhaps wish it were in your power to go back; and this sentiment ought to be considered, as the panegyric of your first parents, the condemnation of your contemporaries, and a source of terror to all those who may have the misfortune of succeeding you.

Chapter 12

Adam Smith

Adam Smith (1723–1790) was a Scottish moral philosopher, and the author of *The Theory of Moral Sentiments* (1759) and *The Wealth of Nations* (1776), the primary foundation of modern economic thought. Smith was a long time professor at the University of Glasgow teaching moral philosophy.

Smith studied at both the University of Glasgow and Oxford University. He concluded that the instruction at Glasgow was much better than at Oxford. His experience at Oxford was not a happy one and he left Oxford before the completion of his scholarship period. In more recent years, Oxford University has improved its educational process.

Among his major contributions to economic thought are:

a. Free markets result in efficient allocations of resources (the "invisible hand" of markets).
b. The importance of division of labor.

The extracts to follow illustrate both of these ideas.

In discussing the manufacturing of pins, Smith concludes:

> "Those ten persons, therefore, could make among them upwards of forty-eight thousand pins in a day. Each person, therefore, making a tenth part of forty-eight

thousand pins, might be considered as making four thousand eight hundred pins in a day. But if they had all wrought separately and independently, and without any of them having been educated to this peculiar business, they certainly could not each of them have made twenty, perhaps not one pin in a day; that is, certainly, not the two hundred and fortieth, perhaps not the four thousand eight hundredth part of what they are at present capable of performing, in consequence of a proper division and combination of their different operations."

On the subject of markets, he states:

"It is not from the benevolence of the butcher, the brewer, or the baker, that we expect our dinner, but from their regard to their own interest."

This is a classic observation.

Smith explains why it is necessary to have a "stock of assets" or accumulated savings:

"As the accumulation of stock is previously necessary for carrying on this great improvement in the productive powers of labor, so that accumulation naturally leads to this improvement. The person who employs his stock in maintaining labor, necessarily wishes to employ it in such a manner as to produce as great a quantity of work as possible. He endeavors, therefore, both to make among his workmen the most proper distribution of employment, and to furnish them with the best machines which he can either invent or afford to purchase."

Smith is a great admirer of the "invisible hand" of the marketplace.

"He generally, indeed, neither intends to promote the public interest, nor knows how much he is promoting it. By preferring the support of domestic to that of foreign industry, he intends only his own security; and by directing that industry in such a manner as its produce may be of the greatest value, he intends only his own gain, and he is in this, as in many other cases, led by an invisible hand to promote an end which was no part of his intention. Nor is it always the worse for the society that it was no part of it. By pursuing his own interest he frequently promotes that of the society more effectually than when he really intends to promote it. I have never known much good done by those who affected to trade for the public good. It is an affectation, indeed, not very common among merchants, and very few words need be employed in dissuading them from it."

Smith, Adam, *Wealth of Nations*, P.F. Collier & Son, New York, 1909, pp. 9–11, 19–23.

1. An Inquiry into the Nature and Causes of the Wealth of Nations Book I — of the Causes of Improvement in the Productive Power of Labor and of the Order According to Which its Produce is Naturally Distributed Among the Different Ranks of the People. Chapter I — Of the Division of Labor

The greatest improvement in the productive powers of labor, and the greater part of the skill, dexterity, and judgment with which it is any where directed, or applied, seem to have been the effects of the division of labor.

The effects of the division of labor, in the general business of society, will be more easily understood, by considering in what manner it operates in some particular manufactures. It is commonly supposed to be carried furthest in some very trifling ones; not perhaps that it really is carried further in them than in others of more importance: but in those trifling manufactures which are destined to supply the small wants of but a small number of people, the whole number of workmen must necessarily be small; and those employed in every different branch of the work can often be collected into the same workhouse, and placed at once under the view of the spectator.

In those great manufactures, on the contrary, which are destined to supply the great wants of the great body of the people, every different branch of the work employs so great a number of workmen, that it is impossible to collect them all into the same workhouse. We can seldom see more, at one time, than those employed in one single branch. Though in such manufactures, therefore, the work may really be divided into a much greater number of parts, than in those of a more trifling nature, the division is not near so obvious, and has accordingly been much less observed.

To take an example, therefore, from a very trifling manufacture; but one in which the division of labor has been very often taken notice of, the trade of the pinmaker; a workman not educated to this business (which the division of labor has rendered a distinct trade), nor acquainted with the use of the machinery employed in it (to the invention of which the same division of labor has probably given occasion), could scarce, perhaps, with his utmost industry, make one pin in a day, and certainly could not make twenty. But in the way in which this business is now carried on, not only the whole work is a peculiar trade, but it is divided into a number of branches, of which the greater part are likewise peculiar trades. One man draws out the wire, another straights it, a third cuts it, a fourth points it, a fifth grinds it at the top for receiving the head; to make the head requires two or three distinct operations; to put it on, is a peculiar business, to whiten the pins is another; it is even a trade by itself to put them into the paper; and the important business of making a pin is, in this manner, divided into about eighteen distinct operations, which, in some manufactories, are all performed by distinct hands, though in others the same man will sometimes perform two or three of them. I have seen a small manufactory of this kind where ten men only were employed, and where some of them consequently performed two or three distinct operations. But though they were very poor, and therefore but indifferently accommodated with the necessary machinery, they could, when they exerted themselves, make among them about twelve pounds of pins in a day. There are in a pound upwards of four thousand pins of a middling size. Those ten persons, therefore, could make among them upwards of forty-eight thousand pins in a day. Each person, therefore, making a tenth part of forty-eight thousand pins, might be considered as making four thousand eight hundred pins in a day. But if they had all wrought separately and independently, and without any of them having been educated to this peculiar business, they certainly could not each of them have made twenty, perhaps not one pin in a day; that is, certainly, not the two hundred and fortieth, perhaps not the four thousand eight hundredth part of what they are at present capable of performing, in consequence of a proper division and combination of their different operations.

2. Chapter II — Of the Principle Which Gives Occasion to the Division of Labor

This division of labor, from which so many advantages are derived, is not originally the effect of any human wisdom, which foresees and intends that general opulence to which it gives occasion. It is the necessary, though very slow and gradual, consequence of a certain propensity in human nature which has in view no such extensive utility; the propensity to truck, barter, and exchange one thing for another.

Whether this propensity be one of those original principles in human nature, of which no further account can be given; or whether, as seems more probable, it be the necessary consequence of the faculties of reason and speech, it belongs not to our present subject to enquire. It is common to all men, and to be found in no other race of animals, which seem to know neither this nor any other species of contracts. Two greyhounds, in running down the same hare, have sometimes the appearance of acting in some sort of concert. Each turns her towards his companion, or endeavors to intercept her when his companion turns her toward himself. This, however, is not the effect of any contract, but of the accidental concurrence of their passions in the same object at that particular time. Nobody ever saw a dog make a fair and deliberate exchange of one bone for another with another dog. Nobody ever saw one animal by its gestures and natural cries signify to another, this is mine, that yours; I am willing to give this for that. When an animal wants to obtain something either of a man or of another animal, it has no other means of persuasion but to gain the favor of those whose service it requires. A puppy fawns upon its dam, and a spaniel endeavors by a thousand attractions to engage the attention of its master who is at dinner, when it wants to be fed by him. Man sometimes uses the same arts with his brethren, and when he has no other means of engaging them to act according to his inclinations, endeavors by every servile and fawning attention to obtain their good will. He has not time, however, to do this upon every occasion. In civilized society he stands at all times in need of the co-operation and assistance of great multitudes, while his whole life is scarce sufficient to gain the friendship of a few persons. In almost every other race of animals each individual, when it is grown up to maturity, is entirely independent, and in its natural state has occasion for the assistance of no other living creature. But man has almost constant occasion for the help of his brethren, and it is in vain for him to expect it from their benevolence only. He will be more likely to prevail if he can interest their self-love in his favor, and show them that it is for their own advantage to do for him what he requires of them. Whoever offers to another a bargain of any kind, proposes to do this: Give me that which I want, and you shall have this which you want, is the meaning of every such offer; and it is in this manner that we obtain from one another the far greater part of those good offices which we stand in need of.

It is not from the benevolence of the butcher, the brewer, or the baker, that we expect our dinner, but from their regard to their own interest. We address ourselves, not to their humanity but to their self-love, and never talk to them of our own necessities but of their advantages. Nobody but a beggar chooses to depend chiefly upon the benevolence of his fellow-citizens. Even a beggar does not depend upon it entirely. The charity of well-disposed people, indeed, supplies him with the whole fund of his subsistence. But though this principle ultimately provides him with all the necessaries of life which he has occasion for, it neither does nor can provide him with them as he has occasion for them. The greater part of his occasional wants are supplied in the same manner as those of other people, by treaty, by barter, and by purchase. With the money which one man gives him he purchases food. The old clothes which another bestows upon him he exchanges for other old clothes which suit him better, or for lodging, or for food, or for money, with which he can buy either food, clothes, or lodging, as he has occasion.

As it is by treaty, by barter, and by purchase, that we obtain from one another the greater part of those mutual good offices which we stand in need of, so it is this same trucking disposition which originally gives occasion to the division of labor. In a tribe of hunters or shepherds a particular person makes bows and arrows, for example, with more readiness and dexterity than any other. He frequently exchanges them for cattle or for venison with his companions; and he finds at last that he can in this manner get more cattle and venison, than if he himself went to the field to catch them. From a regard to his own interest, therefore, the making of bows and arrows grows to be his chief business, and he becomes a sort of armorer. Another excels in making the frames and covers of their little huts or moveable houses. He is accustomed to be of use in this way to his neighbors, who reward him in the same manner with cattle and with venison, till at last he finds it his interest to dedicate himself entirely to this employment, and to become a sort of house-carpenter. In the same manner a third becomes a smith or a brazier; a fourth a tanner or dresser of hides or skins, the principal part of the clothing of savages. And thus the certainty of being able to exchange all that surplus part of the produce of his own labor, which is over and above his own consumption, for such parts of the produce of other men's labor as he may have occasion for, encourages every man to apply himself to a particular occupation and to cultivate and bring to perfection whatever talent or genius he may possess for that particular species of business.

The difference of natural talents in different men is, in reality, much less than we are aware of; and the very different genius which appears to distinguish men of different professions, when grown up to maturity, is not upon many occasions so much the cause, as the effect of the division of labor. The difference between the most dissimilar characters, between a philosopher and a common street porter, for example, seems to arise not so much from nature, as from habit, custom, and education. When they came into the world, and for the first six or eight years of their existence, they were, perhaps, very much alike, and neither their parents nor playfellows could perceive any remarkable difference. About that age, or soon after, they come to be employed in very different occupations. The difference of talents comes then to be taken notice of, and widens by degrees, till at last the vanity of the philosopher is willing to acknowledge scarce any resemblance. But without the disposition to truck, barter, and exchange, every man must have procured to himself every necessary and conveniency of life which he wanted. All must have had the same duties to perform, and the same work to do, and there could have been no such difference of employment as could alone give occasion to any great difference of talents.

As it is this disposition which forms that difference of talents, so remarkable among men of different professions, so it is this same disposition which renders that difference useful. Many tribes of animals acknowledged to be all of the same species, derive from nature a much more remarkable distinction of genius, than what, antecedent to custom and education, appears to take place among men. By nature a philosopher is not in genius and disposition half so different from a street porter, as a mastiff is from a greyhound, or a greyhound from a spaniel, or this last from a shepherd's dog. Those different tribes of animals, however, though all of the same species, are of scarce any use to one another. The strength of the mastiff is not in the least supported either by the swiftness of the greyhound, or by the sagacity of the spaniel, or by the docility of the shepherd's dog. The effects of those different geniuses and talents, for want of the power or disposition to barter and exchange, cannot be brought into a common stock, and do not in the least contribute to the better accommodation and conveniency of the species. Each animal is still obliged to support and defend itself, separately and independently, and derives no sort of advantage from that variety of talents with which nature has distinguished its fellows. Among men, on the contrary, the most dissimilar geniuses are of use to one another; the different produces of their respective talents, by the general disposition to truck, barter, and exchange, being brought, as it were, into a common stock, where every man may purchase whatever part of the produce of other men's talents he has occasion for.

3. Book II — Of the Nature, Accumulation, and Employment of Stock

3.1. *Introduction*

In that rude state of society in which there is no division of labor, in which exchanges are seldom made, and in which every man provides every thing for himself, it is not necessary that any stock should be accumulated or stored up beforehand, in order to carry on the business of the society. Every man endeavors to supply by his own industry his own occasional wants as they occur. When he is hungry, he goes to the forest to hunt; when his coat is worn out, he clothes himself with the skin of the first large animal he kills: and when his hut begins to go to ruin, he repairs it, as well as he can, with the trees and the turf that are nearest it.

But when the division of labor has once been thoroughly introduced, the produce of a man's own labor can supply but a very small part of his occasional wants. The far greater part of them are supplied by the produce of other men's labor, which he purchases with the produce, or, what is the same thing, with the price of the produce of his own. But this purchase cannot be made till such time as the produce of his own labor has not only been completed, but sold. A stock of goods of different kinds, therefore, must be stored up somewhere sufficient to maintain him, and to supply him with the materials and tools of his work, till such time, at least, as both these events can be brought about. A weaver cannot apply himself entirely to his peculiar business, unless there is beforehand stored up somewhere, either in his own possession or in that of some other person, a stock sufficient to maintain him, and to supply him with the materials and tools of his work, till he has not only completed but sold his web. This accumulation must, evidently, be previous to his applying his industry for so long a time to such a peculiar business.

As the accumulation of stock must, in the nature of things, be previous to the division of labor, so labor can be more and more subdivided in proportion only as stock is previously more and more accumulated. The quantity of materials which the same number of people can work up, increases in a great proportion as labor comes to be more and more subdivided; and as the operations of each workman are gradually reduced to a greater degree of simplicity, a variety of new machines come to be invented for facilitating and abridging those operations. As the division of labor advances, therefore, in order to give constant employment to an equal number of workmen, an equal stock of provisions, and a greater stock of materials and tools than what would have been necessary in a ruder state of things, must be accumulated beforehand. But the number of workmen in every branch of business generally increases with the division of labor in that branch, or rather it is the increase of their number which enables them to class and subdivide themselves in this manner.

As the accumulation of stock is previously necessary for carrying on this great improvement in the productive powers of labor, so that accumulation naturally leads to this improvement. The person who employs his stock in maintaining labor, necessarily wishes to employ it in such a manner as to produce as great a quantity of work as possible. He endeavors, therefore, both to make among his workmen the most proper distribution of employment, and to furnish them with the best machines which he can either invent or afford to purchase. His abilities in both these respects are generally in proportion to the extent of his stock, or to the number of people whom it can employ. The quantity of industry, therefore, not only increases in every country with the increase of the stock which employs it, but, in consequence of that increase, the same quantity of industry produces a much greater quantity of work.

Such are in general the effects of the increase of stock upon industry and its productive powers.

4. Chapter II — Of Restraints Upon the Importation from Foreign Countries of Such Goods as can be Produced at Home

By restraining, either by high duties, or by absolute prohibitions, the importation of such goods from foreign countries as can be produced at home, the monopoly of the home market is more or less secured to the domestic industry employed in producing them. Thus the prohibition of importing either live cattle or salt provisions from foreign countries secures to the graziers of Great Britain the monopoly of the home market for butcher's meat. The high duties upon the importation of corn, which in times of moderate plenty amount to a prohibition, give a like advantage to the growers of that commodity. The prohibition of the importation of foreign woolens is equally favorable to the woolen manufacturers. The silk manufacture, though altogether employed upon foreign materials, has lately obtained the same advantage. The linen manufacture has not yet obtained it, but is making great strides towards it. Many other sorts of manufacturers have, in the same manner, obtained in Great Britain, either altogether, or very nearly a monopoly against their countrymen. The variety of goods of which the importation into Great Britain is prohibited, either absolutely, or under certain circumstances, greatly exceeds what can easily be suspected by those who are not well acquainted with the laws of the customs.

That this monopoly of the home-market frequently gives great encouragement to that particular species of industry which enjoys it, and frequently turns towards that employment a greater share of both the labor and stock of the society than would otherwise have gone to it, cannot be doubted. But whether it tends either to increase the general industry of the society, or to give it the most advantageous direction, is not, perhaps, altogether so evident.

The general industry of the society never can exceed what the capital of the society can employ. As the number of workmen that can be kept in employment by any particular person must bear a certain proportion to his capital, so the number of those that can be continually employed by all the members of a great society, must bear a certain proportion to the whole capital of that society, and never can exceed that proportion. No regulation of commerce can increase the quantity of industry in any society beyond what its capital can maintain. It can only divert a part of it into a direction into which it might not otherwise have gone; and it is by no means certain that this artificial direction is likely to be more advantageous to the society than that into which it would have gone of its own accord.

Every individual is continually exerting himself to find out the most advantageous employment for whatever capital he can command. It is his own advantage, indeed, and not that of the society, which he has in view. But the study of his own advantage naturally, or rather necessarily leads him to prefer that employment which is most advantageous to the society.

First, every individual endeavors to employ his capital as near home as he can, and consequently as much as he can in the support of domestic industry; provided always that he can thereby obtain the ordinary, or not a great deal less than the ordinary profits of stock.

Thus, upon equal or nearly equal profits, every wholesale merchant naturally prefers the home-trade to the foreign trade of consumption, and the foreign trade of consumption to the carrying trade. In the home-trade his capital is never so long out of his sight as it frequently is in the foreign trade of consumption. He can know better the character and situation of the person whom he trusts, and if he should happen to be deceived, he knows better the laws of the country from which he must seek redress. In the carrying trade, the capital of the merchant is, as it were, divided between two foreign countries, and no part of it is ever necessarily brought home, or placed under his own immediate view and command. The capital which an Amsterdam merchant employs in carrying corn from Konnigsberg to Lisbon, and fruit and wine from Lisbon to Konnigsberg, must generally be the one-half of it at Konnigsberg and the other half at Lisbon. No part of it need ever come to Amsterdam. The natural residence of such a merchant should either be at Konnigsberg or Lisbon, and it can only be some very particular circumstances which can make him prefer the residence of Amsterdam. The uneasiness, however, which he feels at being separated so far from his capital, generally determines him to bring part both of the Konnigsberg goods which he destines for the market of Lisbon, and of the Lisbon goods which he destines for that of Konnigsberg, to Amsterdam; and though this necessarily subjects him to a double charge of loading and unloading, as well as to the payment of some duties and customs, yet for the sake of having some part of his capital always under his own view and command, he willingly submits to this extraordinary charge; and it is in this manner that every country which has any considerable share of the carrying trade, becomes always the emporium, or general market, for the goods of all the different countries whose trade it carries on. The merchant, in order to save a second loading and unloading, endeavors always to sell in the home-market as much of the goods of all those different countries as he can, and thus, so far as he can, to convert his carrying trade into a foreign trade of consumption. A merchant, in the same manner, who is engaged in the foreign trade of consumption, when he collects goods for foreign markets, will always be glad, upon equal or nearly equal profits, to sell as great a part of them at home as he can. He saves himself the risk and trouble of exportation, when, so far as he can, he thus converts his foreign trade of consumption into a home-trade. Home is in this manner the center, if I may say so, round which the capitals of the inhabitants of every country are continually circulating, and towards which they are always tending, though by particular causes they may sometimes be driven off and repelled from it towards more distant employments. But a capital employed in the home-trade, it has already been shown, necessarily puts into motion a greater quantity of domestic industry, and gives revenue and employment to a greater number of the inhabitants of the country, than an equal capital employed in the foreign trade of consumption: and one employed in the foreign trade of consumption has the same advantage over an equal capital employed in the carrying trade. Upon equal, or only nearly equal profits, therefore, every individual naturally inclines to employ his capital in the manner in which it is likely to afford the greatest support to domestic industry, and to give revenue and employment to the greatest number of people of his own country.

Secondly, every individual who employs his capital in the support of domestic industry, necessarily endeavors so to direct that industry, that its produce may be of the greatest possible value.

The produce of industry is what it adds to the subject or materials upon which it is employed. In proportion as the value of this produce is great or small, so will likewise be the profits of the employer. But it is only for the sake of profit that any man employs a capital in the support of industry; and he will always, therefore, endeavor to employ it in the support of that industry of which the produce is likely to be of the greatest value, or to exchange for the greatest quantity either of money or of other goods.

But the annual revenue of every society is always precisely equal to the exchangeable value of the whole annual produce of its industry, or rather is precisely the same thing with that exchangeable value. As every individual, therefore, endeavors as much as he can both to employ his capital in the support of domestic industry, and so to direct that industry that its produce may be of the greatest value; every individual necessarily labors to render the annual revenue of the society as great as he can. He generally, indeed, neither intends to promote the public interest, nor knows how much he is promoting it. By preferring the support of domestic to that of foreign industry, he intends only his own security; and by directing that industry in such a manner as its produce may be of the greatest value, he intends only his own gain, and he is in this, as in many other cases, led by an invisible hand to promote, an end which was no part of his intention. Nor is it always the worse for the society that it was no part of it. By pursuing his own interest he frequently promotes that of the society more effectually than when he really intends to promote it. I have never known much good done by those who affected to trade for the public good. It is an affectation, indeed, not very common among merchants, and very few words need be employed in dissuading them from it.

What is the species of domestic industry which his capital can employ, and of which the produce is likely to be of the greatest value, every individual, it is evident, can, in his local situation, judge much better than any statesman or lawgiver can do for him. The statesman, who should attempt to direct private people in what manner they ought to employ their capitals, would not only load himself with a most unnecessary attention, but assume an authority which could safely be trusted, not only to no single person, but to no council or senate whatever, and which would no-where be so dangerous as in the hands of a man who had folly and presumption enough to fancy himself fit to exercise it.

To give the monopoly of the home-market to the produce of domestic industry, in any particular art or manufacture, is in some measure to direct private people in what manner they ought to employ their capitals, and must, in almost all cases, be either a useless or a hurtful regulation. If the produce of domestic can be brought there as cheap as that of foreign industry, the regulation is evidently useless. If it cannot, it must generally be hurtful. It is the maxim of every prudent master of a family, never to attempt to make at home what it will cost him more to make than to buy. The taylor does not attempt to make his own shoes, but buys them of the shoemaker. The shoemaker does not attempt to make his own clothes, but employs a taylor. The farmer attempts to make neither the one nor the other, but employs those different artificers. All of them find it for their interest to employ their whole industry in a way in which they have some advantage over their neighbors, and to purchase with a part of its produce, or what is the same thing, with the price of a part of it, whatever else they have occasion for.

Chapter 13

George Washington

George Washington (1732–1799) is justifiably called "Father of His Country" and was the first President of the United States (1789–1797). He was also the first Commander of the Continental Army (1775–1783) and led it to victory.

A reading of Washington's farewell address (1797) offering advice for the future American leaders brings the greatness of the man to life. We have included some thoughtful excerpts. Consider the following where "they" refers to the words of Washington's address.

"But if I may even flatter myself that they may be productive of some partial benefit, some occasional good; that they may now and then recur to moderate the fury of party spirit; to warn against the mischiefs of foreign intrigue; to guard against the impostures of pretended patriotism; this hope will be a full recompense for the solicitude for your welfare by which they have been dictated."

At the height of his intellectual capabilities, Washington voluntarily gave up the most powerful position America had to offer. There is a lesson there for top managers and the leaders of countries.

Washington, George, "Farewell Address, Delivered in 1797," in G.M. Whitman, *American Orators and Oratory*, Fairbanks, Palmer & Co., Chicago, 1884, pp. 51, 57–59.

1. Farewell Address

Delivered in 1797.

Friends and Fellow-Citizens:

The period for a new election of a citizen to administer the executive government of the United States being not far distant, and the time having actually arrived when your thoughts must be employed in designating the person who is to be clothed with that important trust, it appears to me proper, especially as it may conduce to a more distinct expression of the public voice, that I should now apprise you of the resolution I have formed, to decline being considered among the number of those out of whom the choice is to be made.

It is substantially true that virtue or morality is a necessary spring of popular government. The rule, indeed, extends with more or less force to every species of free government. Who that is a sincere friend to it can look with indifference upon attempts to shake the foundation of the fabric?

Promote, then, as an object of primary importance, institutions for the general diffusion of knowledge. In proportion as the structure of a government gives force to public opinion, it is essential that public opinion should be enlightened.

As a very important source of strength and security, cherish public credit. One method of preserving it, is to use it as sparingly as possible, avoiding occasions of expense by cultivating peace, but remembering, also, that timely disbursements, to prepare for danger, frequently prevent much greater disbursements to repel it; avoiding likewise the accumulation of debt, not only by shunning occasions of expense, but by vigorous exertions, in time of peace, to discharge the debts which unavoidable wars have occasioned, not ungenerously throwing upon posterity the burdens which we ourselves ought to bear. The execution of these maxims belongs to your representatives; but it is necessary that public opinion should co-operate. To facilitate to them the performance of their duty, it is essential that you should practically bear in mind that, toward the payment of debts, there must be revenue; that, to have revenue, there must be taxes; that no taxes can be devised which are not more or less inconvenient and unpleasant; that the intrinsic embarrassment, inseparable from the selection of the proper objects (which is always a choice of difficulties), ought to be a decisive motive for a candid construction of the conduct of the government in making it, and for a spirit of acquiescence in the measures for obtaining revenue which the public exigencies may at any time dictate.

Observe good faith and justice toward all nations; cultivate peace and harmony with all; religion and morality enjoin this conduct; and can it be that good policy does not equally enjoin it? It will be worthy of a free, enlightened, and, at no distant period, a great nation, to give to mankind the magnanimous and too novel example of a people always guided by an exalted justice and benevolence. Who can doubt but that, in the course of time and things, the fruits of such a plan would richly repay any temporary advantages which might be lost by a steady adherence to it? Can it be that Providence has connected the permanent felicity of a nation with its virtue? The experiment, at least, is recommended by every sentiment which ennobles human nature. Alas! it is rendered impossible by its vices!

In the execution of such a plan, nothing is more essential than that permanent, inveterate antipathies against particular nations, and passionate attachment for others, should be excluded; and that, in the place of them, just and amicable feelings toward all should be cultivated. The nation which indulges toward another an habitual hatred, or an habitual fondness, is, in some degree, a slave. It is a slave to its animosity or to its affection, either of which is sufficient to lead it astray from its duty and its interest. Antipathy in one nation against another, disposes each more readily to offer insult and injury, to lay hold of slight causes of umbrage, and to be haughty and intractable when accidental or trifling occasions of dispute occur.

Europe has a set of primary interests, which, to us, have none, or a very remote relation. Hence, she must be engaged in frequent controversies, the causes of which are essentially foreign to our concerns. Hence, therefore, it must be unwise in us to implicate ourselves, by artificial ties, in the ordinary vicissitudes of her politics, or the ordinary combinations and collisions of her friendships or enmities.

Our detached and distant situation invites and enables us to pursue a different course. If we remain one people, under an efficient government, the period is not far off when we may defy material injury from external annoyance; when we may take such an attitude as will cause the neutrality we may at any time resolve upon, to be scrupulously respected; when belligerent nations, under the impossibility of making requisitions upon us, will not lightly hazard the giving us provocation; when we may choose peace or war, as our interest, guided by justice, shall counsel.

Why forego the advantages of so peculiar a situation? Why quit our own to stand upon foreign ground? Why, by interweaving our destiny with that of any part of Europe, entangle our peace and prosperity in the toils of European ambition, rivalship, interest, humor or caprice?

It is our true policy to steer clear of permanent alliances with any portion of the foreign world; so far, I mean, as we are now at liberty to do it; for let me not be understood as capable of patronizing infidelity to existing engagements. I hold the maxim no less applicable to public than to private affairs, that honesty is always the best policy. I repeat, therefore, let those engagements be observed in their genuine sense. But, in my opinion, it is unnecessary, and would be unwise to extend them.

Taking care always to keep ourselves, by suitable establishments, on a respectable defensive posture, we may safely trust to temporary alliances for extraordinary emergencies.

Harmony and a liberal intercourse with all nations, are recommended by policy, humanity, and interest. But even our commercial policy should hold an equal and impartial hand; neither seeking nor granting exclusive favors nor preferences; consulting the natural course of things; diffusing and diversifying by gentle means the stream of commerce, but forcing nothing; establishing, with powers so disposed, in order to give trade a stable course, to define the rights of our merchants, and to enable the government to support them, conventional rules of intercourse, the best that present circumstances and natural opinion will permit, but temporary, and liable to be, from time to time, abandoned or varied, as experience and circumstances shall dictate; constantly keeping in view that it is folly in one nation to look for disinterested favors from another; that it must pay, with a portion of its independence, for whatever it may accept under that character; that, by such acceptance, it may place itself in the condition of having given equivalents for nominal favors, and yet of being reproached with ingratitude for not giving more. There can be no greater error than to expect or calculate upon real favors from nation to nation. It is an illusion which experience must cure, which a just pride ought to discard.

In offering to you, my countrymen, these counsels of an old, affectionate friend, I dare not hope they will make the strong and lasting impression I could wish — that they will control the usual current of the passions, or prevent our nation from running the course which has hitherto marked the destiny of nations. But if I may even flatter myself that they may be productive of some partial benefit, some occasional good; that they may now and then recur to moderate the fury of party spirit; to warn against the mischiefs of foreign intrigue; to guard against the impostures of pretended patriotism; this hope will be a full recompense for the solicitude for your welfare by which they have been dictated.

Chapter 14

John Adams

John Adams was born in 1735 and died in 1826. For many years, he lived in Braintree, Massachusetts and in 1766 at the age of 31 he moved his family to Boston. He was one of the primary leaders in the struggle of the American colonies for independence and a practicing lawyer. He was the first Vice President and the second President of the United States. He worked with Thomas Jefferson to draft the Declaration of Independence (other members of the drafting committee were Benjamin Franklin, Roger Sherman, and Robert R. Livingston). As a member of the Continental Congress, he was the leading spokesman for Independence for the thirteen colonies.

As a young lawyer of 35 years, he defended eight British soldiers involved in the Boston Massacre of 1770. Thanks to his efforts, six of the soldiers were acquitted and two were convicted of manslaughter (they had been charged with murder). He accepted the assignment to defend the British soldiers even though he knew he was taking a very unpopular position. The task was not going to be desirable either economically or politically, but he did the job and did it well. It was the right thing to do.

His speech "Independence" was not a great speech but it made clear Adams' desire for the independence of the American colonies and the creation of a new free country. His arguments are strong and logical. He first appealed to the emotions of his listeners. “The injustice of England has driven us to arms…” He then invoked loyalty to Washington: “may my right hand forget her cunning and my tongue cleave to the roof of my mouth if I hesitate or waiver in the support I give him.” He closes with: “independence now; and independence forever!” Adams was dedicated to the causes of freedom and liberty and offered his life to those causes.

Adams, John. “Independence,” in G.M. Whitman, *American Orators and Oratory*, Fairbanks, Palmer & Co., Chicago, 1884, pp. 27–28.

1. Independence

Mr. Adams' Speech Favoring the Declaration of Independence, delivered in 1776.

Mr. President, Sink or swim, live or die, survive or perish, I give my hand and my heart to this vote. It is true, indeed, that in the beginning we aimed not at independence. But there's a divinity which shapes our ends. The injustice of England has driven us to arms, and, blinded to her own interest for our good, she has obstinately persisted, till independence is now within our grasp. We have but to reach forth to it, and it is ours.

Why then, should we defer the declaration? Is any man so weak as now to hope for a reconciliation with England, which shall leave either safety to the country and its liberties, or safety to his own life and his own honor? Are not you, sir, who sit in that chair, is not he, our venerable colleague near you, are you not both already the proscribed and predestined objects of punishment and of vengeance? Cut off from all hope of royal clemency, what are you, what can you be, while the power of England remains, but outlaws?

If we postpone independence, do we mean to carry on, or to give up the war? Do we mean to submit to the measures of Parliament, Boston port bill, and all? Do we mean to submit, and consent that we ourselves shall be ground to powder, and our country and its rights trodden down in the dust? I know we do not mean to submit. We never shall submit.

Do we intend to violate that most solemn obligation ever entered into by men — that plighting, before God, of our sacred honor to Washington, when, putting him forth to incur the dangers of war, as well as the political hazards of the times, we promised to adhere to him, in every extremity, with our fortunes and our lives? I know there is not a man here who would not rather see a general conflagration sweep over the land, or an earthquake sink it, than one jot or tittle of that plighted faith fall to the ground.

For myself, having, twelve months ago, in this place, moved you that George Washington be appointed commander of the forces, raised or to be raised, for defense of American liberty, may my right hand forget her cunning, and my tongue cleave to the roof of my mouth, if I hesitate or waver in the support I give him. The war, then, must go on. We must fight it through. And if the war must go on, why put off longer the Declaration of Independence? That measure will strengthen us. It will give us character abroad.

The nations will then treat with us, which they never can do while we acknowledge ourselves subjects, in arms against our sovereign. Nay, I maintain that England herself will sooner treat for peace with us on the footing of independence, than consent, by repealing her acts, to acknowledge that her whole conduct toward us has been a course of injustice and oppression. Her pride will be less wounded by submitting to that course of things which now predestinates our independence, than by yielding the points in controversy to her rebellious subjects. The former she would regard as the result of fortune; the latter she would feel as her own deep disgrace. Why, then — why, then sir, do we not, as soon as possible, change this from a civil to a national war? And since we must fight it through, why not put ourselves in a state to enjoy all the benefits of victory, if we gain the victory?

If we fail, *it* can be no worse for us. But we shall not fail. The cause will raise up armies; the cause will create navies. The people, the people, if we are true to them, will carry us, and will carry themselves, gloriously through this struggle. I care not how fickle other people have been found. I know the people of these colonies, and I know that resistance to British aggression is deep and settled in their hearts, and cannot be eradicated. Every colony, indeed, has expressed its willingness to follow, if we but take the lead. Sir, the Declaration will inspire the people with increased courage. Instead of a long and bloody war for restoration of privileges, for redress of grievances, for chartered immunities, held under a British king, set before them the glorious object of entire independence, and it will breathe into them anew the breath of life.

Read this Declaration at the head of the army; every sword will be drawn from its scabbard, and the solemn vow uttered to maintain it, or to perish on the bed of honor. Publish it from the pulpit; religion will approve it, and the love of religious liberty will cling round it, resolved to stand with it, or fall with it. Send it to the public halls; proclaim it there; let them hear it who heard the first roar of the enemy's cannon; let them see it who saw their brothers and their sons fall on the field of Bunker Hill, and in the streets of Lexington and Concord, and the very walls will cry out in its support.

Sir, I know the uncertainty of human affairs, but I see, I see clearly through this day's business. You and I, indeed, may rue it. We may not live to the time when this declaration shall be made good. We may die; die, colonists; die, slaves; die, it may be, ignominiously, and on the scaffold. Be it so. Be it so. If it be the pleasure of Heaven that my country shall require the poor offering of my life, the victim shall be ready, at the appointed hour of sacrifice, come when that hour may. But while I do live, let me have a country, or at least the hope of a country, and that a free country.

But whatever may be our fate, be assured, be assured that this declaration will stand. It may cost treasure, and it may cost blood; but it will stand, and it will richly compensate for both. Through the thick gloom of the present, I see the brightness of the future, as the sun in heaven. We shall make this a glorious, an immortal day. When we are in our graves, our children will honor it. They will celebrate it with thanksgiving, with festivity, with bonfires and illuminations. On its annual return, they will shed tears, copious, gushing tears, not of subjection and slavery, not of agony and distress, but of exultation, of gratitude, and of joy.

Sir, before God, I believe the hour is come. My judgment approves this measure, and my whole heart is in it.

All that I have, and all that I am, and all that I hope, in this life, I am now ready here to stake upon it; and I leave off as I begun, that, live or die, survive or perish, I am for the Declaration. It is my living sentiment, and by the blessing of God, it shall be my dying sentiment; independence *now*; and independence forever!

Chapter 15

Patrick Henry

Patrick Henry (1736–1799) was the first and sixth Governor of Virginia (in office 1776–1779 and 1784–1786). He is best known for the speech given March 23, 1776 in the House of Burgesses, Richmond, Virginia. The speech ended with "Give me Liberty or give me Death."

Patrick Henry had six children with his first wife and 11 children with his second wife. He voted against ratification of the U.S. Constitution in 1788 as a representative to the Virginia Convention. He was an anti-Federalist. But by the late 1790s, seeing the radicalism of the French Revolution, Henry shifted and supported the Federal system.

Henry, Patrick, "An Appeal to Arms" and "Give Me Liberty, or Give Me Death," in *The Patriotic Anthology,* introduced by Carl Van Doren, New York, Literary Guild of America, Inc., 1941, pp. 82–85.

1. An Appeal to Arms

Mr. President, this is no time for ceremony. The question before the house is one of awful moment to this country. For my own part, I consider it as nothing less than a question of freedom or slavery.

And in proportion to the magnitude of the subject ought to be the freedom of the debate.

It is only in this way that we can hope to arrive at truth, and fulfil the great responsibility which we hold to God and our country.

Should I keep back my opinions at this time, through fear of giving offence, I should consider myself as guilty of treason towards my country, and of an act of disloyalty towards the majesty of Heaven, which I revere above all earthly kings.

Mr. President, it is natural to man to indulge in the illusions of Hope. We are apt to shut our eyes against a painful truth and listen to the song of that siren, till she transforms us into beasts.

Is this the part of wise men engaged in a great and arduous struggle for liberty? Are we disposed to be of the numbers of those, who having eyes, see not, and having ears, hear not, the things which so nearly concern their temporal salvation? For my part, whatever anguish of spirit it may cost, I am willing to know the whole truth; to know the worst and to provide for it!

I have but one lamp by which my feet are guided; and that is the lamp of experience. I know of no way of judging of the future but by the past. And judging by the past, I wish to know what there has been in the conduct of the British ministry, for the last ten years, to justify those hopes with which gentlemen have been pleased to solace themselves and the House? Is it that insidious smile with which our petition has 'been lately received? Trust it not, Sir; it will prove a snare to your feet!

Suffer not yourselves to be betrayed by a kiss!

Ask yourselves how this gracious reception of our petition comports with those warlike preparations which cover our waters, and darken our land.

Are fleets and armies necessary to a work of love and reconciliation? Have we shown ourselves so unwilling to be reconciled, that force must be called in to win back our love? Let us not deceive ourselves, Sir.

These are the implements of war and subjugation — the last arguments to which Kings resort.

I ask, Sir, what means this martial array, if its purpose be not to force us to submission?

Can gentlemen assign any other possible motive for it? Has Great Britain any enemy in this quarter of the world, to call for all this accumulation of navies and armies? No, Sir, she has none. They are meant for us; they can be meant for no other. They are sent over to bind and rivet upon us those chains which the British ministry have been so long forging.

And what have we to oppose to them? Shall we try argument? Sir, we have been trying that for the last ten years. Have we, anything new to offer upon the subject? Nothing. We have held the subject in every light of which it is capable; but it has been all in vain. Shall we resort to entreaty and humble supplication? What terms shall we find, which have not been already exhausted? Let us not, I beseech you, Sir, deceive ourselves longer.

Sir, we have done everything that could be done, to avert the storm that is now coming on. We have petitioned, we have remonstrated, we have supplicated, we have prostrated ourselves before the Throne, and have implored its interposition to arrest the tyrannical hands of the Ministry and Parliament.

Our petitions have been slighted; our remonstrances have produced additional violence, and insult; our supplications have been disregarded; and we have been spurned with contempt, from the foot of the Throne.

In vain, after these things may we indulge the fond hope of peace and reconciliation.

There is no longer any room for hope.

If we wish to be free, if we mean to preserve inviolable those inestimable privileges for which we have been so long contending, if we mean not basely to abandon the noble struggle in which we have been so long engaged, and which we have pledged ourselves never to abandon until the glorious object of our contest shall be obtained, we must fight; I repeat it, Sir, we must fight! An appeal to arms, and to the God of Hosts, is all that is left us!

2. Give Me Liberty, or Give Me Death

They tell us, Sir, that we are weak, unable to cope with so formidable an adversary. But when shall we be stronger? Will it be the next week, or the next year? Will it be when we are totally disarmed, and when a British guard shall be stationed in every house? Shall we gather strength by irresolution and inaction? Shall we acquire the means of effectual resistance by lying supinely on our backs, and hugging the delusive phantom of hope, until our enemies shall have bound us hand and foot? Sir, we are not weak, if we make a proper use of those means which the God of nature hath placed in our power.

Three millions of People, armed in the holy cause of liberty, and in such a country as that which we possess, are invincible by any force which our enemy can send against us. Besides, Sir, we shall not fight our battles alone. There is a just God who presides over the destinies of Nations, and who will raise up friends to fight our battles for us. The battle, Sir, is not to the strong alone, it is to the vigilant, the active, the brave. Besides, Sir, we have no election. If we were base enough to desire it, it is now too late to retire from the contest. There is no retreat but in submission and slavery! Our chains are forged! Their clanking may be heard on the plains of Boston! The war is inevitable; and let it come! I repeat, sir, let it come!

It is in vain, Sir, to extenuate the matter. Gentlemen may cry, peace, peace! But there is no peace. The war is actually begun! The next gale that sweeps from the North will, bring to our ears the clash of resounding arms! Our brethren are already in the field! Why stand we here idle? What is it that Gentlemen wish? What would they have? Is life so dear, or peace so sweet, as to be purchased at the price of chains and slavery? Forbid it, Almighty God! I know not what course others may take, but as for me, give me liberty, or give me death!

Chapter 16

Thomas Jefferson

Thomas Jefferson (1743–1826) was the third President of the United States (1801–1809) and the second Vice President, and first Secretary of State. He was the principal author of the Declaration of Independence.

Jefferson had many talents (scientist, statesman, founder of the University of Virginia, etc.). But as a person who could express the ideals of a new country he was without peer.

Consider Jefferson's Inaugural Address (1801):

> "All, too, will bear in mind this sacred principle, that, though the will of the majority is in all cases to prevail, that will, to be rightful, must be reasonable; that the minority possess their equal rights, which equal law must protect, and to violate would be oppression."

How many countries would do well to adopt this thought as a guideline for their actions?

Jefferson then defines the function of government:

> "Still one thing more, fellow citizens: a wise and frugal government, which shall restrain men from injuring one another, shall leave them otherwise free to regulate their own pursuits of industry and improvement, and shall not take from the mouth of labor the bread it has

earned. This is the sum of good government, and this is necessary to close the circle of our felicities."

As Jefferson defines the relationship of the government and the country's citizens, so must the leaders of industry define the relationship of a corporate enterprise and its workers. See the chapters on Brandeis, Carnegie, Douglas, and Young.

Jefferson, Thomas, "Inaugural Address," in G.M. Whitman, *American Orators and Oratory*, Fairbanks, Palmer & Co., Chicago, 1884, pp. 65–67.

1. Inaugural Address

Delivered in 1801.

Friends and fellow citizens: Called to undertake the duties of the first executive office of *our* country, I avail myself of the presence of that portion of my fellow-citizens which is here assembled, to express my grateful thanks for the favor with which they have been pleased to look toward me, to declare a sincere consciousness that the task is above my talents, and that I approach it with those anxious and awful presentiments, which the greatness of the charge, and the weakness of my powers, so justly inspire.

During the contest of opinion through which we have passed, the animation of discussion and of exertions has sometimes worn an aspect which might impose on strangers unused to think freely, and to speak and to write what they think; but this being now decided by the voice of the nation, announced according to the rules of the Constitution, all will of course arrange themselves under the will of the law, and unite in common efforts for the common good. All, too, will bear in mind this sacred principle, that, though the will of the majority is in all cases to prevail, that will, to be rightful, must be reasonable; that the minority possess their equal rights, which equal law must protect, and to violate would be oppression. Let us then, fellow-citizens, unite with one heart and one mind, let us restore to social intercourse that harmony and affection, without which liberty, and even life itself, are but dreary things. And let us reflect, that, having banished from our land that religious intolerance under which mankind so long bled and suffered, we have yet gained little, if we countenance a political intolerance as despotic, as wicked, and capable of as bitter and bloody persecutions. During the throes and convulsions of the ancient world, during the agonizing spasms of infuriated man, seeking through blood and slaughter his long-lost liberty, it was not wonderful that the agitation of the billows should reach even this distant and peaceful shore; that this should be more felt and feared by some, and less by others; that this should divide opinions as to measures of safety; but every difference of opinion is not a difference of principle. We have called by different names brethren of the same principle. We are all Republicans; we are all Federalists. If there be any among us who would wish to dissolve this Union, or to change its republican form, let them stand undisturbed as monuments of the safety with which error of opinion may be tolerated, where reason is left free to combat it. I know indeed, that some honest men fear that a republican government cannot be strong; that this government is not strong enough. But would the honest patriot, in the full tide of successful experiment, abandon a government which has so far kept us free and firm, on the theoretic and visionary fear that this government, the world's best hope, may, by possibility, want energy to preserve itself? I trust not. I believe this, on the contrary, the strongest government on earth. I believe it the only one where every man, at the call of the laws, would fly to the standard of the law, and would meet invasions of the public order as his own personal concern. Sometimes it is said that man cannot be trusted with the government of himself. Can he then be trusted with the government of others; or have we found angels in the forms of kings to govern him? Let history answer this question.

Still one thing more, fellow-citizens: a wise and frugal government, which shall restrain men from injuring one another, shall leave them otherwise free to regulate their own pursuits of industry and improvement, and shall not take from the mouth of labor the bread it has earned. This is the sum of good government, and this is necessary to close the circle of our felicities.

About to enter, fellow-citizens, on the exercise of duties which comprehend everything dear and valuable to you, it is proper that you should understand what I deem the essential principles of our government, and consequently those which ought to shape its administration. I will compress them within the narrowest compass they will bear, stating the general principles, but not all its limitations. Equal and exact justice to all men, of whatever State or persuasion, religious or political; peace, commerce, and honest friendship with all nations, entangling alliances with none; the support of the State governments in all their rights, as the most competent administrations for our domestic concerns, and the surest bulwarks against anti-Republican tendencies; the preservation of the general government in its whole constitutional vigor, as the sheet anchor of our peace at home and safety abroad; a jealous care of the right of election by the people; a mild and safe corrective of abuses, which are lopped by the sword of revolution, where peaceable remedies are unprovided; absolute acquiescence in the decisions of the majority, the vital principle of republics, from which is no appeal but to force, the vital principle and immediate parent of despotism; a well-disciplined militia, our best reliance in peace, and for the first moments of war, till regulars may relieve them; the supremacy of the civil over the military authority; economy in the public expense, that labor may be lightly burdened; the honest payment of our debts, and sacred preservation of the public faith; encouragement of agriculture, and of commerce as its handmaid; the diffusion of information, and arraignment of all abuses at the bar of public reason; freedom of religion; freedom of the press; and freedom of person, under the protection of the habeas corpus; and trial by juries, impartially selected. These principles form the bright constellation which has gone before us, and guided our steps through an age of revolution and reformation. The wisdom of our sages and blood of our heroes have been devoted to their attainment; they should be the creed of our political faith; the text of civil instruction; the touchstone by which to try the services of those we trust; and should we wander from them, in moments of error or alarm, let us hasten to retrace our steps, and to regain the road which alone leads to peace, liberty, and safety.

Chapter 17

Thomas Paine

Thomas Paine (1737–1809) was born in England and came to the British American colonies in 1774. His pamphlet, *Common Sense*, was published and distributed in 1776. It advocated that the colonies declare independence from the Kingdom of Great Britain.

Paine was an author, inventor, and one of the Founding Fathers of the United States because of his writings, especially *Common Sense* and *The American Crisis* (1776–1783).

Paine, Thomas, "These are the Times That Try Men's Souls," in *The Patriotic Anthology,* introduced by Carl Van Doren, New York, Literary Guild of America, Inc., 1941, pp. 71–73.

1. These are the Times That Try Men's Souls

These are the times that try men's souls. The summer soldier and the sunshine patriot will, in this crisis, shrink from the service of their country, but he that stands it *now* deserves the love and thanks of man and woman. Tyranny, like hell, is not easily conquered, yet we have this consolation with us, that the harder the conflict, the more glorious the triumph. What we obtain too cheap, we esteem too lightly; it is dearness only that gives everything its value. Heaven knows how to put a proper price upon its goods, and it would be strange indeed, if so celestial an article as freedom should not be highly rated. Britain, with an army to enforce her tyranny, has declared that she has a right (*not only to* ***tax***) but "to ***bind*** *us in* ***all cases whatsoever***," and if being *bound in that manner*, is not slavery, then is there not such a thing as slavery upon earth. Even the expression is impious; for so unlimited a power can belong only to God.

Whether the independence of the continent was declared too soon, or delayed too long, I will not now enter into as an argument; my own simple opinion is, that had it been eight months earlier, it would have been much better. We did not make a proper use of last winter, neither could we, while we were in a dependent state. However, the fault, if it were one, was all our own; we have none to blame but ourselves. But no great deal is lost yet. All that Howe has been doing for this month past, is rather a ravage than a conquest, which the spirit of the Jerseys, a year ago, would have quickly repulsed, and which time and a little resolution will soon recover.

I have as little superstition in me as any man living, but my secret opinion has ever been, and still is, that God Almighty will not give up a people to military destruction, or leave them unsupportedly to perish, who have so earnestly and so repeatedly sought to avoid the calamities of war, by every decent method which wisdom could invent. Neither have I so much of the infidel in me, as to suppose that He has relinquished the government of the world, and given us up to the care of devils; and as I do not, I cannot see on what grounds the king of Britain can look up to heaven for help against us: a common murderer, a highwayman, or a housebreaker, has as good a pretence as he.

The times that tried men's souls are over and the greatest and completest revolution the world ever knew, gloriously and happily accomplished.

But to pass from the extremes of danger to safety; from the tumult of war to the tranquility of peace, though sweet in contemplation, requires a gradual composure of the senses to receive it. Even calmness has the power of stunning, when it opens too instantly upon us. The long and raging hurricane that should cease in a moment, would leave us in a state rather of wonder than enjoyment; and some moments of recollection must pass, before we could be capable of tasting the felicity of repose. There are but few instances, in which the mind is fitted for sudden transitions: it takes in its pleasures by reflection and comparison and those must have time to act, before the relish for new scenes is complete.

In the present case, the mighty magnitude of the object, the various uncertainties of fate it has undergone, the numerous and complicated dangers we have suffered or escaped, the eminence we now stand on, and the vast prospect before us, must all conspire to impress us with contemplation.

To see it in our power to make a world happy, to teach mankind the art of being so, to exhibit, on the theater of the universe a character hitherto unknown, and to have, as it were, a new creation intrusted to our hands, are honours that command reflection, and can neither be too highly estimated, nor too gratefully received.

In this pause then of recollection, while the storm is ceasing, and the long agitated mind vibrating to a rest, let us look back on the scenes we have passed, and learn from experience what is yet to be done.

Never, I say, had a country so many openings to happiness as this. Her setting out in life, like the rising of a fair morning, was unclouded and promising. Her cause was good. Her principles just and liberal. Her temper serene and firm. Her conduct regulated by the nicest steps, and everything about her wore the mark of honor. It is not every country (perhaps there is not another in the world) that can boast so fair an origin. Even the first settlement of America corresponds with the character of the revolution. Rome, once the proud mistress of the universe, was originally a band of ruffians. Plunder and rapine made her rich, and her oppression of millions made her great. But America need never be ashamed to tell her birth, nor relate the stages by which she rose to empire.

Chapter 18

Ralph Waldo Emerson

Ralph Waldo Emerson (1803–1882) was an American (New England) writer and poet famous for his essays. He was an important orator of his time period and today readers find his essays to be thought provoking.

It is fun to read Emerson's essays and pick out a favorite sentence or two or three.

Emerson's writings are full of stimulating thoughts and pungent quotes. This essay, "Self-Reliance," starts: "To believe your own thought..." and ends with the famous "A foolish consistency is the hobgoblin of little minds, adored by little statesmen." In between, is much to be learned.

Emerson tells us to have more faith in our individuality. He rejects conformity. "Do your own thing" is consistent with Emerson's advice, but he goes on: "A man is relieved and gay when he has put his heart into his work and done his best."

One generalization is the need for flexibility. Do not be a slave to past thoughts, yours or someone else's.

The message of Emerson's essay, "Compensation," is clear. Justice is done now. We cannot escape the immediate consequences of our actions. There are two sides to all actions (dualism). Do you believe it? Think about it. Accountants practice it.

"The dice of God are always loaded."

Emerson, Ralph Waldo. "Self-Reliance," and "Compensation," and "Power" in *Essays*, by Ralph Waldo Emerson, New York, P.F. Collier & Son, 1903, Vol. 7, pp. 27–29, 30–35, 58–64, Vol. 9, pp. 47–48, 50–52.

1. Self-Reliance

I read the other day some verses written by an eminent painter which were original and not conventional. Always the soul hears an admonition in such lines, let the subject be what it may. The sentiment they instill is of more value than any thought they may contain. To believe your own thought, to believe that what is true for you in your private heart, is true for all men, that is genius. Speak your latent conviction and it shall be the universal sense; for always the inmost becomes the outmost, and our first thought is rendered back to us by the trumpets of the Last Judgment. Familiar as the voice of the mind is to each, the highest merit we ascribe to Moses, Plato, and Milton, is that they set at naught books and traditions, and spoke not what men, but what they, thought. A man should learn to detect and watch that gleam of light which flashes across his mind from within, more than the luster of the firmament of bards and sages. Yet he dismisses without notice his thought, because it is his. In every work of genius we recognize our own rejected thoughts: they come back to us with a certain alienated majesty. Great works of art have no more affecting lesson for us than this. They teach us to abide by our spontaneous impression with good humored inflexibility than most when the whole cry of voices is on the other side. Else, tomorrow a stranger will say with masterly good sense precisely what we have thought and felt all the time, and we shall be forced to take with shame our own opinion from another.

There is a time in every man's education when he arrives at the conviction that envy is ignorance; that imitation is suicide; that he must take himself for better, for worse, as his portion; that though the wide universe is full of good, no kernel of nourishing corn can come to him but through his toil bestowed on that plot of ground which is given to him to till. The power which resides in him is new in nature, and none but he knows what that is which he can do, nor does he know until he has tried. Not for nothing one face, one character, one fact makes much impression on him, and another none. It is not without pre-established harmony, this sculpture in the memory. The eye was placed where one ray should fall, that it might testify of that particular ray. Bravely let him speak the utmost syllable of his confession. We but half express ourselves, and are ashamed of that divine idea which each of us represents. It may be safely trusted as proportionate and of good issues, so it be faithfully imparted, but God will not have his work made manifest by cowards. It needs a divine man to exhibit anything divine. A man is relieved and gay when he has put his heart into his work and done his best; but what he has said or done otherwise, shall give him no peace. It is a deliverance which does not deliver. In the attempt his genius deserts him; no muse befriends; no invention, no hope...

The objection to conforming to usages that have become dead to you, is that it scatters your force. It loses your time and blurs the impression of your character. If you maintain a dead church, contribute to a dead Bible society, vote with a great party either for the Government or against it, spread your table like base housekeepers — under all these screens I have difficulty to detect the precise man you are. And, of course, so much force is withdrawn from your proper life. But do your thing, and I shall know you. Do your work, and you shall reinforce yourself. A man must consider what a blind-man's-buff is this game of conformity. If I know your sect, I anticipate your argument. I hear a preacher announce for his text and topic the expediency of one of the institutions of his church. Do I not know beforehand that not possibly can he, say a new and spontaneous word? Do I not know that with all this ostentation of examining the grounds of the institution, he will do no such thing? Do I not know that he is pledged to himself not to look but at one side; the permitted side, not as a man, but as a parish minister? He is a retained attorney, and these airs of the bench are the emptiest affectation. Well, most men have bound their eyes with one or another handkerchief, and attached themselves to some one of these communities of opinion. This conformity makes them not false in a few particulars, authors of a few lies, but false in all particulars. Their every truth is not quite true. Their two is not the real two, their four not the real four; so that every word they say chagrins us, and we know not where to begin to set them right. Meantime nature is not slow to equip us in the prison uniform of the party to which we adhere. We come to wear one cut of face and figure, and acquire by degrees the gentlest asinine expression. There is a mortifying experience in particular which does not fail to wreck itself also in the general history; I mean, "the foolish face of praise," the forced smile which we put on in company where we do not feel at ease in answer to conversation which does not interest us. The muscles, not spontaneously moved, but moved by a low usurping willfulness, grow tight about the outline of the face and make the most disagreeable sensation, a sensation of rebuke and warning which no brave young man will suffer twice.

For non-conformity the world whips you with its displeasure. And therefore a man must know how to estimate a sour face. The bystanders look askance on him in the public street or in the friend's parlor. If this aversation had its origin in contempt and resistance like his own, he might well go home with a sad countenance; but the sour faces of the multitude, like their sweet faces, have no deep cause, disguise no god, but are put on and off as the wind blows, and a newspaper directs. Yet is the discontent of the multitude more formidable than that of the senate and the college. It is easy enough for a firm man who knows the world to brook the rage of the cultivated classes. Their rage is decorous and prudent, for they are timid as being very vulnerable themselves. But when to their feminine rage the indignation of the people is added, when the ignorant and the poor are aroused, when the unintelligent brute force that lies at the bottom of society is made to growl and mow, it needs the habit of magnanimity and religion to treat it godlike as a trifle of no concernment.

The other terror that scares us from self-trust is our consistency; a reverence for our past act or word, because the eyes of others have no other data for computing our orbit than our past acts, and we are loath to disappoint them.

But why should you keep your head over your shoulder? Why drag about this monstrous corpse of your memory, lest you contradict somewhat you have stated in this or that public place? Suppose you should contradict yourself;

what then? It seems to be a rule of wisdom never to rely on your memory alone, scarcely even in acts of pure memory, but bring the past for judgment into the thousand-eyed present, and live ever in a new day. Trust your emotion. In your metaphysics you have denied personality to the Deity; yet when the devout motions of the soul come, yield to them heart and life, though they should clothe God with shape and color. Leave your theory as Joseph his coat in the hand of the harlot, and flee.

A foolish consistency is the hobgoblin of little minds, adored by little statesmen and philosophers and divines. With consistency a great soul has simply nothing to do.

2. Compensation

Ever since I was a boy, I have wished to write a discourse on Compensation: for, it seemed to me when very young, that, on this subject, life was ahead of theology, and the people knew more than the preachers taught. The documents too, from which the doctrine is to be drawn, charmed my fancy by their endless variety, and lay always before me, even in sleep; for they are the tools in our hands, the bread in our basket, the transactions of the street, the farm, and the dwelling-house, the greetings, the relations, the debts and credits, the influence of character, the nature and endowment of all men. It seemed to me also that in it might be shown men a ray of divinity, the present action of the Soul of this world, clean from all vestige of tradition, and so the heart of man might be bathed by an inundation of eternal love, conversing with that which he knows was always and always must be, because it really is now. It appeared, moreover, that if this doctrine could be stated in terms with any resemblance to those bright intuitions in which this truth is sometimes revealed to us, it would be a star in many dark hours and crooked passages in our journey that would not suffer us to lose our way.

I was lately confirmed in these desires by hearing a sermon at church. The preacher, a man esteemed for his orthodoxy, unfolded in the ordinary manner the doctrine of the Last Judgment. He assumed that judgment is not executed in this world; that the wicked are successful; that the good are miserable; and then urged from reason and from Scripture a compensation to be made to both parties in the next life. No offense appeared to be taken by the congregation at this doctrine. As far as I could observe, when the meeting broke up, they separated without remark on the sermon.

Yet what was the import of this teaching? What did the preacher mean by saying that the good are miserable in the present life? Was it that houses and lands, offices, wine, horses, dress, luxury, are had by unprincipled men, while the saints are poor and despised; and that a compensation is to be made to these last hereafter, by giving them the like gratifications another day, bank-stock and doubloons, venison and champagne? This must be the compensation intended; for, what else? Is it that they are to have leave to pray and praise, to love and serve men? Why, that they can do now. The legitimate inference the disciple would draw, was: "We are to have *such* a good time as the sinners have now;" or, to push it to its extreme import, "You sin now; we shall sin by-and-by; we would sin now, if we could; not being successful, we expect our revenge tomorrow."

The fallacy lay in the immense concession that the bad are successful; that justice is not done now. The blindness of the preacher consisted in deferring to the base estimate of the market of what constitutes a manly success, instead of confronting and convicting the world from the truth; announcing the presence of the Soul; the omnipotence of the Will: and so establishing the standard of good and ill, of success and falsehood, and summoning the dead to its present tribunal.

The same dualism underlies the nature and conditions of man. Every excess causes a defect; every defect an excess. Every sweet hath its sour; every evil its good. Every faculty which is a receiver of pleasure, has an equal penalty put on its abuse. It is to answer for its moderation with its life. For every grain of wit there is a grain of folly. For every thing you have missed, you have gained something else; and for everything you gain, you lose something. If riches increase, they are increased that use them. If the gatherer gathers too much, nature takes out of the man what she puts into his chest; swells the estate, but kills the owner. Nature hates monopolies and exceptions. The waves of the sea do not more speedily seek a level from their loftiest tossing, than the varieties of condition tend to equalize themselves. There is always some leveling circumstance that puts down the overbearing, the strong, the rich, the fortunate, substantially on the same ground with all others. Is a man too strong and fierce for society, and by temper and position a bad citizen, a morose ruffian with a dash of the pirate in him; nature sends him a troop of pretty sons and daughters who are getting along in the dame's classes at the village school, and love and fear for them smoothes his grim scowl to courtesy. Thus she contrives to intenerate the granite and felspar, takes the boar out and puts the lamb in, and keeps her balance true.

The farmer imagines power and place are fine things. But the President has paid dear for his White House. It has commonly cost him all his peace and the best of his manly attributes. To preserve for a short time so conspicuous an appearance before the world, he is content to eat dust before the real masters who stand erect behind the throne. Or, do men desire the more substantial and permanent grandeur of genius? Neither has this an immunity. He who by force of will or of thought is great, and overlooks thousands, has the responsibility of overlooking. With every influx of light, comes new danger. Has he light? He must bear witness to the light, and always outrun that sympathy which gives him such keen satisfaction, by his fidelity to new revelations of the incessant soul. He must hate father and mother, wife and child. Has he all that the world loves and admires and covets? He must cast behind him their admiration, and afflict them by faithfulness to his truth, and become a by-word and a hissing.

This Law writes the laws of cities and nations. It will not be balked of its end in the smallest iota, it is in vain to build or plot or combine against it. Things refuse to be mismanaged long. *Res noluxt diu male administrari.* Though no checks to a new evil appear, the checks exist and will appear. If the government is cruel, the governor's life is not safe. If you tax too high, the revenue will yield nothing. If you make the criminal code sanguinary, juries will not convict. Nothing arbitrary, nothing artificial can endure. The true life and satisfactions of man seem to elude the utmost rigors or felicities of condition, and to establish themselves with great indifferency under all varieties of circumstance. Under all governments the influence of character remains the same — in Turkey and in New England about alike. Under the primeval despots of Egypt, history honestly confesses that man must have been as free as culture could make him.

Thus is the universe alive. All things are moral. That soul which within us is a sentiment, outside of us is a law. We feel its inspirations; out there in history we can see its fatal strength. It is almighty. All nature feels its grasp. "It is in the world and the world was made by it." It is eternal, but it enacts itself in time and space. Justice is not postponed. A perfect equity adjusts its balance in all parts of life. The dice of God are always loaded. The world looks like a multiplication table or a mathematical equation, which, turn it how you will, balances itself. Take what figure you will, its exact value, no more nor less, still returns to you. Every secret is told, every crime is punished, every virtue rewarded, every wrong redressed, in silence and certainty. What we call retribution, is the universal necessity by which the whole appears wherever a part appears. If you see smoke, there must be fire. If you see a hand or a limb, you know that the trunk to which it belongs, is there behind.

Every act rewards itself, or, in other words, integrates itself in a twofold manner; first, in the thing, or, in real nature; and secondly, in the circumstance, or, in apparent nature. Men call the circumstance the retribution. The causal retribution is in the thing, and is seen by the soul. The retribution in the circumstance, is seen by the understanding; it is inseparable from the thing, but is often spread over a long time, and so does not become distinct until after many years. The specific stripes may follow late after the offense, but they follow because they accompany it. Crime and punishment grow out of one stem. Punishment is a fruit that unsuspected ripens within the flower of the pleasure which concealed it. Cause and effect, means and ends, seed and fruit, cannot be severed; for the effect already blooms in the cause, the end pro-exists in the means, the fruit in the seed.

3. Power

There is not yet any inventory of a man's faculties, and more than a bible of his opinions. Who shall set a limit to the influence of a human being? There are men, who, by their sympathetic attractions, carry nations with them, and lead the activity of the human race. And if there be such a tie, that, wherever the mind of man goes, nature will accompany him, perhaps there are men whose magnetisms are of that force to draw material and elemental powers, and where they appear, immense instrumentalities organize around them. Life is a search after power; and this is an element with which the earth is so saturated, there is no chink or crevice in which it is not lodged, that no honest seeking goes unrewarded. A man should prize events and possessions as the ore in which this fine mineral is found; and he can well afford to let events and possessions, and the breath of the body go, if their value has been added to him in the shape of power. If he have secured the elixir, he can spare the wide gardens from which it was distilled. A cultivated man, wise to know and bold to perform, is the end to which nature works, and the education of the will is the flowering and result of all this geology and astronomy. All successful men have agreed in one thing: they were *causationists.* They believed that things went not by luck, but by law; that there was not a weak or a cracked link in the chain that joins the first and last of things. A belief in causality, or strict connection between every trifle and the principle of being, and, in consequence, belief in compensation, or, that nothing is got for nothing, characterizes all valuable minds and must control every effort that is made by an industrious one. The most valiant men are the best believers in the tension of the laws. "All the great captains," said Bonaparte, "have performed vast achievements by conforming with the rules of the art — by adjusting efforts to obstacles."

All power is of one kind, a sharing of the nature of the world. The mind that is parallel with the laws of nature will be in the current of events, and strong with their strength. One man is made of the same stuff of which events are made; is in sympathy with the course of things; can predict it. Whatever befalls, befalls him first; so that he is equal to whatever shall happen. A man who knows men, can talk well on politics, trade, law, war, religion. For, everywhere, men are led in the same manners.

The advantage of a strong pulse is not to be supplied by any labor, art, or concert. It is like the climate, which easily rears a crop, which no glass, or irrigation, or tillage, or manures, can elsewhere rival. It is like the opportunity of a city like New York, or Constantinople, which needs no diplomacy to force capital or genius or labor to it. They come of themselves, as the waters flow to it. So a broad, healthy, massive understanding seems to lie on the shore of unseen rivers, of unseen oceans, which are covered with barks, that, night and day, are drifted to this point. That is poured into its lap, which other men lie plotting for. It is in everybody's secret; anticipates everybody's discovery; and if it do not command every fact of the genius and the scholar, it is because it is large and sluggish, arid does not think them worth the exertion which you do.

This affirmative force is in one, and is not in another, as one horse has the spring in him, and another in the whip. "On the neck of the young man," said Hafiz, "sparkles no gem so gracious as enterprise." Import into any stationary district, as into an old Dutch population in New York or Pennsylvania, or among the planters of Virginia, a colony of hardy Yankees, with seething brains, heads full of steam-hammer, pulley, crank, and toothed wheel, and everything begins to shine with values. What enhancement to all the water and land in England, is the arrival of James Watt or Brunel! In every company, there is not only the active and passive sex, but, in both men and women, a deeper and more important *sex of mind,* namely the inventive or creative class of both men and women, and the uninventive or accepting class. Each *plus* man represents his set, and, if he have the accidental advantage of personal ascendency, which implies neither more nor less of talent, but merely the temperamental or taming eye of a soldier or a schoolmaster, (which one has, and one has not, as one has a black moustache and one a blond,) then quite easily and without any envy or resistance all his coadjutors and feeders will admit his right to absorb them. The merchant works by bookkeeper and cashier; the lawyer's authorities are hunted up by clerks; the geologist reports the surveys of his subalterns; Commander Wilkes appropriates the results of all the naturalists attached to the Expedition; Thorwaldsen's statue is finished by stonecutters; Dumas has journeymen; and Shakespeare was theatre-manager and used the labor of many young men, as well as the play-books.

There is always room for a man of force, and he makes room for many. Society is a troop of thinkers, and the best heads among them take the best places. A feeble man can see the farms that are fenced and tilled, the houses that are built. The strong man sees the possible houses and farms. His eye makes estates, as fast as the sun breeds clouds.

Chapter 19

Abraham Lincoln

Abraham Lincoln (1809–1865) was the 16th President of the United States (1861–1865). Born in a Kentucky log cabin, he died (was assassinated) in Washington, D.C. Before his election to President, he was a lawyer, an Illinois state legislator, and a member of the United States House of Representatives.

He was one of the greatest of the great American presidents. Lincoln's Gettysburg Address is a fine illustration of his abilities.

Lincoln was inaugurated as president on March 4, 1861. On April 12, 1861, Union troops at Fort Sumter were fired on by supporters of secession. Florida, Mississippi, Alabama, Georgia, Louisiana, and Texas announced their leaving the Union early in 1861. The Confederate States of America selected Jefferson Davis as their President. With the fall of Fort Sumter, the Civil War had begun. Lincoln had one primary objective, the preservation of the Union. The states that seceded wanted to preserve their right to own slaves. It was not until September 22, 1862 (after the battle of Antietam, September 1862) that Lincoln announced the Emancipation Proclamation that freed slaves held in territories under rebel control. In 1865, Congress passed the Thirteenth Amendment to the Constitution that abolished slavery throughout the United States. Lincoln was consistently against the practice of slavery. But his number one priority was to preserve the Union.

Lincoln, Abraham, "Lincoln at Gettysburg," in G.M. Whitman, *American Orators and Oratory*, Chicago, Fairbanks, Palmer & Co., 1884, p. 367.

1. Lincoln at Gettysburg

Mr. Lincoln's Speech at Gettysburg, delivered November 19, 1863.

Four score and seven years ago our fathers brought forth upon this continent a new nation, conceived in liberty, and dedicated to the proposition that all men are created equal.

Now, we are engaged in a great civil war, testing whether that nation, or any nation, so conceived, and so dedicated, can long endure. We are met on a great battle-field of that war. We have come to dedicate a portion of that field as a final resting-place for those who here gave their lives that that nation might live. It is altogether fitting and proper that we should do this.

But, in a large sense, we cannot dedicate, we cannot consecrate, we cannot hallow this ground. The brave men, living and dead, who struggled here, have consecrated far above our poor power to add or detract. The world will little note, nor long remember what we *say* here, but it can never forget what they *did* here. It is for us, the living, rather, to be dedicated here to the unfinished work which they who fought here have thus far so nobly advanced. It is rather for us to be here dedicated to the great task remaining before us, that from these honored dead we take increased devotion for that cause for which they gave the last full measure of devotion; that we here highly resolve that these dead shall not have died in vain; that this nation, under God, shall have a new birth of freedom; and that a government of the people, by the people, and for the people, shall not perish from the earth.

Chapter 20

Karl Heinrich Marx

Karl Marx (1818–1883) was a German philosopher and author whose ideas were the foundation of communism. Whether or not his ideas were right or wrong, they were important to the lives of hundreds of millions of people and are still important.

The Communist Manifesto and *Das Kapital* are his two masterpieces and the concept of class struggle was one of the foundations of Marx's theory. Marx was a theoretician and his theories are not easily understood. Of course, we know that the theories of Marx were rapidly replaced in practice by power. How many communists have read and understood *Das Kapital*?

Note that Marx died in 1883 well before the Russian revolution. His writings did not forecast the unfortunate future of the successful revolt.

Marx, Karl and Engels, Friedrich, *Manifesto of the Communist Party*, New York, International Publishers, 1937, pp. 43–44.

1. IV Position of the Communists in Relation to the Various Existing Opposition Parties

Section II has made clear the relations of the Communists to the existing working class parties, such as the Chartists in England and the Agrarian Reformers in America.

The Communists fight for the attainment of the immediate aims, for the enforcement of the momentary interests of the working class; but in the movement of the present, they also represent and take care of the future of that movement. In France the Communists ally themselves with the Social-Democrats against the conservative and radical bourgeoisie, reserving, however, the right to take up a critical position in regard to phrases and illusions traditionally handed down from the great Revolution.

In Switzerland they support the Radicals, without losing sight of the fact that this party consists of antagonistic elements, partly of Democratic Socialists, in the French sense, partly of radical bourgeoisie.

In Poland they support the party that insists on an agrarian revolution as the prime condition for national emancipation, that party which fomented the insurrection of Cracow in 1846.

In Germany they fight with the bourgeoisie whenever it acts in a revolutionary way, against the absolute monarchy, the feudal squirearchy, and the petty bourgeoisie.

But they never cease, for a single instant, to instill into the working class the clearest possible recognition of the hostile antagonism between bourgeoisie and proletariat, in order that the German workers may straightway use, as so many weapons against the bourgeoisie, the social and political conditions that the bourgeoisie must necessarily introduce along with its supremacy, and in order that, after the fall of the reactionary classes in Germany, the fight against the bourgeoisie itself may immediately begin.

The Communists turn their attention chiefly to Germany, because that country is on the eve of a bourgeois revolution that is bound to be carried out under more advanced conditions of European civilization and with a much more developed proletariat than what existed in England in the 17th and in France in the 18th century, and because the bourgeois revolution in Germany will be but the prelude to an immediately following proletarian revolution.

In short, the Communists everywhere support every revolutionary movement against the existing social and political order of things.

In all these movements they bring to the front, as the leading question in each case, the property question, no matter what its degree of development at the time.

Finally, they labor everywhere for the union and agreement of the democratic parties of all countries.

The Communists disdain to conceal their views and aims. They openly declare that their ends can be attained only by the forcible overthrow of all existing social conditions. Let the ruling classes tremble at a Communist revolution. The proletarians have nothing to lose but their chains. They have a world to win.

Workingmen of all countries, unite!

Chapter 21

Andrew Carnegie

Andrew Carnegie (1835–1911) was an American (of Scottish birth) leader of industry. He created the Carnegie Steel Company which was later to be changed into U.S. Steel Corporation.

Carnegie devoted the last years of his life to philanthropy. He is famous for financing local libraries throughout the United States but he also founded the Carnegie Corporation of New York, Carnegie Endowment for International Peace, Carnegie Mellon University, etc.

In 1892, the famous Homestead Strike took place at Carnegie Steel's plant in Homestead Pennsylvania. The strike lasted 143 days and there were ten deaths and hundreds were injured. The extracts that follow were published in 1908. The thrust of his writings is captured by "the next step toward improved labor conditions is through the stage of shareholding in the industrial world."

Andrew Carnegie accomplished much good in his lifetime and laid the foundation for doing good for as long as history is recorded.

Carnegie, Andrew. *Problems of To-Day, Wealth, Labor, Socialism.* Garden City, New York, Doubleday, Doran & Company, 1932, pp. 43–69.

1. Labor — The Upward March of Labor

The progress of man from the earliest day up to the present has been one steady march upward, now and then in divers regions seemingly checked, receding for the moment, only to be swept onward again like the waves by the advancing tide.

If it were still thought that the Unknown had made man perfect, but with an instinct for his own degradation which ensured his fall, a call to return to the past would not have been astonishing, but when we in our enlightened age know that man is an outgrowth from lower orders of life, and has implanted within him the instinct which compels him to turn his face to the sun and slowly move upward toward that which is better, rejecting in his progress, after test, all that injures or debases, the call upon us by our Socialistic friends to exchange the individualistic civilized present which we have reached after many hundreds of thousands of years of progress, for the system of communism of the savage past, is indeed startling. There is no phase of human existence upon which we look today which does not show encouraging improvement over the past. This progress made, in obedience to the very nature of man, created to ascend, in intelligence, tastes and conduct, has made all the difference between the savage and the civilized being.

Let us never forget that under present conditions the world has grown and is growing better, and we steadily approach nearer the ideal. Never was there so much of the spirit of brotherhood among men, never so much kindness, never so much help extended by men, and especially by women, to their less fortunate fellows. The writer scarcely knows a family intimately of which one or more members are not earnestly engaged spending their time and means in doing good, thus giving not only their wealth, but themselves, to make brighter and better the lives of the less fortunate. There are many of his acquaintances treading the path that leads to making earth a heaven, less solicitous about "heaven our home" than hitherto, but more about making "home our heaven" here in this life.

Many indeed in our day will merit the epitaph:

> "If there's another world, he lives in bliss;
> If there be none, he made the best of this."

It is not, therefore, to the savage past that we should look for guidance. The part of wisdom is to hold fast to that which has proved itself good, and to keep on as we have been doing. Marching upward, the race is not led by the multitude but by the few exceptional natures, just as all orders of vegetation have been and are improved by the exceptional plants, from the sour crab to the apple of today; from the love-apple in America of a past generation to our succulent tomato. Exceptional plants arose, and from these came others. So in the animal kingdom; from the wolf came the collie dog; from a five-toed rude progenitor, the horse. All breeders perpetuate the best.

Now in this progress the laborer has not failed to share with the employer. If we contrast what he is with what he was, the difference is great. He was once slave, then serf who did manual labor; up to a century ago he was still a villein and was sold with the mine — that is, he could not leave it without the consent of the proprietor. Till recent times he was not paid in cash. Now he is a freeman, and sells the labor the mine-owner buys, both equally independent. In Dunfermline some time ago, the writer visited the cottage gardens for which prizes are given, with the Secretary of the Horticultural Society, who is a working coal-miner and a credit to Labor. He remarked that the masters and miners were that day conferring upon the wage question. "Only a hundred years ago," the writer replied, "your forefathers would have been transferred with the mines in case of sale. Now masters and men meet today as equals, buyers, and sellers. What would be thought if the masters proposed a return to the old conditions?" With a twinkle in the eye, never to be forgotten, came the words, "Ay, there wud be twa at that bargain, I'm thinkin'." With their trades unions, cash payments — masters of themselves, and their labor — it is clear that workingmen have shared in the general advance. The wand of progress has not passed them by untouched, nor are we without evidence that the march of their improvement is not to stop.

Following the same course with "Labor" as with "Wealth," the writer will make free use of what he has said in years gone by rather than give his views in new form, since they remain today substantially as they were then expressed.

From "An Employer's View of the Labor Question," *Forum,* April 1886:

> The influence of trades unions upon the relations between the employer and employed has been much discussed. Some establishments in America have refused to recognize the right of the men to form themselves into these unions although I am not aware that any concern in England would dare to take this

position. This policy, however, may be regarded as only a temporary phase of the situation. The right of the working-men to combine and to form trades unions is no less sacred than the right of the manufacturer to enter into associations and conferences with his fellows, and it must be sooner or later conceded. Indeed, it gives one but a poor opinion of the American workman if he permits himself to be deprived of a right which his fellow in England has conquered for himself long since. My experience has been that trades unions upon the whole are beneficial both to Labor and to Capital. They certainly educate the working-men and give them a truer conception of the relations of Capital and Labor than they could otherwise form. The ablest and best workmen eventually come to the front in these organizations; and it may be laid down as a rule that the more intelligent the workman the fewer the contests with employers. It is not the intelligent workman — who knows that Labor without his brother Capital is helpless — but the blatant ignorant man, who regards Capital as the natural enemy of Labor, who does so much to embitter the relations between employer and employed; and the power of this ignorant demagogue arises chiefly from the lack of proper organization among the men through which their real voice can be expressed. This voice will always be found in favor of the judicious and intelligent representative. Of course, as men become intelligent more deference must be paid to them personally and to their rights, and even to their opinions and prejudices; and upon the whole a greater share of profits must be paid in the day of prosperity to the intelligent than to the ignorant workman. He

> cannot be imposed upon so readily. On the other hand, he will be found much readier to accept reduced compensation when business is depressed; and it is better in the long run for Capital to be served by the highest intelligence, and to be made well aware of the fact that it is dealing with men who know what is due to them, both as to treatment and compensation. I therefore recognize in trades unions, or, better still, in organizations of the men of each establishment, who select representatives to speak for them, a means not of further embittering the relations between employer and employed, but of improving them.
>
> It is astonishing how small a sacrifice upon the part of the employer will sometimes greatly benefit the men. I remember that at one of our meetings with a committee, it was incidentally remarked by one speaker that the necessity for obtaining credit at the stores in the neighborhood was a grave tax upon the men. An ordinary workman, he said, could not afford to maintain himself and family for a month, and, as he only received his pay monthly, he was compelled to obtain credit, and to pay exorbitantly for everything; whereas, if he had the cash, he could buy in Pittsburg at 25 per cent less. "Well," I said, "why cannot we overcome that by paying every two weeks?" The reply was, "We did not like to ask it, because we have always understood that it would cause much trouble; but, if you do that, it will be worth an advance of 5 per cent in our wages." We have paid semimonthly since.

To avoid the excessive prices of the small stores I suggested a cooperative society, which was promptly formed, the first in the region.

"Another speaker happened to say that, although they were in the midst of coal, the price charged for small lots delivered at their houses was a certain sum per bushel. The price named was double what our best coal was costing us. How easy for us to deliver to our men such coal as they required, and charge them cost! This was done without a cent's loss to us, but with much gain to the men. Several other points similar to these have arisen, by which their labors might be lightened or products increased, and others suggesting changes in machinery or facilities, which, but for the conferences referred to, would have been unthought of by the employer, and probably never asked for by the men. For these and other reasons I attribute the greatest importance to an organization of the men, through whose duly-elected representatives the managers may be kept informed from time to time of their grievances and suggestions. No matter how able the manager, the clever workman can often show him how beneficial changes can be made in the special branch in which that work-man labors. Unless the relations between manager and workmen are not only amicable but friendly, the owners miss much; nor is any man a first-class manager who has not the confidence and respect, and even the admiration, of his workmen. No man is a true gentleman who does not inspire the affection and devotion of his servants."

Whatever the future may have in store for Labor, the evolutionist, who sees nothing but certain and steady progress for the race, will never attempt to set bounds to its triumphs, even to its final form of complete and universal industrial cooperation, which I hope is some day to be reached.

The following extract is from an address delivered on opening the Library presented to the workmen of Homestead (1898):

> "A partnership of three is required in the industrial world when an enterprise is planned. The first of these, not in importance, but in time, is Capital. Without it nothing costly can be built. From it comes the first breath of life into matter, previously inert.
>
> The structures reared by outside workmen, equipped and ready to begin in any line of industrial activity, the second partner comes into operation. That is Business Ability. Capital has done its part. It has provided all the instruments of production; but unless it can command the services of able men to manage the business, all that Capital has done crumbles into ruin.
>
> Then comes the third partner in the works, last in order of time, but not least, Skilled Labor. If it fail to perform its part, nothing can be accomplished. Capital and Business Ability brought into play without it, are dead. The wheels cannot revolve unless Skilled Labor starts them."

Now, volumes can be written as to which one of the three partners is first, second, or third in importance, and the subject will remain just as it was before. Political economists, speculative philosophers and preachers, have been giving their views on the subject for hundreds of years, but the answer has not yet been found, nor can it ever be, because each of the three is all-important, and every one is equally essential to the other two. Labor, Capital, and Ability are a three-legged stool. There is no first, second, or last. There is no precedence! They are equal members of the great triple alliance which moves the industrial world.

We have seen the position which Labor has reached in our day. Employee and employer meet upon equal terms. It was the writer's province to confer with Labor for twenty-six years, and the more he knew of the working-men the higher they rose in his estimation and regard. Sometimes, but not often, the worker may be misled by extreme men; but, as a rule, a majority can always be depended upon to be fair and reasonable. The following are extracts from an article the writer published in the *Forum,* April and August 1886:

> "A strike or lock-out is, in itself, a ridiculous affair. Whether a failure or a success, it gives no direct proof of its justice or injustice. In this it resembles war between two nations. It is simply a question of strength and endurance between the contestants. The gage of battle or the duel is not more senseless as a means of establishing what is just and fair than an industrial strike or lock-out. It would be folly to conclude that we have reached any permanent adjustment between Capital and Labor until strikes and lock-outs are as much things of the past as the gage of battle or the duel have become in the most advanced communities.
>
> Among the expedients suggested for their better reconciliation, the first place must be assigned to the idea of cooperation, or the plan by which the workers are to become part owners in enterprises, and share their fortunes. There is no doubt that if this could be effected it would have the same beneficial effect upon the workman which the ownership of land has upon the man who has hitherto tilled the land for another. The sense of

> ownership would make of him more of a man as regards himself, and hence more of a citizen as regards the commonwealth."

While public sentiment has rightly and unmistakably condemned violence, even in the form for which there is the most excuse, I would have the public give due consideration to the terrible temptation to which the working-man on a strike is sometimes subjected. To expect that one dependent upon his daily wage for the necessaries of life will stand by peaceably and see a new man employed in his stead is to expect much. This poor man may have a wife and children dependent upon his labor. Whether medicine for a sick child, or even nourishing food for a delicate wife, is procurable, depends upon his steady employment. In all but a very few departments of labor it is unnecessary, and, I think, improper, to subject men to such an ordeal. In the case of railways and a few other employments it is, of course, essential for the public wants that no interruption occur, and in such case substitutes must be employed; but the employer of labor will find it much more to his interest, wherever possible to allow his works to remain idle and await the result of a dispute, than to employ the class of men that can be induced to take the place of other men who have stopped work. Neither the best men as men, nor the best men as workers, are thus to be obtained. There is an unwritten law among the best workmen: "Thou shalt not take thy neighbor's job." No wise employer will lightly lose his old employees. Length of service counts for much in many ways. Calling upon strange men should be the last resort.

The writer never attempted to run works with new men. In his opinion, strikes generally arise not so much owing to disputes about wages as to the lack of knowledge of the one party by the other. The employer does not know the men and their point of view and their troubles, and the men do not know their employer and his troubles. Neither does the employer know the virtues of the working-man, nor the working-man the good qualities of the employer. Each looks only at one side of the problem. Lack of proper recognition of the workers by the employers as fellow-men causes most of the labor disputes. In domestic service, where the two classes, employer and employed, do get to know each other as men and women, there are few quarrels, simply because each finds the other possessed of many endearing traits. Few are the families in which are not found valued servants living in their old age as members of the household, or pensioned and living nearby in their cottages — often visited.

2. The Final Relation Between Capital and Labor Labor and Capital Partners

While we have said that Labor has shared in the progress of the race, considering from whence it started and the position it now occupies, it cannot be claimed that conditions are satisfactory as they exist. In the future, Labor is to rise still higher. The joint-stock form opens the door to the participation of Labor as shareholders in every branch of business. In this, the writer believes, lies the final and enduring solution of the Labor question. The Carnegie Steel Company made a beginning by making from time to time forty-odd young partners, only one was related to the original partners, but all were selected upon their proved merits after long service. None contributed a penny. Their notes were accepted, payable only out of the profits of the business. Great care was taken to admit workers of the mechanical department, which had hitherto been neglected by employers. The first time a superintendent of one of the works was made a partner attracted attention, but as we kept on admitting men who had risen from the ranks as mechanics, we found it more and more advantageous. The superintendents now sat in conference at the board with the managers in the office. From this policy sprang the custom of bonuses awarded yearly to men in subordinate positions who had done exceptional work. This class naturally felt that they were on the upward road to admission as partners; their feet upon the ladder.

The problem presented by the combination of many steelworks into the one United States Steel Corporation was not altogether new, for individual and corporate management have co-existed since joint-stock companies were formed. The former had undoubtedly great advantages over the latter. Able men managing their own works, in competition with large bodies of shareholders employing salaried managers, were certain to distance their corporate competitors, and did so. Nothing can stand against the direct management of owners. The United States Steel Corporation realized this, and as a substitute resolved to adopt the policy of interesting its officers and employees in its shares. Some plan of profit-sharing was soon seen to present the best, and indeed the only, substitute for individual management. This idea the writer highly approved in his Presidential Address to the Iron and Steel Institute in London, in 1903, but ventured to point out one serious defect. The investments in the shares of the company proposed to the men were to be at the risk of the purchasers. We added that "this seems a feature we may, however, expect the Corporation to change as experience is gained." "Every employee a shareholder" would prevent most of the disputes between Capital and Labor, and this chiefly because of the feeling of mutuality which would be created, now, alas, generally lacking. To effect this, every corporation could well afford to sell shares to its saving workmen, giving preference in repayment at cost as a first charge in case of disaster, just as present laws provide first for the mechanic's lien and for homestead exemption. This is due to the working-man, who necessarily buys the shares without knowledge, and he is asked to buy them, not solely for his own advantage, but for the benefit of the company as well — the advantage of both. This view, as expressed by the writer in the Address referred to, we rejoice to say, has been adapted by the Steel Corporation, and its last offer of shares guarantees the men against loss.

The managerial department is given bonuses every year upon the profits of the concern.

All this was hailed by the writer with intense delight, as in his day-dreams he had often meditated upon the plan of employees becoming joint owners with himself and partners. Perhaps he may be permitted to quote from the Address referred to (May, 1903, London):

> "I cannot speak too highly of this experiment, nor give the Steel Company too much credit for making it, since it is declared to be in the experimental stage, and subject to future improvement, as all new schemes should be. Its able and progressive author, Mr. George W. Perkins, is to be heartily congratulated."

Thus we see, gentlemen, that the world moves on step by step toward better conditions. Just as the mechanical world has changed and improved, so the world of labor has advanced from the slavery of the laborer to the day of his absolute independence, and now to this day, when he begins to take his proper place as the capitalist-partner of his employer. We may look forward with hope to the day when it shall be the rule for the workman to be Partner with Capital, the man of affairs giving his business experience, the working-man in the mill his mechanical skill, to the company, both owners of the shares and so far equally interested in the success of their joint efforts, each indispensable, and without whose cooperation success would be impossible. It is a splendid vista along which we are permitted to gaze.

Perhaps I may be considered much too sanguine in this forecast, which no doubt will take time to realize, but as the result of my experience I am convinced that the huge combination, and even the moderate corporation, has no chance in competition with the partnership which embraces the principal officials and has adopted the system of payment by bonus or reward throughout its works. The latter may be relied upon, as a rule, to earn handsome dividends in times of depression, during which the former, conducted upon the old plan; will incur actual loss, and perhaps land in financial embarrassment. In speaking of corporations we must not forget, however, that there are many which are corporations in name only, their management being the life work of few owners. These rank with partnerships, having all the advantages of this form. The true corporation is that whose shares are upon the Stock Exchange, and whose real owners change constantly and are often unknown even to the president and directors, while to the workmen they are mere abstractions. It is impossible to infuse through their ranks the sentiment of personal regard and loyalty in all its wonderful power. The step taken by the United States Steel Corporation is therefore no surprise to me, for I have long believed that such corporations would be compelled to adopt the best attainable substitute for the personal factor of the older system, or suffer. In the sagacious policy of the United States Steel Corporation I see proof of that opinion, nor can I suggest a better form than that it has adopted, always provided the workingman shareholder be secured against loss.

In the percentage allotted by the plan to reward exceptional officials we have for the huge corporation perhaps the best substitute attainable for the magic of partnership, which nothing, however, can approach. The reward of departmental officials may readily be secured under this provision. In the bonus granted yearly upon shares held by the employees we have proof or regard for them which cannot but tell, and the distribution of shares in the concern among them gives an advantage which so far no partnership even has enjoyed. The latter will no doubt adopt the plan, or find some equivalent, for the workman owning shares in absolute security will prove much more valuable than one without such interest, and many incidental advantages will accrue to the company possessed of numerous shareholding employees who may some day see their representative welcomed to the board of directors. This would prove most conducive to harmony, knowledge of each other on the part of owners and workmen being the best preventive of dissatisfaction. If the investment of the workers' savings be made secure, the rapid extension of the plan seems certain, and can be hailed with unalloyed satisfaction; but in its present form it is obviously incapable of general application, since the officials of few corporations could or would incur the responsibility of inducing their workmen to invest in their shares as a security, and few corporations could or should inspire the needed confidence of labor that these are to enjoy an unbroken career of prosperity, for such has not been the history of manufacturing concerns generally, especially in our field, to which we may well apply the well-known lines of Hudibras:

> "Ay me! what perils do environ
> The man that meddles with cold iron."

The idea of making workmen shareholders, and dividing a percentage of the profits among those rendering exceptional service, will probably encounter the opposition of the extremists on both sides, the violent revolutionist of capitalistic conditions, and the narrow, grasping employer whose creed is to purchase his labor as he does his materials, paying the price agreed upon and ending there. But this opposition will, we believe, amount to little. It will even speak well for the new idea if scouted by the extremists and commended by the mass of men who are on neither dangerous edge, but in the middle, where usually lies wisdom.

Meanwhile, here is the germ of a promising plan offered as a solution for one of the pressing problems of our age, which may prove capable of development. Let us receive, study, and discuss it with open mind. That the problem will be solved and that the two factors are some day to live in friendly cooperation, let no one doubt. Human society bears a charmed life. It is immortal, and was born with the inherent power or instinct, as a law of its being, to solve all problems finally in the best form, and among these none more surely than that vexed question of our day, the relations between these Siamese Twins, which must mutually prosper or mutually decay: Employer and Employed, Capital and Labor.

Two and a half million dollars worth of additional stock was offered by the Steel Company to workmen this year (1908) and all taken, and twenty-five thousand more of the employees applied for shares, many for one share only, and these are to be provided, so that nearly one hundred thousand workmen of this company are soon to be shareholders, i.e., part owners having a right to vote with their fellow-proprietors, and sharing in the profits. These workers have their feet upon the ladder, and are bound to rise. They are very likely to save and invest more and more. This is the answer, reached by evolution under present conditions, to pessimists and revolutionists, which our Socialistic friends should ponder well.

The strict political economist of our day may look askance at the idea of a minimum wage and a guarantee for the workmen against loss upon their shares, in companies in which they hold a minority interest; but whatever final form the merger of Labor and Capital may assume in the distant future, these features seem to be essential under present conditions. If taxation should be borne only according to ability to pay, it is not wholly unreasonable that the workman should not be subject to loss, for, having only a minimum wage, he has no ability to incur loss. The exemption of a stated sum from income tax in Britain, and in America the exemption of the small homestead, are examples of this principle.

Should the workmen hold the majority of shares and really manage the business, exemption from sharing loss should cease.

This is only a beginning. The Filene Stores of Boston, a shareholding company employing seven to nine hundred men, has gone farthest of all in the direction of making its employees joint owners. The capital stock is held only by employees, and is returned to the corporation at its value, should the employee leave the service. Every share of stock belongs to some one working in the stores. The most important advance is that all questions are submitted to arbitration, not only complaints or disputes, but wages, scope of work, and tenure of employment. More than four hundred cases of arbitration have arisen, and the result is that both managers and employees have been satisfied that this is the true plan. When an employee is discharged he has the right to appeal to an arbitration board composed of fellow employees of different grades. All wage disputes have been satisfactorily settled. There is a profit-sharing department, having nothing to do with wages, which has been able to distribute varying amounts each year.

There is also a Welfare Committee of the shareholders, which manages a club house and maintains lunch and recreation rooms. The Insurance Committee furnishes five classes of assurance at cost. Two-thirds of the workers are insured. The bank pays 5 per cent, upon deposits of employees, which are guaranteed by the corporation. The Publication Committee issues a monthly paper. Many features of a social and educational nature are enjoyed by the employees throughout the year, and an atmosphere has been produced of great value to the business and to the members.

It may be added that the Filene Stores are not excelled, if equalled, in making profits. Their goods are turned over ten times some years, six or seven times being the average, and the stores are among the foremost and best known in Boston. No doubt the brothers Filene are remarkable men and recognized leaders in this work, but we may expect their example to impress others, particularly since their profit-sharing and stock-owning plans have been vindicated by unusual success, from every point of view, particularly in improving the relations between employers and employees.

We are just at the beginning of profit-sharing, and the reign of working-men proprietors, which many indications point to as the next step forward in the march of wage-paid labor to the higher stage of profit-sharing — joint partnership — workers with the hand and workers with the head paid from profits — no dragging of the latter down, but the raising of the former up.

We never see a fishing fleet sail without hailing it as the finest illustration of the perfect relationship which is one day to prevail between Capital and Labor generally. Every man in the ship from the captain down is a partner, paid by sharing in the profits of the catch, according to the value of his labor. Even the lowest paid, probably a young hand, not yet an able-bodied seaman, could be a partner in the business.

Here is a field capable of immediate and wide extension provided employers agree to fix a minimum wage sufficient to maintain economically the worker's household, and to this it is believed every fair-minded employer would gladly agree.

So far we have a list of 189 manufacturing concerns in the United States which have welfare departments — sales of stock to workmen, or other modes of adding to their wages, or forms recognizing the community of interest between employers and employed.

Gilman, in his book on profit-sharing, published in 1899, gave the following numbers of profit-sharing firms in the different countries of Europe:

France	120
Britain	94
Germany	47
Switzerland	14
Italy	8
Holland	7
Belgium	6
Austria-Hungary	5

It will soon be the exception for employers upon a great scale to ignore this feature. Eighteen of the principal railroad companies in America have established systems of pensions for their employees as extra recompense, the cost borne exclusively by the corporations. The pension feature, like profit-sharing, is making great headway, and promises soon to be universal.

So marches Labor up the heights to equality with the millionaire as his partner in business.

It will be seen that the writer's views are not of yesterday; he has had considerable experience with the labor problem, and thought much over it. Whether the Communists' ideal is to be finally reached upon earth, after man is so changed that self-interest, which is now the mainspring of human action, will give place to heavenly neighbor-interest cannot be known. The future has not been revealed. He who says yes, and he who says no, are equally foolhardy. Neither knows, therefore neither should presume to consider, much less to legislate in their day for a future they can know nothing of. Endowed as man is with the instinct for improvement, fortunately no limit to his march toward perfection can be set, but what perfection is to be we know not. The writer, however, believes one point to be clear, viz. that the next step toward improved labor conditions is through the stage of shareholding in the industrial world, the workman becoming joint owner in the profits of his labor. Payment to slaves and serfs, by providing shelter and food and clothing for them, then by orders upon the stores for articles, up to payment by cash to independent workmen today, each a great step forward, have all been tried, and now the coming day dawns when payment is to be made wholly or in part by profit-sharing, the workman having the status of the share-owning official and a voice in management as joint owner. He will be guaranteed a minimum wage, when finally paid by profits entirely, to keep his mind easy and free for his work, the proper support of himself and of his family being thus ensured.

It may be mentioned that the investments of workmen-partners in the United States Steel Corporation have been very profitable to both the men and the company.

To the sober-minded workmen, we say again, hold fast to that which has proved itself good. Keep marching upon the path of decided and continuous progress, a progress which can be proved by simply glancing backward to conditions under which Labor started, when work was the part of slaves, and contrasting these with its present independent position.

We have traced the progress of Labor upward under present conditions from slavery to partnership with Capital. What the working man has to consider, and consider well, is whether this be not the most advantageous path for him to continue to tread. So far as it has been tried it has proved a decided success, and it can easily be continued since it is proving mutually beneficial to Capital and Labor. One of the greatest advantages, the writer thinks, will be found in drawing men and managers into closer intercourse, so that they become friends and learn each other's virtues, for that both have virtues none knows better than the writer, who has seen both sides of the shield as employee and employer. "We only hate those we do not know," says the French proverb. There is much truth in this. In vast establishments it is very difficult, almost impossible, for workmen and employers to know each other, but when the managers and workmen are joint owners, and both paid wages, as even the president of the company is, we shall see greater intercourse between them. In the case of disputes, it is certain that the workmen-partners have a status nothing else can give. They can attend all shareholders' meetings and have a voice there if desired. Entrance into the partnership class means increased power to workmen. On the other hand, knowledge of the company's affairs, its troubles and disappointments, which come at intervals to the most successful concerns, will teach the workman much that he did not know before.

Co-partnership tends to bring a realizing sense of 'the truth to both Labor and Capital that their interests, broadly considered, are mutual; and as far as the latter is concerned it may finally, in some cases, be all furnished by those engaged in the works, which is the ideal that should be held in view: the workman both Capitalist and Worker, Employee and Employer.

This, however, is not for our time. We are only pioneers, whose duty is to start the movement, leaving to our successors its full and free development as human society advances.

The first company so owned will mark a new era in the relations of Labor and Capital. We may not have to wait long for this experiment, since it is in line with recent developments. The writer has no desire to embark again in business, but nothing would appeal to him so strongly as this ideal. He should like to address a body of workmen, many thousands in number, as all "fellow-partners." He addresses forty-odd at dinner once every year by that endearing term — partners of his youth and dear friends of his old age; only two ever put a dollar in the business. All the others — many of them working-men — earned their shares by brilliant service. Most of them are dollar-millionaires; all are rich.

Thus is Labor soon to attain its deserved place and recompense, and Workman and Capitalist become one; the wage system, except a minimum, being displaced by division of profits.

The foregoing was written before the following by John Stuart Mill, attracted the writer's attention:

> "The form of association, however, which, if mankind continue to improve, must be expected in the end to predominate, is not that which can exist between a capitalist as chief and workpeople without a voice in the management, but the association of the laborers themselves on terms of equality, collectively owning the capital with which they carry on their operations, and working under managers elected and removable by themselves." ("Political Economy" (Mill), People's Edition, p. 465.)

It is most encouraging that so great an authority as Mill foresaw that the ideal condition of the future lay not in State-owned factories and mines, uniform wages to workmen, and the abolition of private capital, as Socialists urge, but in uniting the workman and the capitalist in one and the same person. The writer is convinced that this is to be the highly satisfactory and final solution. The first step in advance has already come in the natural progress of evolution — no revolution necessary — and it is earnestly pressed upon the attention of the intelligent working-man and his leaders, some of whom seem to have been misled into devoting themselves to the advocacy of a system, admittedly unsuited to our day, which requires an organic change in the relations of society, and indeed involves a complete revolution in the nature of man — the task of a thousand years.

The experiment of Labor-and-Capital-Union — Workmen-Capitalists — has exceeded, so far, all expectations. Even the convinced Socialist might, therefore, hail it as at least a step in the right direction, making Labor's position better than before, saying to himself: "Let the future bring what it may, a bird in the hand is often worth more than a whole flock in the bush. Our socialistic remedy is for the future; let us not forget this in our dealings with the present."

Such seems to the writer the part of wisdom.

CHAPTER 22

Alfred Marshall

Born 1842 in London, England, he died in 1924. Marshall was the leading world economist for most of his career.

An expert mathematician, he used his mathematical skills to obtain insights but did not inflict pain on the readers of his texts. His textbook, *Principles of Economics*, was the most popular economics text for the end of the nineteenth century and the first half of the twentieth century. His book, *Economics of Industry* (1892), was the first volume of *Elements of Economics.* The introduction to this book makes clear that his wife was a co-author who did not want her name to appear as an author.

I have chosen to include two of the book's thirteen chapters. More chapters are relevant to the education of a business manager.

Marshall makes clear that the scope of economics extends beyond the accumulation of wealth:

> "Thus 'money' or 'general purchasing power' or 'command over material wealth,' is the center around which economic science clusters; this is so, not because money or material wealth is regarded as the main aim of human effort, nor even as affording the main subject-matter for the study of the economist, but because in this world of ours it is the one convenient means of measuring human motive on a large scale; and if the

> older economists had made this clear, they would have escaped many grievous misrepresentations. The splendid teachings of Carlyle and Ruskin as to the right aims of human endeavor and the right uses of wealth, would not then have been marred by bitter attacks on economics, based on the mistaken belief that that science had no concern with any motive except the selfish desire for wealth, or even that is inculcated a policy of sordid selfishness."[21]

He then makes clear that the desire to make money can and should be defended:

> "But again, the desire to make money does not itself necessarily proceed from motives of a low order, even when it is to be spent on oneself. Money is a means towards ends, and if the ends are noble, the desire for the means is not ignoble. The lad who works hard and saves all he can, in order to be able to pay his way afterwards at a university, is eager for money; but his eagerness is not ignoble. In short, money is general purchasing power, and is sought as a means to all kinds of ends, high as well as low, spiritual as well as material."

The chapter headed "Industrial Organization" stresses the importance of organization on efficiency.

> "Writers on social science from the time of Plato downwards have delighted to dwell on the increased efficiency

---

[21] It is pointed out in *Principles* I. v. 4, that a theory of economics similar to our own might exist in a world in which there was no private property in material wealth, and no money, provided that motives could be measured, as for instance by transferable honors.

which labor derives from organization. Adam Smith gave a vivid description of the advantages of the division of labor; he pointed out how they render it possible for increased numbers to live in comfort on a limited territory; and he argued that the pressure of population on the means of subsistence tends to weed out those races who through want of organization or for any other cause are unable to turn to the best account the advantages of the place in which they live."

Marshall, Alfred, "The Scope of Economics" and "Industrial Organization," in *Economics of Industry*, Alfred Marshall, London and New York, Macmillan and Co., 1892, pp. 33–39, 159–161.

1. Chapter V — The Scope of Economics

There are some who hold that all the aspects of social life are so closely connected, and act and react on one another in so many *ways,* that a special study of any one of them must be futile; and they urge on economists to abandon their distinctive role, and to devote themselves to the general advancement of a unified and all embracing social science. But experience seems to show that the whole range of man's actions in society is too wide and too various to be explained by a single effort.

On the other hand it is the duty of those who are giving their chief work to a limited field, to keep up close and constant correspondence with those who are engaged in neighboring fields. "A person is not likely to be a good economist who is nothing else. Social phenomena acting and reacting on one another, they cannot rightly be understood apart; but this by no means proves that the material and industrial phenomena of society are not themselves susceptible of useful generalizations, but only that these generalizations must necessarily be relative to a given form of civilization and a given stage of social advancement."[22]

But we have still to deal with the question: How wide should be the limits of that part of social science which the economist regards as his special domain? To answer this we must first consider what are the advantages which have enabled economics, though far behind the more advanced physical sciences, yet to outstrip every other branch of social science. For it would seem reasonable to conclude that any broadening of the scope of the science which brings it more closely to correspond with the actual facts, and to take account of the higher aims of life, will be a gain on the balance provided it does not deprive the science of those advantages: but that any further extension beyond that limit would cause more loss than gain.

The advantage which economics has over other branches of social science appears to arise from the fact that, while they deal almost exclusively with the *quality* of human motive, it deals with *quantity* as well as quality; for it concerns itself chiefly with just that class of motives which are measurable, and therefore are specially suited for scientific treatment. An opening is made for the methods and the tests of exact science as soon as the force of a person's motives can be measured by the sum of money, which he will just give up in order to secure a desired satisfaction, or again the sum which is just required to induce him to undergo a certain fatigue.

---

[22] This point is further discussed in *Principles* I. v. 1, with special reference to the controversy between Mill and Comte on the subject.

The most systematic part of people's lives is generally that by which they earn their living. The work of all those engaged in any one occupation can be carefully observed; general statements can be made about it, and tested by comparison with the results of other observations; and finally the services can be measured in money: that is, numerical estimates can be framed as to the amount of money or general purchasing power that is required to supply a sufficient motive for them.

Again, the unwillingness to postpone enjoyment, and thus to save for future use, is measured by the interest that is got by the possession of accumulated wealth. And, lastly, the desire to obtain anything that is ordinarily bought and sold for money, is for that very reason easily measurable by the price that people are willing to pay for it, though here again allowance must be made for differences in the means of different classes of purchasers.

In all this we take as little notice as possible of individual peculiarities of temper and character. We watch the conduct of a whole class of people — sometimes the whole of a nation, sometimes only those living in a certain district, more often those engaged in some particular trade at some time and place: and by the aid of statistics, or in other ways, we ascertain how much money on the average the members of the particular group we are watching, are just willing to pay as the price of a certain thing which they desire, or how much must be offered to them to induce them to undergo a certain effort or abstinence that they dislike. The measurement of motive thus obtained is not indeed perfectly accurate; for if it were, economics would rank with the most advanced of the physical sciences, and not as it actually does with the least advanced.

But yet the measurement is accurate enough to enable experienced persons to forecast fairly well the extent of the results that will follow from changes in which motives of this kind are chiefly concerned. Thus, for instance, they can estimate very closely the payment that will be required to produce an adequate supply of labor of any grade, from the lowest to the highest, for a new trade which it is proposed to start in any place. And, when they visit a factory of a kind that they have never seen before, they can tell within a shilling or two a week what any particular worker is earning, by merely observing how far his is a skilled occupation and what strain it involves on his physical, mental and moral faculties. They can predict with tolerable certainty what rise of price will result from a given diminution of the supply of a certain thing, and how that increased price will react on the supply.

And, starting from simple considerations of this kind, they can go on to analyze the causes which govern the local distribution of different kinds of industry, the terms on which people living in distant places exchange their goods with one another, and so on. They can explain and predict the ways in which fluctuations of credit will affect foreign trade, or again the extent to which the burden of a tax will be shifted from those on whom it is levied on to those for whose wants they cater.

Thus "money" or "general purchasing power" or "command over material wealth," is the center around which economic science clusters; this is so, not because money or material wealth is regarded as the main aim of human effort, nor even as affording the main subject-matter for the study of the economist, but because in this world of ours it is the one convenient means of measuring human motive on a large scale; and if the older economists had made this clear, they would have escaped many grievous misrepresentations. The splendid teachings of Carlyle and Ruskin as to the right aims of human endeavor and the right uses of wealth, would not then have been marred by bitter attacks on economics, based on the mistaken belief that that science had no concern with any motive except the selfish desire for wealth, or even that it inculcated a policy of sordid selfishness.

So far from confining their attention to selfish motives, economists have always given a prominent place to the unselfish sacrifices which men make in order to secure comfortable provision for their families. The grounds for doing this are obvious on the principle which we have adopted. For family affection acts with so much uniformity in any given stage of civilization that its effects can be systematically observed, reduced to law and measured; and it is therefore reasonable for economists to take it always into account; while yet they do not attempt to study the working of many other benevolent and self-sacrificing motives whose action is irregular. But the greater part of those actions, which are due to a feeling of duty and love of one's neighbor, cannot be classed, reduced to law and measured; and it is for this reason, and not because they are not based on self-interest, that the machinery of economics cannot be brought to bear on them.

There is another direction in which the range of economics has been wider than is commonly thought. When the motive to a man's action is spoken of as supplied by the money which he will earn, it is not meant that his mind is closed to all other considerations save those of gain. For even the most purely business relations of life assume honesty and good faith; while many of them take for granted, if not generosity, yet at least the absence of meanness; and the pride which every honest man takes in acquitting himself well, is an important factor of economic efficiency. Again, much of the work by which people earn their living is pleasurable in itself; and there is truth in the contention of socialists that more of it might be made so. Indeed in business work, that seems at first sight unattractive, many persons find a distinct pleasure, which is partly direct, and partly arises from the gratification which the work affords to their instincts of rivalry and power. Just as a race-horse or an athlete strains every nerve to get in advance of his competitors, and delights in the strain; so a manufacturer or a trader is often stimulated much more by the hope of victory over his rivals than by the desire to add something to his fortune.

But again, the desire to make money does not itself necessarily proceed from motives of a low order, even when it is to be spent on oneself. Money is a means towards ends, and if the ends are noble, the desire for the means is not ignoble. The lad who works hard and saves all he can, in order to be able to pay his way afterwards at a university, is eager for money; but his eagerness is not ignoble. In short, money is general purchasing power, and is sought as a means to all kinds of ends, high as well as low, spiritual as well as material.

The earlier English economists paid almost exclusive attention to the motives of individual action. But it must not be forgotten that economists, like all other students of social science, are concerned with individuals chiefly as members of the social organism. As a cathedral is something more than the stones of which it is built, as a person is something more than a series of thoughts and feelings, so the life of society is something more than the sum of the lives of its individual members. It is true that the action of the whole is made up of that of its constituent parts; and that in most economic problems the best starting-point is to be found in the motives that affect the individual, regarded not indeed as an isolated atom, but as a member of some particular trade or industrial group; but it is also true, as German writers have well urged, that economics has a great and an increasing concern in motives connected with the collective ownership of property and the collective pursuit of important aims. Many new kinds of voluntary association are growing up under the influence of other motives besides that of pecuniary gain; and the Co-operative movement in particular is opening to the economist new opportunities of measuring motives whose action it had seemed impossible to reduce to any sort of law.

2. Chapter VIII — Industrial Organization

Writers on social science from the time of Plato downwards have delighted to dwell on the increased efficiency which labor derives from organization. Adam Smith gave a vivid description of the advantages of the division of labor; he pointed out how they render it possible for increased numbers to live in comfort on a limited territory; and he argued that the pressure of population on the means of subsistence tends to weed out those races who through want of organization or for any other cause are unable to turn to the best account the advantages of the place in which they live. Before two more generations had elapsed Malthus' historical account of man's struggle for existence set Darwin thinking as to the effects of the struggle for existence in the animal world. Since that time biology has more than repaid her debt; and economists have learnt much from the profound analogies which have been discovered between industrial organization on the one side and the physical organization of the higher animals on the other. The development of the organism, whether social or physical, involves a greater subdivision of functions between its separate parts on the one hand, and on the other a more intimate connection between them. Each part gets to be less and less self-sufficient, to depend for its well-being more and more on other parts, so that no change can take place in any part of a highly-developed organism without affecting others also.

This increased subdivision of functions, or "differentiation" as it is called, manifests itself with regard to industry in such forms as the division of labor, and the development of specialized skill, knowledge and machinery: while "integration," that is, a growing intimacy and firmness of the connections between the separate parts of the industrial organism, shows itself in such forms as the increase of security of commercial credit, and of tile means and habits of communication by sea and road, by railway and telegraph, by post and printing press. This leads us to consider the main bearings in economics of the law that the struggle for existence causes those organisms to multiply which are best fitted to derive benefit from their environment.

This law is often misunderstood; and taken to mean that those organisms tend to survive which are *best fitted to benefit* the environment. But this is not its meaning. It states that those organisms tend to survive which are *best fitted to utilize* the environment for their own purposes. Now those that utilize the environment most, may turn out to be those that benefit it most. But it must not be assumed in any particular case that they are thus beneficial, without special study of that case.

Adam Smith was aware that competition did not always cause the survival of those businesses and those methods of business which were most advantageous to society; and though he insisted on the general advantages of that minute division of labor and of that subtle industrial organization which were being developed with unexampled rapidity in his time, yet he was careful to indicate points in which the system failed, and incidental evils which it involved. But many of his followers were less careful. They were not contented with arguing that the new industrial organization was obtaining victories over its rivals in every direction, and that this very fact proved that it met a want of the times, and had a good balance of advantages over disadvantages: but they went further and applied the same argument to all its details; they did not see that the very strength of the system as a whole enabled it to carry along with it many incidents which were in themselves evil. For a while they fascinated the world by their romantic accounts of the flawless proportions of that "natural" organization of industry which had grown from the rudimentary germ of self-interest. They depicted each man selecting his daily work with the sole view of getting for it the best pay he could, but with the inevitable result of choosing that in which he could be of most service to others. They argued for instance that, if a man had a talent for managing business, he would be surely led to use that talent for the benefit of mankind: that meanwhile a like pursuit of their own interests would lead others to provide for his use such capital as he could turn to best account; and that his own interest would lead him so to arrange those in his employment that everyone should do the highest work of which he was capable, and no other.

This "natural organization of industry" had a fascination for earnest and thoughtful minds; it prevented them from seeing and removing the evil that was intertwined with the good in the changes that were going on around them; and it hindered them from inquiring whether many even of the broader features of modern industry may not be transitional, having indeed good work to do in their time, as the caste system had in its time: but like it chiefly serviceable in leading the way towards better arrangements for a happier age.

Chapter 23

Russell Conwell

Russell Conwell (1843–1925) was an American Baptist minister, orator, and writer. He was the founder and first president of Temple University.

He is famous for the motivational speech "Acres of Diamonds." He gave this speech over 6,000 times around the world. The speech follows but it is somewhat lengthy and I shortened it. One of the early readers of this book advised against taking anything out. I suggest you try my shortened version and if you like what you read go to Google and download the original.

The point of Conwell's speech is that "every man has the opportunity to make more of himself than he does in his own environment."

Conwell contributed the net proceeds of his speaking to good causes, such as scholarships for needy students and the establishment of Temple University.

John C. Bogle created Vanguard in 1974 and was the senior chairman of Vanguard until 2000. The book, *Enough*, (2009, Wiley) was written by Bogle. On pp. 8–9, he describes the importance of the "Acres of Diamonds" speech to his success. He also references it on pp. 21–22 and on p. 188 where he states that the acres of diamonds "were always there, waiting to be discovered."

Conwell, Russell H., *Acres of Diamonds*, Harper & Brothers Publishers, New York, 1915, pp. 3–59.

1. Acres of Diamonds

When going down the Tigris and Euphrates rivers many years ago with a party of English travelers I found myself under the direction of an old Arab guide whom we hired up at Bagdad, and I have often thought how that guide resembled our barbers in certain mental characteristics. He thought that it was not only his duty to guide us down those rivers, and do what he was paid for doing, but also to entertain us with stories curious and weird, ancient and modern, strange and familiar. Many of them I have forgotten, and I am glad I have, but there is one I shall never forget.

The old guide was leading my camel by its halter along the banks of those ancient rivers, and he told me story after story until I grew weary of his story-telling and ceased to listen. I have never been irritated with that guide when he lost his temper as I ceased listening. But I remember that he took off his Turkish cap and swung it in a circle to get my attention. I could see it through the corner of my eye, but I determined not to look straight at him for fear he would tell another story. But although I am not a woman, I did finally look, and as soon as I did he went right into another story.

Said he, "I will tell you a story now which I reserve for my particular friends." When he emphasized the words "particular friends," I listened, and I have ever been glad I did. I really feel devoutly thankful, that there are 1,674 young men who have been carried through college by this lecture who are also glad that I did listen. The old guide told me that there once lived not far from the River Indus an ancient Persian by the name of Ali Hafed. He said that Ali Hafed owned a very large farm, that he had orchards, grain-fields, and gardens; that he had money at interest, and was a wealthy and contented man. He was contented because he was wealthy, and wealthy because he was contented. One day there visited that old Persian farmer one of those ancient Buddhist priests, one of the wise men of the East. He sat down by the fire and told the old farmer how this world of ours was made. He said that this world was once a mere bank of fog, and that the Almighty thrust His finger into this bank of fog, and began slowly to move His finger around, increasing the speed until at last He whirled this bank of fog into a solid ball of fire. Then it went rolling through the universe, burning its way through other banks of fog, and condensed the moisture without, until it fell in floods of rain upon its hot surface, and cooled the outward crust. Then the internal fires bursting outward through the crust threw up the mountains and hills, the valleys, the plains and prairies of this wonderful world of ours. If this internal molten mass came bursting out and cooled very quickly it became granite; less quickly copper, less quickly silver, less quickly gold, and, after gold, diamonds were made.

Said the old priest, "A diamond is a congealed drop of sunlight." Now that is literally scientifically true, that a diamond is an actual deposit of carbon from the sun. The old priest told Ali Hafed that if he had one diamond the size of his thumb be could purchase the county, and if he had a mine of diamonds he could place his children upon thrones through the influence of their great wealth.

Ali Hafed heard all about diamonds, how much. they were worth, and went to his bed that night a poor man.

He had not lost anything, but he was poor because he was discontented, and discontented because he feared he was poor. He said, "I want a mine of diamonds," and be lay awake all night.

Early in the morning he sought out the priest. I know by experience that a priest is very cross when awakened early in the morning, and when he shook that old priest out of his dreams, Ali Hafed said to him:

"Will you tell me where I can find diamonds?"

"Diamonds! What do you want with diamonds?" "Why, I wish to be immensely rich." "Well, then, go along and find them. That is all you have to do; go and find them, and then you have them." "But I don't know where to go." "Well, if you will find a river that runs through white sands, between high mountains, in those white sands you will always find diamonds." "I don't believe there is any such river." "Oh yes, there are plenty of them. All you have to do is to go and find them, and then you have them." Said Ali Hafed, "I will go."

So he sold his farm, collected his money, left his family in charge of a neighbor, and away he went in search of diamonds. He began his search, very properly to my mind, at the Mountains of the Moon. Afterward he came around into Palestine, then wandered on into Europe, and at last when his money was all spent and he was in rags, wretchedness, and poverty, he stood on the shore of that bay at Barcelona, in Spain, when a great tidal wave came rolling in between the pillars of Hercules, and the poor, afflicted, suffering, dying man could not resist the awful temptation to cast himself into that incoming tide, and be sank beneath its foaming crest, never to rise in this life again.

When that old guide had told me that awfully sad story he stopped the camel I was riding on and went back to fix the baggage that was coming off another camel, and I had an opportunity to muse over his story while he was gone. I remember saying to myself, "Why did he reserve that story for his 'particular friends'?" There seemed to be no beginning, no middle, no end, nothing to it. That was the first story I had ever heard told in my life, and would be the first one I ever read, in which the hero was killed in the first chapter. I had but one chapter of that story, and the hero was dead.

When the guide came back and took up the halter of my camel, he went right ahead with the story, into the second chapter, just as though there had been no break. The man who purchased Ali Hafed's farm one day led his camel into the garden to drink, and as that camel put its nose into the shallow water of that garden brook, Ali Hafed's successor noticed a curious flash of light from the white sands of the stream. He pulled out a black stone having an eye of light reflecting all the hues of the rainbow. He took the pebble into the house and put it on the mantel which covers the central fires, and forgot all about it.

A few days later this same old priest came in to visit Ali Hafed's successor, and the moment he opened that drawing-room door he saw that flash of light on the mantel, and he rushed up to it, and shouted: "Here is a diamond! Has Ali Hafed returned?" "Oh no, Ali Hafed has not returned, and that is not a diamond. That is nothing but a stone we found right out here in our own garden." "But," said the priest, "I tell you I know a diamond when I see it. I know positively that is a diamond."

Then together they rushed out into that old garden and stirred up the white sands with their fingers, and lo! there came up other more beautiful and valuable gems than the first. "Thus," said the guide to me, and, friends, it is historically true, "was discovered the diamond-mine of Golconda, the most magnificent diamond-mine in all the history of mankind, excelling the Kimberly itself. The Kohinoor, and the Orloff of the crown jewels of England and Russia, the largest on earth, came from that mine."

When that old Arab guide told me the second chapter of his story, he then took off his Turkish cap and swung it around in the air again to get my attention to the moral. Those Arab guides have morals to their stories, although they are not always moral. As he swung his hat, he said to me, "Had Ali Hafed remained at home and dug in his own cellar, or underneath his own wheatfields, or in his own garden, instead of wretchedness, starvation, and death by suicide in a strange land, he would have had 'acres of diamonds.' For every acre of that old farm, yes, every shovelful, afterward revealed gems which since have decorated the crowns of monarchs."

When he had added the moral to his story I saw why he reserved it for "his particular friends." But I did not tell him I could see it. It was that mean old Arab's way of going around a thing like a lawyer, to say indirectly what he did not dare say directly, that "in his private opinion there was a certain young man then traveling down the Tigris River that might better be at home in America." I did not tell him I could see that, but I told him his story reminded me of one, and I told it to him quick, and I think I will tell it to you.

I told him of a man out in California in 1847, who owned a ranch. He heard they had discovered gold in southern California, and so with a passion for gold he sold his ranch to Colonel Sutter, and away he went, never to come back. Colonel Sutter put a mill upon a stream that ran through that ranch, and one day his little girl brought some wet sand from the raceway into their home and sifted it through her fingers before the fire, and in that falling sand a visitor saw the first shining scales of real gold that were ever discovered in California. The man who had owned that ranch wanted gold, and he could have secured it for the mere taking. Indeed, thirty-eight millions of dollars has been taken out of a very few acres since then.

As I come here tonight and look around this audience I am seeing again what through these fifty years I have continually seen — men that are making precisely that same mistake. I often wish I could see the younger people, and would that the Academy had been filled to-night with our high-school scholars and our grammar-school scholars, that I could have them to talk to. While I would have preferred such an audience as that, because they are most susceptible, as they have not grown up into their prejudices as we have, they have not gotten into any custom that they cannot break, they have not met with any failures as we have; and while I could perhaps do such an audience as that more good than I can do grownup people, yet I will do the best I can with the material I have. I say to you that you have "acres of diamonds" in Philadelphia right where you now live. "Oh," but you will say, "you cannot know much about your city if you think there are any 'acres of diamonds' here."

Now then, I say again that the opportunity to get rich, to attain unto great wealth, is here in Philadelphia now, within the reach of almost every man and woman who hears me speak tonight, and I mean just what I say. I have not come to this platform even under these circumstances to recite something to you. I have come to tell you what in God's sight I believe to be the truth, and if the years of life have been of any value to me in the attainment of common sense, I know I am right; that the men and women sitting here, who found it difficult perhaps to buy a ticket to this lecture or gathering to-night, have within their reach "acres of diamonds," opportunities to get largely wealthy. There never was a place on earth more adapted than the city of Philadelphia today, and never in the history of the world did a poor man without capital have such an opportunity to get rich quickly and honestly as he has now in our city. I say it is the truth, and I want you to accept it as such; for if you think I have come to simply recite something, then I would better not be here. I have no time to waste in any such talk, but to say the things I believe, and unless some of you get richer for what I am saying to-night my time is wasted.

I say that you ought to get rich, and it is your duty to get rich. How many of my pious brethren say to me, "Do you, a Christian minister, spend your time going up and down the country advising young people to get rich, to get money?" "Yes, of course I do." They say, "Isn't that awful! Why don't you preach the gospel instead of preaching about man's making money?" "Because to make money honestly is to preach the gospel." That is the reason. The men who get rich may be the most honest men you find in the community.

"Oh," but says some young man here tonight, "I have been told all my life that if a person has money he is very dishonest and dishonorable and mean and contemptible."

My friend, that is the reason why you have none, because you have that idea of people. The foundation of your faith is altogether false. Let me say here clearly, and say it briefly, though subject to discussion which I have not time for here, ninety-eight out of one hundred of the rich men of America are honest. That is why they are rich. That is why they are trusted with money. That is why they carry on great enterprises and find plenty of people to work with them. It is because they are honest men.

Says another young man, "I hear sometimes of men that get millions of dollars dishonestly." Yes, of course you do, and so do I. But they are so rare a thing in fact that the newspapers talk about them all the time as a matter of news until you get the idea that all the other rich men got rich dishonestly.

My friend, you take and drive me — if you furnish the auto — out into the suburbs of Philadelphia, and introduce me to the people who own their homes around this great city, those beautiful homes with gardens and flowers, those magnificent homes so lovely in their art, and I will introduce you to the very best people in character as well as in enterprise in our city, and you know I will. A man is not really a true man until he owns his own home, and they that own their homes are made more honorable and honest and pure, and true and economical and careful, by owning the home.

For a man to have money, even in large sums, is not an inconsistent thing. We preach against covetousness, and you know we do, in the pulpit, and oftentimes preach against it so long and use the terms about "filthy lucre" so extremely that Christians get the idea that when we stand in the pulpit we believe it is wicked for any man to have money — until the collection-basket goes around, and then we almost swear at the people because they don't give more money. Oh, the inconsistency of such doctrines as that!

Money is power, and you ought to be reasonably ambitious to have it. You ought because you can do more good with it than you could without it. Money printed your Bible, money builds your churches, money sends your missionaries, and money pays your preachers, and you would not have many of them, either, if you did not pay them. I am always willing that my church should raise my salary, because the church that pays the largest salary always raises it the easiest. You never knew an exception to it in your life. The man who gets the largest salary can do the most good with the power that is furnished to him. Of course he can if his spirit be right to use it for what it is given to him.

I say, then, you ought to have money. If you can honestly attain unto riches in Philadelphia, it is your Christian and godly duty to do so. It is an awful mistake of these pious people to think you must be awfully poor in order to be pious.

A gentleman gets up back there, and says, "Don't you think there are some things in this world that are better than money?" Of course I do, but I am talking about money now. Of course there are some things higher than money. Oh yes, I know by the grave that has left me standing alone that there are some things in this world that are higher and sweeter and purer than money. Well do I know there are some things higher and grander than gold. Love is the grandest thing on God's earth, but fortunate the lover who has plenty of money. Money is power, money is force, money will do good as well as harm. In the hands of good men and women it could accomplish, and it has accomplished, good.

Yet the age is prejudiced against advising a Christian man (or, as a Jew would say, a godly man) from attaining unto wealth. The prejudice is so universal and the years are far enough back, I think, for me to safely mention that years ago up at Temple University there was a young man in our theological school who thought he was the only pious student in that department. He came into my office one evening and sat down by my desk, and said to me: "Mr. President, I think it is my duty sir, to come in and labor with you." "What has happened now?" Said he, "I heard you say at the Academy, at the Pierce School commencement, that you thought it was an honorable ambition for a young man to desire to have wealth, and that you thought it made him temperate, made him anxious to have a good name, and made him industrious. You spoke about man's ambition to have money helping to make him a good man. Sir, I have come to tell you the Holy Bible says that 'money is the root of all evil."

I told him I had never seen it in the Bible, and advised him to go out into the chapel and get the Bible, and show me the place. So out he went for the Bible, and soon he stalked into my office with the Bible open, with all the bigoted pride of the narrow sectarian, or of one who founds his Christianity on some misinterpretation of Scripture. He flung the Bible down on my desk, and fairly squealed into my ear: "There it is, Mr. President; you can read it for yourself." I said to him: "Well, young man, you will learn when you get a little older that you cannot trust another denomination to read the Bible for you. You belong to another denomination. You are taught in the theological school, however, that emphasis is exegesis. Now, will you take that Bible and read it yourself, and give the proper emphasis to it?"

He took the Bible, and proudly read, "The love of money is the root of all evil."

One of my soldiers in the Civil War had been sentenced to death, and I went up to the White House in Washington — sent there for the first time in my life — to see the President. I went into the waiting-room and sat down with a lot of others on the benches, and the secretary asked one after another to tell him what they wanted. After the secretary had been through the line, he went in, and then came back to the door and motioned for me. I went up to that anteroom, and the secretary said: "That is the President's door right over there. Just rap on it and go right in." I never was so taken aback, friends, in all my life, never. The secretary himself made it worse for me, because he had told me how to go in and then went out another door to the left and shut that. There I was, in the hallway by myself before the President of the United States of America's door. I had been on fields of battle, where the shells did sometimes shriek and the bullets did sometimes hit me, but I always wanted to run. I have no sympathy with the old man who says, "I would just as soon march up to the cannon's mouth as eat my dinner." I have no faith in a man who doesn't know enough to be afraid when he is being shot at. I never was so afraid when the shells came around us at Antietam as I was when I went into that room that day; but I finally mustered the courage — I don't know how I ever did — and at arm's-length tapped on the door. The man inside did not help me at all, but yelled out, "Come in and sit down!"

Well, I went in and sat down on the edge of a chair, and wished I were in Europe, and the man at the table did not look up. He was one of the world's greatest men, and was made great by one single rule. Oh, that all the young people of Philadelphia were before me now and I could say just this one thing, and that they would remember it. I would give a lifetime for the effect it would have on our city and on civilization. Abraham Lincoln's principle for greatness can be adopted by nearly all. This was his rule: Whatsoever he had to do at all, he put his whole mind into it and held it all there until that was all done. That makes men great almost anywhere. He stuck to those papers at that table and did not look up at me, and I sat there trembling. Finally, when he had put the string around his papers, he pushed them over to one side and looked over to me, and a smile came over his worn face. He said: "I am a very busy man and have only a few minutes to spare. Now tell me in the fewest words what it is you want." I began to tell him, and mentioned the case, and he said: "I have heard all about it and you do not need to say any more. Mr. Stanton was talking to me only a few days ago about that. You can go to the hotel and rest assured that the President never did sign an order to shoot a boy under twenty years of age, and never will. You can say that to his mother anyhow."

Then he said to me, "How is it going in the field?" I said, "We sometimes get discouraged." And he said: "It is all right. We are going to win out now. We are getting very near the light. No man ought to wish to be President of the United States, and I will be glad when I get through; then Tad and I are going out to Springfield, Illinois. I have bought a farm out there and I don't care if I again earn only twenty-five cents a day. Tad has a mule team, and we are going to plant onions."

Then he asked me, "Were you brought up on a farm?" I said, "Yes; in the Berkshire Hills of Massachusetts." He then threw his leg over the corner of the big chair and said, "I have heard many a time, ever since I was young, that up there in those hills you have to sharpen the noses of the sheep in order to get down to the grass between the rocks." He was so familiar, so everyday, so farmer-like, that I felt right at home with him at once.

He then took hold of another roll of paper, and looked up at me and said, "Good morning." I took the hint then and got up and went out. After I had gotten out I could not realize I had seen the President of the United States at all. But a few days later, when still in the city, I saw the crowd pass through the East Room by the coffin of Abraham Lincoln, and when I looked at the upturned face of the murdered President I felt then that the man I had seen such a short time before, who, so simple a man, so plain a man, was one of the greatest men that God ever raised up to lead a nation on to ultimate liberty. Yet he was only "Old Abe" to his neighbors. When they had the second funeral, I was invited among others, and went out to see that same coffin put back in the tomb at Springfield. Around the tomb stood Lincoln's old neighbors, to whom he was just "Old Abe."

Oh, I learned the lesson then that I will never forget so long as the tongue of the bell of time continues to swing for me. Greatness consists not in the holding of some future office, but really consists in doing great deeds with little means and the accomplishment of vast purposes from the private ranks of life. To be great at all one must be great here, now, in Philadelphia. He who can give to this city better streets and better sidewalks, better schools and more colleges, more happiness and more civilization, more of God, he will be great anywhere. Let every man or woman here, if you never hear me again, remember this, that if you wish to be great at all, you must begin where you are and what you are, in Philadelphia, now. He that can give to his city any blessing, he who can be a good citizen while he lives here, he that can make better homes, he that can be a blessing whether he works in the shop or sits behind the counter or keeps house, whatever be his life, he who would be great anywhere must first be great in his own Philadelphia.

Chapter 24

Elbert Hubbard

Elbert Hubbard (1856–1915) was an American writer, publisher and philosopher. I first read "A Message to Garcia" as a teenager, I liked it then and I like it now.

After the Titanic sank in 1912, Hubbard wrote the heroic story (and death) of the loving couple, Mr. and Mrs. Straus. On May 1, 1915, Mr. and Mrs. Hubbard were on the Lusitania when it was torpedoed and sunk by a German submarine. They died as heroically as Mr. and Mrs. Straus — two brave and loving pairs.

He founded Roycroft, an Arts and Crafts community, in East Aurora, New York in 1895. The Roycroft Press (or The Roycroft Shops) was part of this community. The Roycrofters produced unique books and two magazines. The extract included here is from an original Roycrofter publication.

How many of us can now carry a message to Garcia? The next time someone asks you, on the job, to do something, think about the way that Rowan went about his task.

I like the quote from Thomas A. Edison, "He was a big service to me in telling me the things I knew, but which I did not know I knew, until he told me."

Hubbard in his "Apologia" states "the hero is the man who does his work — who carries the message to Garcia." He wrote his classic in one hour. As Hubbard notes in the Publisher's Preface, over forty million copies of "A Message to Garcia" have been printed. The world loves an uplifting true story.

The version to follow is the original. I have seen versions that have been edited down. In whatever form, it is a memorable tale.

Hubbard, Elbert, *A Message to Garcia and Other Essays*, New York, Thomas Y. Crowell Company, 1917, pp. 5–23.

1. Publisher's Preface

By special arrangement with The Roycrofters we are privileged to republish these papers from the writings of *Fra Elbertus.* In the author's "Apologia" he tells the circumstances of writing "A Message to Garcia", *a* document which is destined for immortality. The two succeeding papers strike the same high note of responsibility and service.

Elbert Hubbard himself exemplified many of his teachings. He was strong, individual, self-made. Born in 1859, at Bloomington, Illinois, he had only a common-school education, but was an omnivorous reader. His experiment in founding The Roycroft Shop, at East Aurora, New York, devoted to the manufacture of de luxe books, simply carried out a lifetime ambition. Because of his somewhat radical theories and his broad-gauge handling of the labor problem, the experiment was watched elsewhere with much interest. He lived to see it an established success.

Mr. Hubbard toiled early and late. While he was building the Roycroft Shop he founded and carried on two magazines, *The Philistine* and *The Fra,* and actually wrote a greater part of their contents. But that was not all. He wrote a series of 182 biographies under the general title of "Little Journeys to the Homes of the Great." This work was continued without a break for fourteen years!

Still fearing that he should rust out rather than wear out, he went on the lecture platform, and in his public speaking — thanks to his well-stored mind — he was as great a success as in his writing. His engagements were limited only by his physical endurance.

Few men have equalled him in energy or in output. He was a human dynamo. His production increased with the years, and was cut short by his untimely end, when the Lusitania was struck by a German torpedo and went down, May 7, 1915.

Says Franklin K. Lane: "He was a twentieth century Franklin in his application of good sense to modern life." And Thomas A. Edison adds: "He was of big service to me in telling me the things I knew, but which I did not know I knew, until he told me."

"A Message to Garcia" has had probably the most striking success of any short essay of recent times. This success came as a surprise to Mr. Hubbard no less than to others who at first did not realize its outstanding merits.

The man who carried the message, and was thus immortalized by Hubbard, was Colonel Andrew Summers Rowan, who at the outbreak of the Spanish-American War was a young lieutenant in the United States Army. When President McKinley asked of Colonel Arthur Wagner, head of the Bureau of Military Intelligence, "Where can I find a man who will carry a message to Garcia?", the reply was prompt.

"There is a young officer here in Washington named Rowan who will carry it for you," answered Colonel Wagner.

"Send him!" the President ordered tersely.

Lieutenant Rowan started within twenty-four hours, and with no other guard except native Cubans, who were furnished him by the patriots as soon as he secretly landed on the island. He penetrated the interior, and succeeded in reaching the revolutionary General. The story which he himself modestly related bristles with colorful incidents. Fortune undoubtedly favored him, but behind it all was the indomitable pluck of a young American who was determined to do his duty. General Miles, then commanding the United States Army, recommended a decoration for his subaltern, saying: "I regard the achievement as one of the most hazardous and heroic deeds in military warfare."

2. Apologia

This literary trifle, "A Message to Garcia", was written one evening after supper, in a single hour. It was on the Twenty-second of February, Eighteen Hundred Ninety-nine, Washington's Birthday, and we were just going to press with the March *Philistine.* The thing leaped hot from my heart, written after a trying day, when I had been endeavoring to train some rather delinquent villagers to abjure the comatose state and get radioactive.

The immediate suggestion, though, came from a little argument over the teacups, when my boy Bert suggested that Rowan was the real hero of the Cuban War. Rowan had gone alone and done the thing — carried the message to Garcia.

It came to me like a flash! Yes, the boy is right, the hero is the man who does his work — who carries the message to Garcia.

I got up from the table, and wrote "A Message to Garcia". I thought so little of it that we ran it in the Magazine without a heading. The edition went out, and soon orders began to come for extra copies of the March *Philistine*, a dozen, fifty, a hundred; and when the American News Company ordered a thousand, I asked one of my helpers which article it was that had stirred up the cosmic dust. "It's the stuff about Garcia," he said.

The next day a telegram came from George H. Daniels, of the New York Central Railroad, thus: "Give price on one hundred thousand Rowan article in pamphlet form — Empire State Express advertisement on back — also how soon can ship."

I replied giving price, and stated we could supply the pamphlets in two years. Our facilities were small and a hundred thousand booklets looked like an awful undertaking.

The result was that I gave Mr. Daniels permission to reprint the article in his own way. He issued it in booklet form in editions of half a million. Two or three of these half-million lots were sent out by Mr. Daniels, and in addition the article was reprinted in over two hundred magazines and newspapers. It has been translated into all written languages.

At the time Mr. Daniels was distributing the "Message to Garcia", Prince Hilakoff, Director of Russian Railways, was in this country. He was the guest of the New York Central, and made a tour of the country under the personal direction of Mr. Daniels. The Prince saw the little book and was interested in it, more because Mr. Daniels was putting it out in such big numbers, probably, than otherwise.

In any event, when he got home he had the matter translated into Russian, and a copy of the booklet given to every railroad employee in Russia.

Other countries then took it up, and from Russia it passed into Germany, France, Spain, Turkey, Hindustan and China. During the war between Russia and Japan, every Russian soldier who went to the front was given a copy of the *Message to Garcia.*

The Japanese, finding the booklets in possession of the Russian prisoners, concluded that it must be a good thing, and accordingly translated it into Japanese.

And on an order of the Mikado, a copy was given to every man in the employ of the Japanese Government, soldier or civilian.

Over forty million copies of "A Message to Garcia" have been printed. This is said to be a larger circulation than any other literary venture has ever attained during the lifetime of the author, in all history — thanks to a series of lucky accidents.

E.H.
East Aurora,
December 1, 1913.

3. A Message to Garcia

In all this Cuban business there is one man who stands out on the horizon of my memory like Mars at perihelion.

When war broke out between Spain and the United States, it was very necessary to communicate quickly with the leader of the Insurgents. Garcia was somewhere in the mountain fastnesses of Cuba — no one knew where. No mail or telegraph message could reach him. The President must secure his co-operation, and quickly.

What to do!

Someone said to the President, "There is a fellow by the name of Rowan who will find Garcia for you, if anybody can."

Rowan was sent for and given a letter to be delivered to Garcia. How the "fellow by the name of Rowan" took the letter, sealed it up in an oilskin pouch, strapped it over his heart, in four days landed by night off the coast of Cuba from an open boat, disappeared into the jungle, and in three weeks came out on the other side of the Island, having traversed a hostile country on foot, and delivered his letter to Garcia, are things I have no special desire now to tell in detail. The point that I wish to make is this: McKinley gave Rowan a letter to be delivered to Garcia; Rowan took the letter and did not ask, "Where is he at?"

By the Eternal! There is a man whose form should be cast in deathless bronze and the statue placed in every college of the land. It is not book-learning young men need, nor instruction about this and that, but a stiffening of the vertebrae which will cause them to be loyal to a trust, to act promptly, concentrate their energies: do the thing — "Carry a message to Garcia."

General Garcia is dead now, but there are other Garcias. No man who has endeavored to carry out an enterprise where many hands were needed, but has been well-nigh appalled at times by the imbecility-of the average man — the inability or unwillingness to concentrate on a thing and do it.

Slipshod assistance, foolish inattention, dowdy indifference, and half-hearted work seem the rule; and no man succeeds, unless by hook or crook or threat he forces or bribes other men to assist him; or mayhap, God in His goodness performs a miracle, and sends him an Angel of Light for an assistant.

You, reader, put this matter to a test:

You are sitting now in your office; six clerks are within call. Summon any one and make this request: "Please look in the encyclopedia and make a brief memorandum for me concerning the life of Correggio."

Will the clerk quietly say, "Yes, sir," and go do the task?

On your life he will not. He will look at you out of a fishy eye and ask one or more of the following questions:

Who was he?

Which encyclopedia?

Where is the encyclopedia? Was I hired for that?

Don't you mean Bismarck?

What's the matter with Charlie doing it?

Is he dead?

Is there any hurry?

Sha'n't I bring you the book and let you look it up yourself?

What do you want to know for?

And I will lay you ten to one that after you have answered the questions, and explained how to find the information, and why you want it, the clerk will go off and get one of the other clerks to help him try to find Garcia — and then come back and tell you there is no such man. Of course I may lose my bet, but according to the Law of Average I will not.

Now, if you are wise, you will not bother to explain to your "assistant" that Correggio is indexed under the C's, not in the K's, but you will smile very sweetly and say, "Never mind," and go look it up yourself. And this incapacity for independent action, this moral stupidity, this infirmity of the will, this unwillingness to cheerfully catch hold and lift — these are the things that put pure Socialism so far into the future. If men will not act for themselves, what will they do when the benefit of their effort is for all?

A first mate with knotted club seems necessary; and the dread of getting "the bounce" Saturday night holds many a worker to his place. Advertise for a stenographer, and nine out of ten who apply can neither spell nor punctuate — and do not think it necessary to.

Can such a one write a letter to Garcia?

"You see that bookkeeper," said the foreman to me in a large factory.

"Yes; what about him?"

"Well, he's a fine accountant, but if I'd send him up town on an errand, he might accomplish the errand all right, and on the other hand, might stop at four saloons on the way, and when he got to Main Street would forget what he had been sent for."

Can such a man be entrusted to carry a message to Garcia?

We have recently been hearing much maudlin sympathy expressed for the "downtrodden denizens of the sweatshop" and the "homeless wanderer searching for honest employment," and with it all often go many hard words for the men in power.

Nothing is said about the employer who grows old before his time in a vain attempt to get frowsy ne'er-do-wells to do intelligent work; and his long, patient striving after "help" that does nothing but loaf when his back is turned. In every store and factory there is a constant weeding-out process going on. The employer is constantly sending away "help" that have shown their incapacity to further the interests of the business, and others are being taken on. No matter how good times are, this sorting continues: only, if times are hard and work is scarce, the sorting is done finer — but out and forever out the incompetent and unworthy go. It is the survival of the fittest. Self-interest prompts every employer to keep the best — those who can carry a message to Garcia.

I know one man of really brilliant parts who has not the ability to manage a business of his own, and yet who is absolutely worthless to anyone else, because he carries with him constantly the insane suspicion that his employer is oppressing, or intending to oppress, him. He cannot give orders, and he will not receive them. Should a message be given him to take to Garcia, his answer would probably be, "Take it yourself!"

Tonight this man walks the streets looking for work, the wind whistling through his threadbare coat. No one who knows him dare employ him, for he is a regular firebrand of discontent. He is impervious to reason, and the only thing that can impress him is the toe of a thick-soled Number Nine boot.

Of course, I know that one so morally deformed is no less to be pitied than a physical cripple; but in our pitying let us drop a tear, too, for the men who are striving to carry on a great enterprise, whose working hours are not limited by the whistle, and whose hair is fast turning white through the struggle to hold in line dowdy indifference, slipshod imbecility, and the heartless ingratitude which, but for their enterprise, would be both hungry and homeless.

Have I put the matter too strongly? Possibly I have; but when all the world has gone a-slumming I wish to speak a word of sympathy for the man who succeeds — the man who, against great odds, has directed the efforts of others, and having succeeded, finds there's nothing in it: nothing but bare board and clothes. I have carried a dinner-pail and worked for day's wages, and I have also been an employer of labor, and I know there is something to be said on both sides. There is no excellence, per se, in poverty; rags are no recommendation; and all employers are not rapacious and high-handed, any more than all poor men are virtuous. My heart goes out to the man who does his work when the "boss" is away, as well as when he is at home. And the man who, when given a letter for Garcia, quietly takes the missive, without asking any idiotic questions, and with no lurking intention of chucking it into the nearest sewer, or of doing aught else but deliver it, never gets "laid off," nor has to go on a strike for higher wages. Civilization is one long, anxious search for just such individuals. Anything such a man asks shall be granted. He is wanted in every city, town and village — in every office, shop, store and factory. The world cries out for such; he is needed and needed badly — the man who can "Carry a Message to Garcia."

Chapter 25

Louis Brandeis

Louis Brandeis (1856–1941) graduated from Harvard Law School and was appointed to the U.S. Supreme Court in 1916 by President Woodrow Wilson (he was the first Jew to be appointed to that court).

He devoted his entire life to public causes (social issues) such as free speech and the right to privacy. It is easy to disagree with many of the economic positions he takes, but one cannot disagree with the moral objectives of his positions.

His positions are often upsetting (inconsistent with the status quo), but always thought provoking. It is interesting that some of his most outrageous positions are somewhat similar to those of Owen D. Young, a great industrialist. However, Brandeis is unique in his conclusions. Consider the following: "Politically, the American working man is free — so far as the law can make him so. But is he really free?" This one sentence starts one thinking. He goes on to state, "There must be a division not only of profits, but a division also of responsibilities." And finally, "Men must have industrial liberty as well as good wages." These are suggestions worthy of debate.

Brandeis, Louis D. "Industrial Democracy" and "Absolutism in Industry" in *The Social and Economic Views of Mr. Justice Brandeis,* collected, with introductory notes by Alfred Lief. New York; Vanguard Press, 1930, pp. 369–370, 380–385.

1. Industrial Democracy

From an address before the National Congress of Charities and Correction, Boston, June 8, 1911.

Politically, the American workingman is free — so far as the law can make him so. But is he really free? Can any man be really free who is constantly in danger of becoming dependent for mere subsistence upon somebody and something else than his own exertion and conduct? Financial dependence is consistent with freedom only where claim to support rests upon right, and not upon favor.

President Cleveland's epigram that "it is the duty of the citizen to support the Government, not of the Government to support the citizen" is only qualifiedly true. Universal suffrage necessarily imposes upon the State the obligation of fitting its governors — the voters — for their task; and the freedom of the individual is as much an essential condition of successful democracy as his education. If the Government permits conditions to exist which make large classes of citizens financially dependent, the great evil of dependence should at least be minimized by the State's assuming, or causing to be assumed by others, in some form, the burden incident to its own shortcomings.

The cost of attaining freedom is usually high; and the cost of providing for the workingman, as an essential of freedom, a comprehensive and adequate system of insurance will prove to be no exception to this general rule. But, however large the cost, it should be fairly faced and courageously met. For the expense of securing indemnity against the financial losses attending accident, sickness, invalidity, premature death, superannuation, and unemployment should be recognized as a part of the daily cost of living, like the more immediate demands for rent, for food, and for clothing. So far as it is a necessary charge, it should be met as a current expense, instead of being allowed to accumulate as a debt with compound interest to plague us hereafter.

2. Absolutism in Industry

From statements before the United States Commission on Industrial Relations, April 16, 1914, and January 23, 1915.

"Siciety and labor should demand continuity of employment, and when we once get to a point where workingmen are paid throughout the year, as the officers of a corporation are paid throughout the year, everyone will recognize that a business cannot be run profitably unless you keep it running, because if you have to pay, whether your men are working or not, your men will work.

It seems to me that industry has been allowed to develop chaotically, mainly because we have accepted irregularity of employment as if it was something inevitable. It is no more inevitable than insistence upon payment for a great many of the overhead charges in a business, whether the business is in daily operation or not.

It seems to me that the intensive study of businesses and of the elimination of wage in business must result in regularizing business. Every man who has undertaken to study the problem of his business in the most effective way has come to recognize that what we must do is to keep the business running all the time, keep it full. If it is a retail business, he makes it his effort to make other days in the week than Saturday a great day; he tries to take periods of the year when people do not naturally buy and make them buy, in the off seasons, in order to keep his plant going during the period in which ordinarily and in other places of business it loses money. Now, that effort must proceed in every business, to try by means of invention, and invention involving large investment, to make the business run throughout the year; that is, to regularize the work, avoid the congestion of the extra-busy season, and avoid the dearth in what has been a slack season.

There must be a division not only of profits, but a division also of responsibilities. The employees must have the opportunity of participating in the decisions as to what shall be their condition and how the business shall be run. They must learn also in sharing that responsibility that they must bear, too, the suffering arising from grave mistakes, just as the employer must. But the right to assist in making the decisions, the right of making their own mistakes, if mistakes there must be, is a privilege which should not be denied to labor. We must insist upon labor sharing the responsibility for the result of the business.

Now, to a certain extent we are getting it in smaller businesses. The grave objection to the large business is that, almost inevitably, the form of organization, the absentee stockholdings, and its remote directorship prevent participation, ordinarily, of the employees in such management. The executive officials become stewards in charge of the details of the operation of the business, they alone coming into direct relation with labor. Thus we lose that necessary cooperation which naturally flows from contact between employers and employees and which the American aspirations for democracy demand. It is in the resultant absolutism that you will find the fundamental cause of prevailing unrest; no matter what is done with the superstructure, no matter how it may be improved in one way or the other, unless we eradicate that fundamental difficulty, unrest will not only continue, but, in my opinion, will grow worse.

"The wide distribution of stock, instead of being a blessing, constitutes, to my mind, one of the gravest dangers to the community. It is absentee landlordism of the worst kind. It is more dangerous, far more dangerous than the absentee landlordism from which Ireland suffered. There, at all events, control was centered in a few individuals. By the distribution of nominal control among ten thousand or a hundred thousand stockholders there is developed a sense of absolute irresponsibility on the part of the person who holds that stock. The few men that are in position continue absolute control without any responsibility except to their stockholders of continuing and possibly increasing the dividends.

Industrial democracy will not come by gift. It has got to be won by those who desire it. And if the situation is such that a voluntary organization like a labor union is powerless to bring about the democratization of a business, I think we have in this fact some proof that the employing organization is larger than is consistent with the public interest. I mean by larger, is more powerful, has a financial influence too great to be useful to the State; and the State must in some way come to the aid of the workingmen if democratization is to be secured.

Men must have industrial liberty as well as good wages.

CHAPTER 26

Thorstein Veblen

Thorstein Bunde Veblen was born in 1857 in Wisconsin and died in 1929. He was a very unique economist who helped develop the institutional economics branch of economic study.

He wrote *The Theory of the Leisure Class* and coined the phrase (and concept) of "conspicuous consumption." He concluded that businessmen made the economic system inefficient. He also had a low opinion of workers and the union movement and opposed Karl Marx's beliefs.

He was not a person who was easy to like. However, the bit of his writings to follow illustrates his great cleverness and imagination in applying economic concepts where we would not expect to find them. He stretches our minds.

Veblen, Thorstein, *The Place of Science in Modern Civilization*, B.W. Heubsch, New York, 1919.

1. An Early Experiment in Trusts

According to Much,[23] following in the main the views of Penka, Wilser, De Lapouge, Sophus Müller, Andreas Hansen, and other spokesmen of the later theories touching

[23] Matthaeus much, *Die Heimat der Judo germanen.*

Aryan origins, the area of characterization of the West-European culture, as well as of that dolicho-blond racial stock that bears this culture, is the region bordering on the North Sea and the Baltic, and its center of diffusion is to be sought on the southern shores of the Baltic. This region is in a manner, then, the primary focus of that culture of enterprise that has reshaped the scheme of life for mankind during the Christian era. Its spirit of enterprise and adventure has carried this race to a degree of material success that is without example in history, whether in point of the extent or of the scope of its achievements. Up to the present the culminating achievement of this enterprise is dominion in business, and its most finished instrument is the quasi-voluntary coalition of forces known as a Trust.

In its method and outward form this enterprise of the Indo-germanic racial stock has varied with the passage of time and the change of circumstances; but in its spirit and objective end it has maintained a singularly consistent character through all the mutations of name and external circumstance that have passed over it in the course of history.

In its earlier, more elemental expression this enterprise takes the form of raiding, by land and sea. A shrewd interpretation might, without particular violence to the facts, find a coalition of forces of the kind which is later known as a Trust in the Barbarian raids spoken of as the *Völkerwanderung.* Such an interpretation would seem remote, however, and not particularly apt. The beginnings of a *bona fide* trust enterprise are of a more businesslike character and have left a record more amenable to the tests of accountancy. A trust, as that term is colloquially understood, is a business organisation.

Now, the line of enterprise, of indigenous growth in the north-European cultural region, which first falls into settled shape as an orderly, organized business is the traffic of those seafaring men of the North known to fame as the Vikings. And it is in this traffic, so far as the records show, that a trust, with all essential features, is first organized. The term "Viking" covers, somewhat euphemistically, two main facts: piracy and slave trade. Without both of these lines of business the traffic could not be maintained in the long run; and both, but more particularly the latter, presume, as an indispensable condition to their successful prosecution, a regular market and an assured demand for the output. It is a traffic in which, in order to get the best results, a relatively large initial investment must be sunk, and the period of turnover — the period of production — is necessarily of some duration; the risk is also considerable. Further, certain technological prerequisites must be met, in the way particularly of shipbuilding, navigation, and the manufacture of weapons; an adequate accumulation of capital goods must be had, coupled with a sagacious spirit of adventure; there must also be an available supply of labor. There appears to have been a concurrence of all these circumstances, together with favorable market conditions, in the south-Baltic region from about the sixth century onward; the circumstances apparently growing gradually more favorable through the succeeding four centuries.

The Viking trade appears to have grown up gradually on the Baltic seaboard, as well as in the Sound country and throughout the fjord region of Norway, as a by-occupation of the farming population. Its beginnings are earlier than any records, so that the earliest traditions speak of it as an institution well understood and fully legitimate. The well-to-do freehold farmers, including some who laid claim to the rank of *jarl*, seem to have found it an agreeable and honorable diversion, as well as a lucrative employment for their surplus wealth and labor supply. From such sporadic and occasional beginnings it passed presently into an independently organized and self-sustaining line of business enterprise, and in the course of time it attained a settled business routine and a defined code of professional ethics. Syndication, of a loose form, had begun as early as the oldest accounts extant, but it is evident from the way in which the matter is spoken of that combination had not at that date — say, about the beginning of the ninth century — long been the common practice. It was not then a matter of course. The early combinations were relatively small and transient. They took the form of "gentlemen's agreements," pools, working arrangements, division of territory, etc., rather than hard and fast syndicates. In those early days a combine would be formed for a season between two or more capitalist-undertakers, for the most part employing their own capital only, without recourse to credit; although credit arrangements occur quite early, but are not very common in the earlier recorded phases of the trade. Such a loose combine, say about the middle of the ninth century, might comprise from two to a dozen boats. What may be called the normal unit in the trade at that time was a boat of perhaps thirty tons' burden, with an effective crew of some eighty men. Boats and crews gradually increase both in size and efficiency for a century and a half after that time.

Syndication, of an increasingly close texture and increasingly permanent effect, appears to have rapidly grown in favor through the ninth and tenth centuries. The reasons for this movement of coalition are plain. The volume of the trade, as well as its territorial extension, increased uninterruptedly. The technique of the trade was gradually improved, and the equipment and management were improved and reduced to standard forms. The tonnage employed at any given time can, of course, not be ascertained with anything like a confident approximation; but its steady increase is unmistakable. Year by year the boats and crews increase in average size as well as in number, until by the middle of the tenth century the number of men and ships engaged, as well as the volume of capital invested in the trade, are probably larger than the corresponding figures for any other form of lucrative enterprise at that time. It is, at that time, altogether the best-organized line of enterprise in the West-European region in respect of its business management, and the most efficient and progressive in respect of its equipment and technology. At a conservative guess, the aggregate number of ships engaged about the middle of the tenth century must have appreciably exceeded six hundred, and may have reached one thousand; with crews which had also grown gradually larger until they may by this time have averaged 150 or 200 men. There was consequently what would in modern phrase be called an "overproduction" of piratical craft — overinvestment in the Viking trade and consequent cut-throat competition. The various coalitions came into violent conflict, and many of them went under, with great resultant loss of capital, impoverishment of well-to-do families, hardship and demoralization of the entire trade.

Added to these untoward conditions within the trade was the open disfavor of the crown, in each of the three Scandinavian kingdoms. The traffic had long passed out of the stage at which it had offered a lucrative opening for farmers' sons who were tired of the farm and eager to find excitement, reputation, and creature comforts in that wider human contact and busier life for which the tedium of the farm had sharpened their appetites. The larger capitalists alone could succeed as organizers or directors of a Viking concern under the changed conditions. The common run of well-to-do farmers had neither the tangible assets nor the "good-will" requisite to the successful promotion of a new company of freebooters. At the best, their sons could enter the business only as employees and with but a very uncertain outlook to speedy promotion to an executive position. On the other hand, as the trade became better organized in stronger hands, with a larger equipment, and as the competition within the trade grew more severe, the blackmail from which much of the profits of the trade was drawn grew more excessive and more uncertain, both as to its amount and as to the manner and incidents with which it was levied. As competition grew severe and the small Vikings practically disappeared, and as the demoralization that goes with cut-throat competition set in, the livelihood of the common people, at whose expense the Vikings lived, grew progressively more precarious, and even their domestic peace and household industry grew insecure. Popular sentiment was running strongly against the whole traffic. So much so, indeed, as to threaten the tenure of courts and sovereigns if the popular hardship incident to the continuance of the trade were not abated.

The politicians, therefore, made a strenuous show of effort to regulate, or even to repress, the Viking organizations. Outright and indiscriminate repression was scarcely a feasible remedy, certainly not an agreeable one. The Viking companies were a source of strength to the country, both in that they might be drawn on for support in case of war and in that they brought funds into the country. The remedy to which the politicians turned, by preference, therefore, was a regulation of the companies in such a manner as to let "the foreigners pay the tax," to adapt a modern phrase. If the freebooters of a given state could be induced, by stringent regulations, to prey upon the people of the neighboring states, and particularly if they worked at cross-purposes with similar companies of freebooters domiciled in such neighboring states, it was then plain to the sagacious politicians of those days that the companies might be more of a blessing than a curse. On trial it was found that this policy of control gave at the best but very dubious results, and consequently the repressive hand of the authorities perforce fell with increasingly rigorous pressure on the Viking organizations, particularly on the smaller ones which were scarcely of national importance. The competition in the trade was too severe to admit of a consistent avoidance of excesses and irregularities on the part of the Vikings, and these irregularities obliged the authorities to interfere.

Under these circumstances it is plain that no Viking combine could hope to prosper in the long run unless it were strong enough to take an international position and to maintain a practical monopoly of the trade. "International" in these premises means within the Scandinavian countries. In the days of its finest development the Viking trade was domiciled in the Scandinavian countries, almost exclusively. This means the two Scandinavian peninsulas, with Iceland, the Faroes, Orkneys, Hebrides, and the Scandinavian portions of Scotland. To this, for completeness of statement, is to be added a stretch of Wendish seaboard on the south of the Baltic and a negligible patch of German territory. The trade, so far as regards its home offices, to use a modern phrase, gathered in the main about two chief centers: the Orkneys and the south end of the Baltic. Outlying regions, such as the Norwegian fjord country and the Hebrides, are by no means negligible, but the two regions named above are after all the chief seats of the traffic; and of these two centers the Baltic — chiefly Danish — region is in many respects the more notable. Its Viking traffic is better, more regularly organized, is carried on with a more evident sense of a solidarity of interests and a more consistent view to a long-term prosperity. As one might say, looking at the matter from the modern standpoint, it has more of a look of stability and conservative management, such as belongs to an investment business, and has less of a speculative air, than the trade that centers in the western isles.

Perhaps it is just on this account, because of its greater stability of interests and more conservative animus, that the traffic of this region responds with greater alacrity to the pressure of excessive competition and political interference, and so enters on a policy of larger and closer coalition. It may be added that many of the great captains of adventure in this region are men of good family and substantial standing in the community. As may often happen in a like conjuncture, when the irksomeness of this competitive situation in the Baltic was fast becoming intolerable, there arose a man of far-seeing sagacity and settled principles, of executive ability and businesslike integrity, who saw the needs of the hour and the available remedy, and who saw at the same glance his own opportunity of gain. This man was Pálnatoki, the descendant of an honorable line of country gentlemen in the island of Funen, whose family had from time immemorial borne an active and prudent part in the trade, and had been well seen at court and in society. He was a man of mature experience, with a large investment in the traffic, and with a body of "good-will" that gave him perhaps his most decisive advantage.

During the reign of Harald Gormsson, about the middle of the tenth century, Pálnatoki seems to have cast about for a basis on which to promote an international coalition of Vikings, such as would put an end to headlong competition in the trade and would at the same time be placed above the accidents of national politics. To this end it was necessary to find a neutral ground on which to establish the home office of the concern. Such a medieval-Scandinavian New Jersey was the Wendish kingdom at the south of the Baltic.

Jómsborg (on the island of Wollin, at the mouth of the Oder) seems to have been a resort of Vikings before Pálnatoki organized his company there and strengthened the harbor, which may have been fortified by those who held it before him. Here the new company was incorporated under a special franchise from the Wendish crown, with the stipulation that it was to do business only outside the Wendish territories. The tangible assets of the corporation were the harbor and fortified town of Jómsborg, together with the ships and other equipment of such Vikings as were admitted to fellowship; its intangible assets were its franchise and the good-will of the promoter and the underlying companies. Its by-laws were very strict, both as to the discipline of the personnel and as to the distribution of earnings. The promoter, who was the first president of the corporation, was given extreme powers for the enforcement of the by-laws, and throughout his long incumbency of office he exercised his powers with the greatest discretion and with a most salutary effect.

This neutral, international corporation of piracy rapidly won a great prestige. In modern phrase, its intangible assets grew rapidly larger. Backed by the competitive pressure which the new corporation was able to bring upon the smaller companies and syndicates, this prestige of the Jomsvikings brought a steady run of applications for admission into the trust. The trust's policy was substantially the same as has since become familiar in other lines of enterprise, with the difference that in those early days the competitive struggle took a less sophisticated form. Outstanding syndicates and private firms were given the alternative of submission to the trust's terms or retirement from the traffic. There was great hardship among the outstanding concerns, especially among that large proportion of them that were unable to meet the scale of requirements imposed on applicants for admission into the trust. The qualifications both as to equipment and personnel were extremely strict, so that a large percentage of the applicants were excluded; and the unfortunates who failed of admission found themselves in a doubtful position that grew more precarious with every year that passed. Practically, such concerns were either frozen out of the business or forced into a liquidation which permanently wound up their affairs and terminated their corporate existence.

The accounts extant are of course not reliable in minute details, being not strictly contemporary, nor are they cast in such modern terms as would give an easy comparison with present-day facts. The chief documents in the case are *Jómsvikingasaga*, *Saxo Grammaticus*, *Heimskringla*, and *Olafssaga Tryggvasonar*; but nearly the whole of the saga literature bears on the development of the Viking trade, and characteristic references to the

Jómsviking trust occur throughout. The evidence afforded by these accounts converges to the conclusion that toward the close of the tenth century the trust stood in a high state of prosperity and was in a position virtually to dictate the course of the traffic for all that portion of the Viking trade that centered in the Baltic. Its prestige and influence were strong wherever the traffic extended, even in the region of the western isles and in the fjord country of Norway. It had even come to be a factor of first-rate consequence in international politics, and its power was feared and courted by those two sovereigns who established the Danish rule in England, as well as by their Swedish, Norwegian, and Russian contemporaries. It is probably not an overstatement to say that the Danish conquest of England would not have been practicable except for the alliance of the trust with Svend, which enabled him to turn his attention from the complications of Scandinavian politics to his English interests.

The extent of the trust's material equipment at the height of its prosperity is a matter of surmise rather than of statistical information. Some notion of its strength may be gathered from the statement that the fortified harbor of Jómsborg included within its castellated seawall an inclosed basin capable of floating three hundred ships at anchor. In the great raid against the kingdom of Norway, whose failure inaugurated the disintegration of the trust, the number of ships sent out is variously given by different authorities. The *Jómsvikingasaga* says that they numbered one hundred. This fleet, however, was made up of craft selected from among the ships that were under the immediate command of four of the great captains of adventure. The fleet, as it lay in the Sound before the final selection, is said to have numbered 185, but the context shows that this fleet was but a fraction of the aggregate Jómsviking tonnage. Of this disastrous expedition but a fraction returned; yet various later expeditions of the Jómsvikings are mentioned in which some scores of their ships took part.

The trust having become an international power, it undertook to shape the destiny of nations and dynasties, and it broke under the strain. It, or its directors, took a contract to bring Norway into subjection to the Danish crown. Partly through untoward accidents, partly through miscalculation and hurried preparations, it failed in this undertaking, which brought the affairs of the trust to a spectacular crisis. From this disaster it never recovered. With the opening of the eleventh century the Viking trust fell into abeyance, and in a few years it disappeared from the field. There are several good reasons for its failure. On the death of its founder the management had passed into the hands of Sigvaldi, a man of less sagacity and less integrity as well as of more unprincipled personal ambition, and somewhat given to flighty ventures in the field of politics. It was Sigvaldi's overweening personal ambition that committed the corporation to the ill-advised expedition against Norway. The trust, moreover, being supreme within its field, the discipline grew lax and its exactions grew arbitrary, sometimes going to unprovoked excesses. As one might say, too little thought was given to "economies of production," and the charges were pushed beyond "what the traffic would bear." But for all that, in spite of its meddling in politics, and in spite of jobbery and corruption in its management, the trust still had a fair outlook for continued success, except that the bottom dropped out of the trade. For better or worse, the slave-trade in the north of Europe collapsed on the introduction of Christianity, at least so far as regards the trade in Christians; and without a slave market the Viking enterprise had no chance of reasonable earnings. At the same time, the risk and hardships of the traffic — the "cost of production" — grew heavier as the countries to the south became better able to defend their shores. The passenger traffic failed almost entirely, and the goods traffic was in a disorganized and unprofitable state. The costs were fast becoming prohibitive, even to men so enterprising and necessitous as the Norwegian freebooters. The situation changed in such a way as to leave the trust out.

Some show of corporate existence was still maintained for a short period after the trust's great crisis, but there was an end of discipline and authoritative control. The minor concerns and private establishments that had once formed part of the trust continued in the trade on an independent footing, but with decreasing regularity and with diminishing strength. As the equipment wore out it was not replaced, and the trade lapsed. The great captains of the industry, like Sigvaldi, Thorkel Haraldson, Sigurd Kápa, and Vagn Akason, turned their holdings to the service of the dynastic politics which were then engaging the attention of the northern countries. Much of this body of enterprise and wealth was exhausted in working out the imperialistic schemes of expansion of Svend and Knut the Great; and what was left over shared the fortunes of the other available forces of the Scandinavian countries, being dissipated in political dissensions, extortionate government organizations, and the establishment of a church and a nobility.

CHAPTER 27

Alfred North Whitehead

Alfred North Whitehead (1861–1947) was born in England "of yeoman stock" and died in the United States. He attended Cambridge University as a student and taught there as a fellow and acknowledged a large obligation to that University for "social and intellectual training."[24] His first writings and teachings were mathematical but he then proceeded to philosophy. He co-authored *Principia Mathematica* with his ex-student Bertrand Russell. At age 63, he left the Imperial College, London to become a professor at Harvard. He had a significant interest in the young business school across the Cambridge river.

On Foresight

Whitehead defines "foresight" to be an essential element of success in a business activity. To help explain foresight he contrasts understanding and routine and defines the need for each and their limits.

"Rigid maxims, a rule-of-think routine, and cast-iron particular doctrines will be the ruin of many people." I also like a flexible approach to management.

[24] A. N. Whitehead, *Essays in Science and Philosophy*, Philosophical Library, New York, 1948.

Requisites for Social Progress

Authors sometimes write great thoughts. Whitehead did for me with the following:

> "The great conquerors, from Alexander to Caesar, and from Caesar to Napoleon, influenced profoundly the lives of subsequent generations. But the total effect of this influence shrinks to insignificance, if compared to the entire transformation of human habits and human mentality produced by the long line of men of thought from Thales to the present day, men individually powerless, but ultimately the rulers of the world."

I would have inserted after "profoundly" and before "the lives" the words "but not always in a positive fashion."

Whitehead, Alfred North, *An Introduction to Business Adrift*, by W.B. Donham, Whittlesey House, McGraw-Hill, New York, 1931.

1. On Foresight

At the outset, I must disclaim the foolish notion that it is possible for anyone, devoid of personal experience of business, to provide useful suggestions for its detailed conduct. There is no substitute for first-hand practice. I am using the word "business" in the largest sense of that term, in which it includes a variety of activities. But any useful theory about them, capable of immediate application to specific instances, must depend on a direct knowledge of the relevant reactions of men and women composing that society, or group of nations, within which the business in question is to flourish.

There remains, however, the question of the general type of mentality which in the present condition of the world will promote the general success of a business community. Such a type is, of course, very complex. But I pick out one unquestioned element in it, namely Foresight, and will discuss the conditions for its development and its successful exercise.

We shall comprehend better the varieties of individual understanding which go to complete this general equipment of an ideal business community, if we commence by considering the contrast between understanding and routine.

Routine is the god of every social system; it is the seventh heaven of business, the essential component in the success of every factory, the ideal of every statesman. The social machine should run like clockwork. Every crime should be followed by an arrest, every arrest by a judicial trial, every trial by a conviction, every conviction by a punishment, every punishment by a reformed character. Or, you can conceive an analogous routine concerning the making of a motor car, starting with the iron in the ore, and the coal in the mine, and ending with the car driving out of the factory and with the president of the corporation signing the dividend warrants, and renewing his contracts with the mining corporations. In such a routine everyone from the humblest miner to the august president is exactly trained for his special job. Every action of miner or president is the product of conditioned reflexes, according to current physiological phraseology. When the routine is perfect, understanding can be eliminated, except such minor flashes of intelligence as are required to deal with familiar accidents, such as a flooded mine, a prolonged drought, or an epidemic of influenza.

A system will be the product of intelligence. But when the adequate routine is established, intelligence vanishes and the system is maintained by a coordination of conditioned reflexes. What is then required from the humans is receptivity of special training. No one, from president to miner, need understand the system as a whole. There will be no foresight, but there will be complete success in the maintenance of the routine.

Now it is the beginning of wisdom to understand that social life is founded upon routine. Unless society is permeated, through and through, with routine, civilization vanishes. So many sociological doctrines, the products of acute intellects, are wrecked by obliviousness to this fundamental sociological truth. Society requires stability, foresight itself presupposes stability, and stability is the product of routine.

But there are limits to routine, and it is for the discernment of these limits, and for the provision of the consequent action, that foresight is required.

The two extremes of complete understanding and of complete routine are never realized in human society. But of the two, routine is more fundamental than understanding, that is to say, routine modified by minor flashes of short range intelligence. Indeed the notion of complete understanding controlling action is an ideal in the clouds, grotesquely at variance with practical life. But we have under our eyes countless examples of societies entirely dominated by routine. The elaborate social organizations of insects appear to be thorough going examples of routine. Such organizations achieve far-reaching, complex purposes: they involve a differentiation of classes, from cows to serfs, from serfs to workers, from workers to warriors, from warriors to janitors, and from janitors to queens. Such organizations have regard to needs in a distant future, especially if the comparatively short space of life of the individual insect is taken into account as the unit of measurement.

It is at this point that we recur to the title of this article, Foresight. We require such an understanding of the present conditions, as may give us some grasp of the novelty which is about to produce a measurable influence on the immediate future. Yet the doctrine, that routine is dominant in any society that is not collapsing, must never be lost sight of. Thus the grounds, in human nature and in the successful satisfaction of purpose,—these grounds for the current routine, must be understood; and at the same time the sorts of novelty just entering into social effectiveness have got to be weighed against the old routine.

The older political economy reigned supreme for about a hundred years from the time of Adam Smith, because in its main assumptions it did apply to the general circumstances of life as led, then and for innumerable centuries in the past. These circumstances were then already passing away. But it still remained a dominant truth that in commercial relations men were dominated by well-conditioned reactions to completely familiar stimuli.

In the present age, the element of novelty which life affords is too prominent to be omitted from our calculations. A deeper knowledge of the varieties of human nature is required to determine the reaction, in its character and its strength, to those elements of novelty which each decade of years introduces into social life. The possibility of this deeper knowledge constitutes the Foresight, of which I am speaking.

But we are faced with a fluid, shifting situation in the immediate future Rigid maxims, a rule-of-thumb routine, and cast-iron particular doctrines will be the ruin of many people. The business of the future must be controlled by a somewhat different type of men to that of previous centuries. The type is already changing, and has already changed so far as the leaders are concerned. The Business Schools of Universities are concerned with spreading this type throughout the nations by aiming at the production of the requisite type of mentality.

I will conclude by a sketch of the Business Mind of the future. In the first place, it is fundamental that there be a power of conforming to routine, of supervising routine, of constructing routine, and of understanding routine both as to its internal structure and as to its external purposes. Such a power is the bedrock of all practical efficiency.

But for the production of the requisite Foresight, something more is wanted. This extra endowment can only be described as a philosophic power of understanding the complex flux of the varieties of human societies; for instance the habit of noting varieties of character, of demands on life, of serious purposes, of frivolous amusements. Such instinctive grasp of the relevant features of social currents is of supreme importance. For example, the time-span of various types of social behavior is of the essence of their effect on policy. A widespread type of religious interest, with its consequent behaviors, has a dominant life of about a hundred years, while a fashion of dress survives any time between three months and three years. Methods of agriculture change slowly. But the scientific world seems to be on the verge of far-reaching biological discoveries. Thus the assumption of slow changes in agriculture must be scanned vigilantly.

This example of time-spans can be generalized. The quantitative aspect of social changes is of the essence of business relations. Thus the habit of transforming observation of qualitative changes into quantitative estimates should be a characteristic of business mentality. I have said enough to show that the modern business mentality requires many elements of discipline, scientific and sociological. But the great fact remains that details of relevant knowledge cannot be foreseen. Thus even for mere success, and apart from any question of intrinsic quality of life, an unspecialized aptitude for eliciting generalizations from particulars and for seeing the divergent illustration of generalities in diverse circumstances is required.

Such a reflective power is essentially a philosophic habit: it is the survey of society from the standpoint of generality. This habit of general thought, undaunted by novelty, is the gift of philosophy.

But the motive of success is not enough. It produces a short-sighted world which destroys the sources of its own prosperity. The cycles of trade depression which afflict the world warn us that business relations are infected through and through with the disease of short-sighted motives. The robber barons did not conduce to the prosperity of Europe in the Middle Ages, though some of them died prosperously in their beds. Their example is a warning to our civilization.

Also we must not fall into the fallacy of thinking of the business world in abstraction from the rest of the community. The business world is one main part of the very community which is the subject-matter of our study. The behavior of the community is largely dominated by the business mind. A great society is a society in which its men of business think greatly of their functions. Low thoughts mean low behavior, and after a brief orgy of exploitation, low behavior means a descending standard of life. The general greatness of the community, qualitatively as well as quantitatively, is the first condition for steady prosperity, buoyant, self-sustained, and commanding credit.

The Greek philosopher who laid the foundation of all our finer thoughts ended his most marvelous dialogue with the reflection that the ideal state could never arrive till philosophers are kings. Today, in an age of democracy, the kings are the plain citizens pursuing their various avocations. There can be no successful democratic society till general education conveys a philosophic outlook.

Mankind is now in one of its rare moods of shifting its outlook. The mere compulsion of tradition has lost its force. It is the business of philosophers, students, and practical men to re-create and re-enact a vision of the world, conservative and radical, including those elements of reverence and order without which society lapses into riot, a vision penetrated through and through with unflinching rationality. Such a vision is the knowledge which Plato identified with virtue.

Epochs for which, within the limits of their development, this vision has been widespread, are the epochs unfading in the memory of mankind. There is now no choice before us: either we must succeed in providing a rational coordination of impulses and thoughts, or for centuries civilization will sink into a mere welter of minor excitements. We must produce a great age, or see the collapse of the upward striving of our race.

2. Requisites for Social Progress

It has been the purpose of these lectures to analyze the reactions of science in forming that background of instinctive ideas which control the activities of successive generations. Such a background takes the form of a certain vague philosophy as to the last word about things, when all is said. The three centuries, which form the epoch of modern science, have revolved round the ideas of *God*, *mind*, *matter*, and also of *space* and *time* in their characters of expressing *simple location* for matter. Philosophy has on the whole emphasized *mind*, and has thus been out of touch with science during the two latter centuries. But it is creeping back into its old importance owing to the rise of psychology and its alliance with physiology. Also, this rehabilitation of philosophy has been facilitated by the recent breakdown of the seventeenth century settlement of the principles of physical science. But, until that collapse, science seated itself securely upon the concepts of matter, space, time, and latterly, of energy. Also there were arbitrary laws of nature determining locomotion. They were empirically observed, but for some obscure reason were known to be universal. Anyone who in practice or theory disregarded them was denounced with unsparing vigor. This position on the part of scientists was pure bluff, if one may credit them with believing their own statements. For their current philosophy completely failed to justify the assumption that the immediate knowledge; inherent in any present occasion throws any light either on its past, or its future.

Another great fact confronting the modern world is the discovery of the method of training professionals, who specialize in particular regions of thought and thereby progressively add to the sum of knowledge within their respective limitations of subject. In consequence of the success of this professionalizing of knowledge, there are two points to be kept in mind, which differentiate our present age from the past. In the first place, the rate of progress is such that an individual human being, of ordinary length of life, will be called upon to face novel situations which find no parallel in his past. The fixed person for the fixed duties, who in older societies was such a godsend, in the future will be a public danger. In the second place, the modern professionalism in knowledge works in the opposite direction so far as the intellectual sphere is concerned. The modern chemist is likely to be weak in zoology, weaker still in his general knowledge of the Elizabethan drama, and completely ignorant of the principles of rhythm in English versification. It is probably safe to ignore his knowledge of ancient history. Of course I am speaking of general tendencies; for chemists are no worse than engineers, or mathematicians, or classical scholars. Effective knowledge is professionalized knowledge, supported by a restricted acquaintance with useful subjects subservient to it.

This situation has its dangers. It produces minds in a groove. Each profession makes progress, but it is progress in its own groove. Now to be mentally in a groove is to live in contemplating a given set of abstractions. The groove prevents straying across country, and the abstraction abstracts from something to which no further attention is paid. But there is no groove of abstractions which is adequate for the comprehension of human life. Thus in the modern world, the celibacy of the medieval learned class has been replaced by a celibacy of the intellect which is divorced from the concrete contemplation of the complete facts. Of course, no one is merely a mathematician, or merely a lawyer. People have lives outside their professions or their businesses. But the point is the restraint of serious thought within a groove. The remainder of life is treated superficially, with the imperfect categories of thought derived from one profession.

It is very arguable that the science of political economy, as studied in its first period after the death of Adam Smith (1790), did more harm than good. It destroyed many economic fallacies, and taught how to think about the economic revolution then in progress. But it riveted on men a certain set of abstractions which were disastrous in their influence on modern mentality. It de-humanized industry. This is only one example of a general danger inherent in modern science. Its methodological procedure is exclusive and intolerant, and rightly so. It fixes attention on a definite group of abstractions, neglects everything else, and elicits every scrap of information and theory which is relevant to what it has retained. This method is triumphant, provided that the abstractions are judicious. But, however triumphant, the triumph is within limits. The neglect of these limits leads to disastrous oversights. The anti-rationalism of science is partly justified, as a preservation of its useful methodology; it is partly mere irrational prejudice. Modern professionalism is the training of minds to conform to the methodology. The historical revolt of the seventeenth century, and the earlier reaction towards naturalism, were examples of transcending the abstractions which fascinated educated society in the Middle Ages. These early ages had an ideal of rationalism, but they failed in its pursuit. For they neglected to note that the methodology of reasoning requires the limitations involved in the abstract.

Accordingly, the true rationalism must always transcend itself by recurrence to the concrete in search of inspiration. A self-satisfied rationalism is in effect a form of anti-rationalism. It means an arbitrary halt at a particular set of abstractions. This was the case with science.

Almost equally dangerous is the Gospel of Uniformity. The differences between the nations and races of mankind are required to preserve the conditions under which higher development is possible. One main factor in the upward trend of animal life has been the power of wandering. Perhaps this is why the armor-plated monsters fared badly. They could not wander. Animals wander into new conditions. They have to adapt themselves or die. Mankind has wandered from the trees to the plains, from the plains to the seacoast, from climate to climate, from continent to continent, and from habit of life to habit of life. When man ceases to wander, he will cease to ascend in the scale of being. Physical wandering is still important, but greater still is the power of man's spiritual adventures — adventures of thought, adventures of passionate feeling, adventures of aesthetic experience. A diversification among human communities is essential for the provision of the incentive and material for the Odyssey of the human spirit. Other nations of different habits are not enemies: they are godsends. Men require of their neighbors something sufficiently akin to be understood, something sufficiently different to provoke attention, and something great enough to command admiration. We must not expect, however, all the virtues. We should even be satisfied if there is something odd enough to be interesting.

Modern science has imposed on humanity the necessity for wandering. Its progressive thought and its progressive technology make the transition through time, from generation to generation, a true migration into uncharted seas of adventure. The very benefit of wandering is that it is dangerous and needs skill to avert evils. We must expect, therefore, that the future will disclose dangers. It is the business of the future to be dangerous; and it is among the merits of science that it equips the future for its duties. The prosperous middle classes, who ruled the nineteenth century, placed an excessive value upon placidity of existence. They refused to face the necessities for social reform imposed by the new industrial system, and they are now refusing to face the necessities for intellectual reform imposed by the new knowledge. The middle class pessimism over the future of the world comes from a confusion between civilization and security. In the immediate future there will be less security than in the immediate past, less stability. It must be admitted that there is a degree of instability which is inconsistent with civilization. But, on the whole, the great ages have been unstable ages.

The moral of the tale is the power of reason, its decisive influence on the life of humanity. The great conquerors, from Alexander to Caesar, and from Caesar to Napoleon, influenced profoundly the lives of subsequent generations. But the total effect of this influence shrinks to insignificance, if compared to the entire transformation of human habits and human mentality produced by the long line of men of thought from Thales to the present day, men individually powerless, but ultimately the rulers of the world.

Chapter 28

O. Henry

O. Henry (1862–1910) was the pen name of American writer William Sydney Porter. O. Henry wrote short stories famous for their humor and clever endings.

Porter's life was short and he suffered numerous tragedies. His mother died of tuberculosis when he was three. His wife, Athol, gave birth to a son who died a few hours after birth. Nine years after their marriage, Athol died from tuberculosis. He had troubles with the law (three years in jail) and drinking too much then followed.

Two of his stories are included. "The Gift of the Magi" is a classic moving short story. Do not be surprised (or ashamed) if it brings tears to your eyes. I also included "The Unknown Quantity" since it incorporates some relevant business and economic factors and I liked it. It is also romantic.

Henry, O., "The Gift of the Magi" and "The Unknown Quantity," William Lyon Phelps, *The Complete Works of O. Henry,* edited by William Lyon Phelps, Garden City, New York, Doubleday, Doran & Company, Inc., 1937, pp. 8–12, 1492–1495.

1. The Gift of the Magi

One dollar and eighty-seven cents. That was all. And sixty cents of it was in pennies. Pennies saved one and two at a time by bulldozing the grocer and the vegetable man and the butcher until one's cheeks burned with the silent imputation of parsimony that such close dealing implied. Three times Della counted it. One dollar and eighty-seven cents. And the next day would be Christmas.

There was clearly nothing to do but flop down on the shabby little couch and howl. So Della did it. Which instigates the moral reflection that life is made up of sobs, sniffles, and smiles, with sniffles predominating.

While the mistress of the home is gradually subsiding from the first stage to the second, take a look at the home. A furnished flat at $8 per week. It did not exactly beggar description, but it certainly had that word on the lookout for the mendicancy squad.

In the vestibule below was a letter-box into which no letter would go, and an electric button from which no mortal finger could coax a ring. Also appertaining thereunto was a card bearing the name "Mr. James Dillingham Young."

The "Dillingham" had been flung to the breeze during a former period of prosperity when its possessor was being paid $30 per week. Now, when the income was shrunk to $20, the letters of "Dillingham" looked blurred, as though they were thinking seriously of contracting to a modest and unassuming D. But whenever Mr. James Dillingham Young came home and reached his flat above he was called "Jim" and greatly hugged by Mrs. James Dillingham Young, already introduced to you as Della. Which is all very good.

Della finished her cry and attended to her cheeks with the powder rag. She stood by the window and looked out dully at a gray cat walking a gray fence in a gray backyard. Tomorrow would be Christmas Day, and she had only $1.87

with which to buy Jim a present. She had been saving every penny she could for months, with this result. Twenty dollars a week doesn't go far. Expenses had to be greater than she had calculated. They always are. Only $1.87 to buy a present for Jim. Her Jim. Many a happy hour she had spent planning for something nice for him. Something fine and rare and sterling — something just a little bit near to being worthy of the honor of being owned by Jim.

There was a pier-glass between the windows of the room. Perhaps you have seen pier-glass in an $8 flat. A very thin and very agile person may, by observing his reflection in a rapid sequence of longitudinal strips, obtain a fairly accurate conception of his looks. Della, being slender, had mastered the art.

Suddenly she whirled from the window and stood before the glass. Her eyes were shining brilliantly, but her face had lost its color within twenty seconds. Rapidly she pulled down her hair and let it fall to its full length.

Now, there were two possessions of the James Dillingham Youngs in which they both took mighty pride. One was Jim's gold watch that had been his father's and his grandfather's; the other was Della's hair. Had the Queen of Sheba lived in the flat across the airshaft, Della would have let her hair hang out the window some day to dry just to depreciate Her Majesty's jewels and gifts. Had King Solomon been the janitor, with all his treasures piled up in the basement, Jim would have pulled out his watch every time he passed, just to see him pluck at his beard from envy.

So now Della's beautiful hair fell about her rippling and shining like a cascade of brown waters. It reached below her knee and made itself almost a garment for her. And then she did it up again nervously and quickly. Once she faltered for a minute and stood still while a tear or two splashed on the worn carpet.

On went her old brown jacket; on went her brown hat. With a whirl of skirts and with the brilliant sparkle still in her eyes, she fluttered out the door and down the stairs to the street.

Where she stopped the sign read: "Mme. Sofronie. Hair Goods of All Kinds." One flight up Della ran, and collected herself, panting. Madame, large, too white, chilly, hardly looked the "Sofonie."

"Will you buy my hair?" asked Della.

"I buy hair," said Madame. "Take yer hat off and let's have a sight at the looks of it."

Down rippled the brown cascade.

"Twenty dollars," said Madame, lifting the mass with a practiced hand.

"Give it to me quick," said Della.

Oh, and the next two hours tripped by on rosy wings. Forget the hashed metaphor. She was ransacking the stores for Jim's present.

She found it at last. It surely had been made for Jim and no one else. There was no other like it in any of the stores, and she had turned all of them inside out. It was a platinum fob chain simple and chaste in design, properly proclaiming its value by substance alone and not by meretricious ornamentation — as all good things should do. It was even worthy of The Watch. As soon as she saw it she knew that it must be Jim's. It was like him. Quietness and value — the description applied to both. Twenty-one dollars they took from her for it, and she hurried home with the 87 cents. With that chain on his watch Jim might be properly anxious about the time in any company. Grand as the watch was, he sometimes looked at it on the sly on account of the old leather strap that he used in place of a chain.

When Della reached home her intoxication gave way a little to prudence and reason. She got out her curling irons and lighted the gas and went to work repairing the ravages made by generosity added to love. Which is always a tremendous task, dear friends — a mammoth task.

Within forty minutes her head was covered with tiny, close-lying curls that made her look wonderfully like a truant school boy. She looked at her reflection in the mirror long, carefully, and critically.

"If Jim doesn't kill me," she said to herself, "before he takes a second look at me, he'll say I look like a Coney Island chorus girl. But what could I do — oh! what could I do with a dollar and eighty-seven cents?"

At 7 o'clock the coffee was made and the frying-pan was on the back of the stove hot and ready to cook the chops.

Jim was never late. Della doubled the fob chain in her hand and sat on the corner of the table near the door that he always entered. Then she heard his step on the stair away down on the first flight, and she turned white for just a moment. She had a habit of saying little silent prayers about the simplest everyday things, and now she whispered: "Please God, make him think I am still pretty."

The door opened and Jim stepped in and closed it. He looked thin and very serious. Poor fellow, he was only twenty-two — and to be burdened with a family! He needed a new overcoat and he was without gloves.

Jim stopped inside the door, as immovable as a setter at the scent of quail. His eyes were fixed upon Della, and there was an expression in them that she could not read, and it terrified her. It was not anger, nor surprise, nor disapproval, nor horror, nor any of the sentiments that she had been prepared for. He simply stared at her fixedly with that peculiar expression on his face.

Della wriggled off the table and went for him.

"Jim, darling," she cried, "don't look at me that way. I had my hair cut off and sold it because I couldn't have lived through Christmas without giving you a present. It'll grow out again — you won't mind, will you? I just had to do it. My hair grows awfully fast. Say 'Merry Christmas!' Jim, and let's be happy. You don't know what a nice — what a beautiful, nice gift I've got for you."

"You've cut off your hair?" asked Jim, laboriously, as if he had not arrived at that patent fact yet even after the hardest mental labor.

"Cut it off and sold it," said Della. "Don't you like me just as well, anyhow? I'm me without my hair, ain't I?"

Jim looked about the room curiously.

"You say your hair is gone?" he said, with an air almost of idiocy. "You needn't look for it," said Della. "It's sold, I tell you — sold and gone, too. It's Christmas Eve, boy. Be good to me, for it went for you. Maybe the hairs of my head were numbered," she went on with a sudden serious sweetness, "but nobody could ever count my love for you. Shall I put the chops on, Jim?"

Out of his trance Jim seemed quickly to wake. He enfolded his Della. For ten seconds let us regard with discreet scrutiny some inconsequential object in the other direction. Eight dollars a week or a million a year — what is the difference? A mathematician or a wit would give you the wrong answer. The magi brought valuable gifts, but that was not among them. This dark assertion will be illuminated later on.

Jim drew a package from his overcoat pocket and threw it upon the table.

"Don't make any mistake, Dell," he said, "about me. I don't think there's anything in the way of a haircut or a shave or a shampoo that could make me like my girl any less. But if you'll unwrap that package you may see why you had me going a while at first."

White fingers and nimble tore at the string and paper. And then an ecstatic scream of joy; and then, alas! a quick feminine change to hysterical tears and wails, necessitating the immediate employment of all the comforting powers of the lord of the flat.

For there lay The Combs — the set of combs, side and back, that Della had worshipped for long in a Broadway window. Beautiful combs, pure tortoise shell, with jewelled rims — just the shade to wear in the beautiful vanished hair. They were expensive combs, she knew, and her heart had simply craved and yearned over them without the least hope of possession. And now, they were hers, but the tresses that should have adorned the coveted adornments were gone.

But she hugged them to her bosom, and at length she was able to look up with dim eyes and a smile and say: "My hair grows so fast, Jim!"

And then Della leaped up like a little singed cat and cried, "Oh, oh!"

Jim had not yet seen his beautiful present. She held it out to him eagerly upon her open palm. The dull precious metal seemed to flash with a reflection of her bright and ardent spirit.

"Isn't it a dandy, Jim? I hunted all over town to find it. You'll have to look at the time a hundred times a day now. Give me your watch. I want to see how it looks on it."

Instead of obeying, Jim tumbled down on the couch and put his hands under the back of his head and smiled.

"Dell," said he, "let's put our Christmas presents away and keep 'em a while. They're too nice to use just at present. I sold the watch to get the money to buy your combs. And now suppose you put the chops on."

The magi, as you know, were wise men — wonderfully wise men — who brought gifts to the Babe in the manger. They invented the art of giving Christmas presents. Being wise, their gifts were no doubt wise ones, possibly bearing the privilege of exchange in case of duplication. And here I have lamely related to you the uneventful chronicle of two foolish children in a flat who most unwisely sacrificed for each other the greatest treasures of their house. But in a last word to the wise of these days let it be said that of all who give gifts these two were the wisest. Of all who give and receive gifts, such as they are wisest. Everywhere they are wisest. They are the magi.

2. The Unknown Quantity

The poet Longfellow — or was it Confucius, the inventor of wisdom? — remarked:

"*Life is real, life is earnest;*
And things are not what they seem."

As mathematics are — or is: thanks, old subscriber! — the only just rule by which questions of life can be measured, let us, by all means, adjust our theme to the straight edge and the balanced column of the great goddess Two-and-Two-Makes-Four. Figures — unassailable sums in addition — shall be set over against whatever opposing element there may be.

A mathematician, after scanning the above two lines of poetry, would say: "Ahem! young gentlemen, if we assume that X plus — that is, that life is real — then things (all of which life includes) are real. Anything that is real is what it seems. Then if we consider the proposition that 'things are not what they seem,' why —"

But this is heresy, and not poesy. We woo the sweet nymph Algebra; we would conduct you into the presence of the elusive, seductive, pursued, satisfying, mysterious X.

Not long before the beginning of this century, Septimus Kinsolving, an old New Yorker, invented an idea. He originated the discovery that bread is made from flour and not from wheat futures. Perceiving that, the flour crop was short, and that the Stock Exchange was having no perceptible effect on the growing wheat, Mr. Kinsolving cornered the flour market.

The result was that when you or my landlady (before the war she never had to turn her hand to anything; Southerners accommodated) bought a five-cent loaf of bread you laid down an additional two cents, which went to Mr. Kinsolving as a testimonial to his perspicacity.

A second result was that Mr. Kinsolving quit the game with $2,000,000 profer-rake-off.

Mr. Kinsolving's son Dan was at college when the mathematical experiment in breadstuffs was made. Dan came home during vacation and found the old gentleman in a red dressing-gown reading "Little Dorrit" on the porch of his estimable red brick mansion in Washington Square. He had retired from business with enough extra two-cent pieces from bread buyers to reach, if laid side by side, fifteen times around the earth and lap as far as the public debt of Paraguay.

Dan shook hands with his father, and hurried over to Greenwich Village to see his old high-school friend, Kenwitz. Dan had always admired Kenwitz. Kenwitz was pale, curly haired, intense, serious, mathematical, studious, altruistic, socialistic, and the natural foe of oligarchies. Kenwitz had foregone college, and was learning watch-making in his father's jewelry store. Dan was smiling, jovial, easy-tempered and tolerant alike of kings and rag pickers. The two fore-gathered joyously, being opposites. And then Dan went back to college, and Kenwitz to his mainsprings — and to his private library in the rear of the jewelry shop.

Four years later Dan came back to Washington Square with the accumulations of B.A. and two years of Europe thick upon him. He took a filial look at Septimus Kinsolving's elaborate tombstone in Greenwood, and a tedious excursion through typewritten documents with the family lawyer; and then, feeling himself a lonely and hopeless millionaire, hurried down to the old jewelry store across Sixth Avenue.

Kenwitz unscrewed a magnifying glass from his eye, routed out his parent from a dingy rear room, and abandoned the interior of watches for outdoors. He went with Dan, and they sat on a bench in Washington Square. Dan had not changed much; he was stalwart, and had a dignity that was inclined to relax into a grin. Kenwitz was more serious, more intense, more learned, philosophical, and socialistic.

"I know about it now," said Dan, finally. "I pumped it out of the eminent legal lights that turned over to me poor old dad's collection of bonds and boodle. It amounts to $2,000,000, Ken. And I am told that he squeezed it out of the chaps that pay their pennies for loaves of bread at the little bakeries around the corner. You've studied economics, Ken, and you know all about monopolies, and the masses, and octopuses and the rights of laboring people. I never thought about those things before. Football and trying to be white to my fellow-man were about the extent of my college curriculum.

"But since I came back and found out how Dad made his money: I've been thinking. I'd like awfully well to pay back those chaps who had to give too much money for bread. I know it would buck the line of my income for a good many yards; but I'd like to make it square with 'em. Is there any way it can be done, old Ways and Means?"

Kenwitz's big black eyes glowed fierily. His thin, intellectual face took on almost a sardonic cast. He caught Dan's arm with the grip of a friend and a judge.

"You can't do it!" he said, emphatically. "One of the chief punishments of you men of ill-gotten wealth is that when you do repent you find that you have lost the power to make reparation or restitution. I admire your good intentions, Dan, but you can't do anything. Those people were robbed of their precious pennies. It's too late to remedy the evil. You can't pay them back."

"Of course," said Dan, lighting his pipe, "we couldn't hunt up every one of the duffers and hand 'em back the right change. There's an awful lot of 'em buying bread all the time. Funny taste they have — I never cared for bread especially, except for a toasted cracker with the Roquefort. But we might find a few of 'em and chuck some of Dad's cash back where it came from. I'd feel better if I could. It seems tough for people to be held up for a soggy thing like bread. One wouldn't mind standing a rise in broiled lobsters or deviled crabs. Get to work and think, Ken, I want to pay back all of that money I can."

"There are plenty of charities," said Kenwitz, mechanically.

"Easy enough," said Dan, in a cloud of smoke. "I suppose I could give the city a park, or endow an asparagus bed in a hospital. But I don't want Paul to get away with the proceeds of the gold brick we sold Peter. It's the bread shorts I want to cover, Ken."

The thin fingers of Kenwitz moved rapidly.

"Do you know how much money it would take to pay back the losses of consumers during that corner in flour?" he asked.

"I do not," said Dan, stoutly. "My lawyer tells me that I have two millions."

"If you had a hundred millions," said Kenwitz, vehemently, "you couldn't repair a thousandth part of the damage that has been done. You cannot conceive of the accumulated evils produced by misapplied wealth. Each penny that was wrung from the lean purses of the poor reacted a thousandfold to their harm. You do not understand. You do not see how hopeless is your desire to make restitution. Not in a single instance can it be done."

"Back up, philosopher!" said Dan. "The penny has no sorrow that the dollar cannot heal."

"Not in one instance," repeated Kenwitz. "I will give you one, and let us see. Thomas Boyne had a little bakery over there in Varick Street. He sold bread to the poorest people. When the price of flour went up he had to raise the price of bread. His customers were too poor to pay it, Boyne's business failed and he lost his $1,000 capital — all he had in the world"

Dan Kinsolving struck the park bench a mighty blow with his fist.

"I accept the instance," he cried. "Take me to Boyne I will repay his thousand dollars and buy him a new bakery."

"Write your check," said Kenwitz, without moving, "and then begin to write checks in payment of the train of consequences. Draw the next one for $50,000. Boyne went insane after his failure and set fire to the building from which he was about to be evicted. The loss amounted to that much. Boyne died in an asylum."

"Stick to the instance," said Dan. "I haven't noticed any insurance companies on my charity list."

"Draw your next check for $100,000," went on Kenwitz, "Boyne's son fell into bad ways after the bakery closed, and was accused of murder. He was acquitted last week after a three-years' legal battle, and the state draws upon taxpayers for that much expense."

"Back to the bakery!" exclaimed Dan, impatiently. "The Government doesn't need to stand in the bread line."

"The last item of the instance is — come and I will show you," said Kenwitz, rising.

The socialistic watchmaker was happy. He was a millionaire-baiter by nature and a pessimist by trade. Kenwitz would assure you in one breath that money was but evil and corruption, and that your brand new watch needed cleaning and a new racket-wheel.

He conducted Kinsolving southward out of the square and into ragged, poverty-haunted Varick Street. Up the narrow stairway of a squalid brick tenement he led the penitent offspring of the Octopus. He knocked on a door, and a clear voice called to them to enter.

In that almost bare room a young woman sat sewing at a machine. She nodded to Kenwitz as to a familiar acquaintance. One little stream of sunlight through the dingy window burnished her heavy hair to the color of an ancient Tuscan's shield. She flashed a rippling smile at Kenwitz and a look of somewhat flustered inquiry.

Kinsolving stood regarding her clear and pathetic beauty in heart-throbbing silence. Thus they came into the presence of the last item of the Instance.

"How many this week, Miss Mary?" asked the watchmaker. A mountain of coarse gray shirts lay upon the floor.

"Nearly thirty dozen," said the young woman, cheerfully. "I've made almost $4. I'm improving, Mr. Kenwitz. I hardly know what to do with so much money." Her eyes turned, brightly soft, in the direction of Dan. A little pink spot came out on her round, pale cheek.

Kenwitz chuckled like a diabolic raven.

"Miss Boyne," he said, "let me present Mr. Kinsolving, the son of the man who put bread up five years ago. He thinks he would like to do something to aid those who were inconvenienced by that act."

The smile left the young woman's face. She rose and pointed her forefinger toward the door. This time she looked Kinsolving straight in the eye, but it was not a look that gave delight.

The two men went down into Varick Street. Kenwitz, letting all his pessimism and rancor and hatred of the Octopus come to the surface, gibed at the moneyed side of his friend in an acrid torrent of words. Dan appeared to be listening, and then turned to Kenwitz and shook hands with him warmly.

"I'm obliged to you, Ken, old man," he said, vaguely, "a thousand times obliged."

"Mein Gott! You are crazy!" cried the watchmaker, dropping his spectacles for the first time in years.

Two months afterward Kenwitz went into a large bakery on lower Broadway with a pair of gold-rimmed eye-glasses that he had mended for the proprietor.

A lady was giving an order to a clerk as Kenwitz passed her.

"These loaves are ten cents," said the clerk.

"I always get them at eight cents uptown," said the lady. "You need not fill the order. I will drive by there on my way home."

The voice was familiar. The watchmaker paused.

"Mr. Kenwitz!" cried the lady, heartily. "How do you do?"

Kenwitz was trying to train his socialistic and economic comprehension on her wonderful fur boa and the carriage waiting outside.

"Why, Miss Boyne!" he began.

"Mrs. Kinsolving," she corrected. "Dan and I were married a month ago."

Chapter 29

George Santayana

George Santayana was born in Spain (1863), lived most of his life in the United States, and died in 1952 (aged 88) in Rome, Italy. He was a great philosopher, poet, and a one-time novelist (one novel).

He taught at Harvard University during a time period when its philosophy department was outstanding. His Harvard students included T.S. Eliot, W.E.B. DuBois, Walter Lippmann, and Gertrude Stein.

Among his most influential books were *The Life of Reason* (five volumes), *Scepticism and Animal Faith* and *The Realms of Being* (four volumes).

Though he lived a large percentage of his life in the United States, he never became an American citizen. He lived in fascist Italy for two decades.

The one remark that many of us have heard and understood is "those who cannot remember the past are condemned to repeat it."

Edman, Irwin, *The Philosophy of Santayana*, The Modern Library, Random House, 1935, p. 596.

1. The Last Puritan, A Memoir in the Form of a Novel Epilogue

Mario, a character in the novel, and the author are conversing about the book.

"Shall I tear the book up, or will it do as a fable?"

"As a fable you may publish it. It's all your invention; but perhaps there's a better philosophy in it than in your other books."

"How so?"

"Because now you're not arguing or proving or criticizing anything, but painting a picture. The trouble with you philosophers is that you misunderstand your vocation. You ought to be poets, but you insist on laying down the law for the universe, physical and moral, and are vexed with one another because your inspirations are not identical."

"Are you accusing me of dogmatism? Do I demand that everybody should agree with me?"

"Less loudly, I admit, than most philosophers. Yet when you profess to be describing a fact, you can't help antagonizing those who take a different view of it, or are blind altogether to that sort of object. In this novel, on the contrary, the argument is dramatized, the views become human persuasions, and the presentation is all the truer for not professing to be true. You have said it somewhere yourself, though I may misquote the words: After life is over and the world has gone up in smoke, what realities might the spirit in us still call its own without illusion save the form of those very illusions which have made up our story?"

Chapter 30

Irving Fisher

Irving Fisher was born in 1867 in New York State and died in 1947. Milton Friedman called Fisher the greatest American economist.

The book (written by Fisher) that is the source of the attached pages is titled, *The Nature of Capital and Income*, and this title reflects Fisher's primary academic interests.

The 1929 stock market crash did harm to Fisher's reputation as an economist (he thought and wrote that the stock market was not too high) but it can be argued that Fisher's analysis was correct. He was a very intelligent person who lived in a crazy world.

It is common knowledge that Fisher, a Yale University economics professor, advised the Yale investment officer in 1929 and Yale lost the majority of its endowment. This knowledge is wrong. Yale was well diversified in 1929 and had a very conservative portfolio. Fisher on his own behalf invested in stocks aggressively and lost his entire wealth.

In the extract, Fisher gives a brilliant justification for the existence of speculation.

"The indiscriminant prejudice against all speculation, which is so often met with, is beside the point; for, were there no speculators, the same risks would have to be borne by those less fitted to bear them."

He goes on to say that the public "enter the market in a purely gambling spirit." Thus Fisher opens the door for some speculation to be actually gambling. The result is "they produce evil consequences for the non-participating public."

Fisher then explains the chief cause of panics and crises. It is interesting that several of today's financial economists are discovering what Fisher explained well in 1906. We can learn a lot by reading what the leading scholars of yesterday had to say. Of course, that is the motivation behind the structuring of this book. Read on. It is difficult to improve on the writing of Irving Fisher.

Fisher, Irving, *The Nature of Capital and Income*, London, Macmillan Company, 1906, pp. 295–300.

1. The Risk Element

Where risks cannot be reduced to a statistical basis, and therefore cannot be insured against, recourse is often had to the shifting of the risk into the hands of those who are willing to take it. Such persons are speculators. A speculator is usually one in whom the caution factor is not so pronounced as in the ordinary individual. In extreme cases he tends to become a simple gambler. The distinction between a speculator and a gambler, however, is usually fairly well marked. A gambler seeks and makes risks which it is not necessary to assume, whereas the speculator is one who merely volunteers to assume those risks of business which must inevitably fall somewhere. A speculator is also usually fitted for his work by special knowledge, so that the risk *to him*, owing to superior foresight, is at the outset less than it would be to others. The indiscriminate prejudice against all speculation, which is so often met with, is beside the point; for, were there no speculators, the same risks would have to be borne by those less fitted to bear them. The chief evils of speculation flow from the participation of the general public, who lack the special knowledge, and enter the market in a purely gambling spirit. In addition to suffering the usual evil consequences of gambling, they produce evil consequences for the non-participating public by causing factitious fluctuations in the values of the products or property in which they speculate.

The evils of speculation are particularly acute when, as generally happens with the investing public, the forecasts are not made independently. Were it true that each individual speculator made up his mind independently of every other as to the future course of events, the errors of some would probably be offset by those of others. But, as a matter of fact, the mistakes of the common herd are usually in the same direction. Like sheep, they all follow a single leader. How easily they are led is shown by the effect on the stock market in the year 1904, when Thomas Lawson published scare-head advertisements in the newspapers advising the public to sell certain securities.

A chief cause of crises, panics, runs on banks, etc., is that risks are not independently reckoned, but are a mere matter of imitation. A crisis is a time of general and forced liquidation. In other words, it differs from any other period in two particulars, viz, that the liquidations are more numerous, and that they are for the most part forced upon the debtors by the creditors because of threatened or actual bankruptcy. Neither of these conditions could exist unless there had been at a prior time a general miscalculation of the future. Both creditors and debtors must have made a wrong forecast when their ill-fated agreements were entered into. Hence a crisis is the penalty which must be paid when a previous *general error in prediction* is discovered. Such a general error *may* be due to the coincidence of a number of independent mistakes of individuals; but it almost always *is* due to lack of independence — to the principle of imitation. The error, whatever it is, when committed by a person of influence, is like an infection; it is caught by hundreds of others and transmitted to thousands. A great mob of easily led investors, eagerly searching for "straight tips" which may bring instant wealth, make their mistake in common, and when the mistake is disastrous they try, *en masse*, to escape. A sudden rush of all the passengers on a ferry-boat to one side will produce a "list" in the boat's position, and sometimes cause it to capsize, though the independent movement of the individual passengers will seldom or never produce disaster. So also the sudden general realization of unforeseen danger on the part of the investing public may submerge the craft of credit and those whom it has hitherto borne along in safety. In short, a general crisis bears the relation to individual bankruptcies which a general conflagration bears to individual fires. The key to the study of either crises or conflagrations is the existence, in place of independent hazards, of *interdependent* ones. So far as conflagrations are concerned the principle of interdependence is distinctly recognized by students of fire insurance, and in consequence, each company strives to keep its own fire risks independent of each other, by not having too many in the same locality; but so far as crises are concerned, the principle has not yet been sufficiently emphasized by students of economic history.

The same principle applies to the phenomenon of a run on a bank. The opinions of the bank's solvency are not formed independently but interdependently. A year or more ago the newspapers reported that, a policeman and a crowd of people being collected on the steps of one of the Wilkes-Barre savings banks to escape the rain, two Hungarian depositors who were passing jumped to the conclusion that the bank had been attacked by burglars, and circulated the disturbing news in the Hungarian colony, with the result that when the bank opened for business many depositors made a run upon it.

We see, then, that where speculation is imitative, it is dangerous alike to those who engage in it and to the public. Where, on the other hand, speculation is based on independent knowledge, its utility is usually enormous. It operates both to *reduce* risk by means of utilizing the special knowledge of speculators, and also to *shift* risk from those who lack this knowledge to those who possess it. The consequence is that normally speculative property will gravitate into the hands of those most able to forecast its true income.

Modern production has been called capitalistic-speculative production, owing to the fact that it is managed by "captains of industry," who are specially fitted at once to forecast and to mould the future within the special realms in which they operate. The industries of transportation and manufacturing particularly are under the lead of an educated and trained speculative class, whose function it is to assume for themselves the main risks, and leave the ordinary investor, who is not so equipped, to cooperate as a mere "lender" or silent partner. Yet it often happens that they betray the confidence placed in them, and continue to throw the burden of risk on those whom they pretend to shield.

In the special field more usually known as "speculative," — namely, that in which attempts are made to forecast prices in the great exchange markets, — we find a similar class who are specially trained. These speculators are either "bulls" or "bears"; that is, they speculate either for a rise or a fall. Those who believe that wheat or any other article is likely to rise in value and hence yield more than the "rate of interest," will hold it, or if they do not own it, will buy it or obtain an option on it. Such an option is known as a "call," and is put in force at a later time, at a price fixed in advance and considered low. On the other hand, those who believe that prices will fall will sell out their present holdings, or may sell "short," agreeing to supply such holdings at a later time at a fixed price which they consider high. Such a contract to sell is often made in the form of an option, in which case it is known as a "put."

To show how such contracts will shift risks, a few examples will suffice. A building contractor who had taken a large contract was asked if he were not taking large risks, since he could not foreknow the cost of building. He replied, "No, I am taking no risks at all except on 'labor'; I have made contracts to be supplied with all materials when needed, at fixed prices." Those who made these contracts thus assumed the risk of fluctuation in price in the special materials in which they dealt, relieving the contractor of the necessity of informing himself of the special market conditions for stone, brick, timber, etc., and enabling him to make a closer bid for the contract, inasmuch as there was less need of the element of caution. The public, of course, get the benefit of such a shifting of risk in the form of reduced cost of building. Similar results follow from most other "short" sales. Again, a woolen manufacturer need not carry so large a stock of wool if he can make a contract by which some one will sell short, or agree to supply the wool at fixed prices and at certain dates. He can afford to use up his present stock fearlessly, with the certainty that when it is gone he can obtain a new supply. Without such a contract, he would be under the necessity of carrying a large and idle stock.

An important method of shifting risks is "hedging," whereby a dealer, for instance in transporting wheat, may be relieved of the risk of a change in price. He buys wheat in the West intending to ship it to New York and sell it there at enough to cover cost of transportation and a small profit. In consequence of a sudden fall in price he might find all his profit wiped out; or he might, on the other hand, by a rise in price, make much more than normal profits. But, being of a cautious disposition, he prefers an intermediate course, — a small profit which is sure, rather than the chances of both gain and loss. Consequently he "hedges." He enters into some speculative market, knowing that it will move in sympathy with the New York market, and there he "speculates" for a fall, or sells "short." In case the price in New York falls, what he loses on the wheat which he has transported he gains through his speculative short selling. Contrariwise, if the price rises, what he gains on his wheat transported he loses in the speculative market. In other words, he is, as it were, betting on both sides of the market at once, and therefore eliminating all risk, so that he only obtains his normal profit, commission, or percentage on the actual wheat handled, having imposed the burden of risk of speculation on the speculative dealers to whom he sold short.

The effect of hedging on those who engage in it, such as the wheat dealers, is evidently to enable them to work on a smaller margin of profit. In consequence the public receives a benefit in lowered prices. The case is thus very similar to those respectively of the builder and of the woolen manufacturer. Short selling, binding the future to the past, enables the specialist to guarantee to the general public a definite foreseen series of events. The beneficial effect to the public, in saving useless stocks and reserves, in producing more intelligent direction of enterprises, and in encouraging accumulation through greater certainty of its future benefits, is both obvious and great. Risk is one of the direst economic evils, and all of the devices which aid in overcoming it — whether increased guaranties, safeguards, foresight, insurance, or legitimate speculation — represent a great boon to humanity.

Chapter 31

W.E.B. DuBois

William Edward Burghardt DuBois (1868–1963) was born in Massachusetts and died in Ghana in self-imposed exile. In the best sense of the term, DuBois was an intellectual who devoted his life to improve the conditions of the black people. It is important to note that he stridently fought both Marcus Garvey and Booker T. Washington who had the same basic goals. DuBois was a prolific talented author and orator and a very influential scholar.

In his later years, he was a member of the left-wing American Labor Party and he died a member of the Communist Party. He was a member of the ideal Communist Party and not the actual party that was present on earth and the cause of so much pain and suffering.

The extract from one of his books illustrates well his scholarship and writing ability.

Du Bois, W. E. Burghardt. *Black Folk, Then and Now, An Essay in the History and Sociology of the Negro Race*, New York, Henry Holt and Company, 1939, pp. 196–198.

1. The Black United States

There were half a million slaves in the confines of the United States when the Declaration of Independence declared "that all men are created equal; that they are endowed by their Creator with certain unalienable rights; that among these are life, liberty, and the pursuit of happiness." The land that thus magniloquently heralded its advent into the family of nations had supported the institution of human slavery for one hundred and fifty-seven years and was destined to cling to it desperately eighty-seven years longer. The greatest experiment in Negro slavery as the base of a modern industrial system was made on the mainland of North America and in the confines of the present United States.

There were in the United States and its dependencies, in 1930, 11,891,143 persons of acknowledged Negro descent, not including the considerable infiltration of Negro blood which is not acknowledged and often not known. Today the number of persons called Negroes is probably about thirteen millions. These persons are almost entirely descendants of African slaves, brought to America from the sixteenth to the nineteenth centuries.

The importation of Negroes to the mainland of North America was small until the British obtained the coveted privilege of the Asiento in 1713. After the Asiento treaty the Negro population in the confines of the United States increased in the eighteenth century from about 50,000 in 1710 to 220,000 in 1750 and 462,000 in 1770. When the colonies became independent, the foreign slave trade was soon made illegal; but illicit trade, annexation of territory and natural increase enlarged the Negro population from a little over a million at the beginning of the nineteenth century to four and a half millions at the outbreak of the Civil War and to about ten and a quarter millions in 1914.

The present so-called Negro population of the United States is:

1. A mixture of the various African populations: Bantu, Sudanese, Nilotic and West Coast Negroes; some dwarfs, and some traces of Semitic blood.
2. A mixture of Negro and American Indian blood.
3. A mixture of Negro with the blood of white Americans through a system of concubinage of colored women in slavery days, together with some legal intermarriage then and later.

The census figures as to mulattoes[25] have been from time to time officially acknowledged to be understatements. This blending of the races has led to interesting human types, but there has been little scientific study of the matter. In general the Negro population in the United States is brown in color, darkening to almost black and shading off in the other direction to yellow and white, and in some cases indistinguishable from the white population.

It has been estimated on admittedly partial data that less than twenty-five per cent of American Negroes are of unmixed African descent, the balance having in varying degrees Indian and white blood.[26]

The slaves, landing from 1619 onward, were usually transported from the West Indian marts, after acclimatization and training in systematic plantation work. They were received by the colonies at first as laborers, on the same plane as other laborers. For a long time there was

---

[25] Eleven to fifteen per cent, 1850 to 1890.

[26] Cf. Herskovits, *The American Negro*.

in law no distinction between the indented white servant from England and the black servant from Africa, except in the term of their service. Even here the distinction was not always observed, some of the whites being kept beyond term of their service and Negroes now and then securing their freedom.

The opposition to slavery had from the first been largely stilled when it was stated that this was a method of converting the heathen to Christianity. The corollary was that when a slave was converted he became free. Up to 1660 or thereabouts it seemed accepted in most colonies and in the English West Indies, that baptism into a Christian Church would legally free a Negro slave. Masters, therefore, were reluctant in the seventeenth century to have their slaves receive Christian instruction. Maryland declared in 1663 that Negro slaves should serve durante vita, but it was not until 1667 that Virginia finally plucked up courage to attack the issue squarely and declared by law: "Baptism doth not alter the condition of the person as to his bondage or freedom, in order that diverse masters freed from this doubt may more carefully endeavor the propagation of Christianity."

During the seventeenth and eighteenth centuries there was a considerable forced slave trade of whites from Europe under the guise of indentured servants. It met, however, not only the monopoly of feudal labor, but the new demand for labor purchase in the expanding industries of Europe. And, on the other hand, these very industries were encouraged and enlarged by the raw material raised in America by slave labor. The profits of the slave trade and of the plantations, together with the ease of obtaining black slaves through the systematic organization of the trade, increased the importation of black slave labor, while white free labor gradually replaced indentured workers.

The African family and clan life were disrupted in this transplantation; the communal life and free use of land were impossible; the power of the chief was transferred to the master, bereft of the usual blood ties and ancient reverence. The African language survived only in occasional words and phrases. African religion, both fetish and Islam, was transformed. Fetish survived in certain rites and even here and there in blood sacrifice, carried out secretly and at night; but more often in open celebration which gradually became transmuted into Catholic and Protestant Christian rites. The slave preacher replaced to some extent the African medicine man and gradually, after a century or more, the Negro Church arose as the center and almost the only social expression of Negro life in America. Nevertheless, there can still be traced not only in words and phrases but in customs, literature and art, and especially in music and dance, something of the African heritage of the black folk in America. Further study will undoubtedly make this survival and connection clearer.

Chapter 32

Mohandas Karamchand Gandhi (Mahatma Gandhi)

Gandhi was born in 1869 and died (assassinated) in 1948 at the age of 78. He is officially called the Father of the Nation of India because he led the struggle for independence.

He received his advanced education at University College of London and the University of London. He studied law.

Gandhi expounded a philosophy of total nonviolence but did advocate peaceful civil disobedience. He first applied this strategy in South Africa in an attempt to obtain civil rights for the Indian population of that country. When he moved to India in 1915, he continued his struggle for independence from Britain. He spent time in jail both in South Africa and India.

He always advocated tolerance between people of different beliefs and races. Truth and love were the highest valued virtues. He advocated a simple life and vegetarianism.

In 1946, Gandhi was strongly opposed to the partition of India into two separate countries (one being Pakistan). But to avoid civil war, Gandhi reluctantly agreed to the two-country solution.

A Hindu nationalist shot Gandhi on 30 January 1948. The likely reason was that Gandhi had supported a payment by India to Pakistan. Contrary to Gandhi's non-violent beliefs, the killer was tried and executed on 15 November 1949.

"Satyagraha" was the word chosen by Gandhi for his variation of passive resistance. Gandhi never realized how fortunate he was that his adversary was Great Britain. While obviously Great Britain still had a long way to go in recognizing the rights of people of different races, Gandhi did not have to cope with the brutality of Nazi Germany.

Martin Luther King adopted Gandhi's passive strategy in a very effective manner. One has to wonder what other uses, say in industry, where passive resistance combined with truth and love could be used effectively.

Gandhi, M. K., *An Autobiography or The Story of My Experiments With Truth*, by M. K. Gandhi, translated by Mahadev Desai, Ahmedabad, Navajivan Publishing House, 1927, pp. 389–390.

1. The Birth of Satyagraha

Events were so shaping themselves in Johannesburg as to make this self-purification on my part as preliminary as it were to Satyagraha. I can now see that all the principal events of my life, culminating in the vow of *brahmacharya,* were secretly preparing me for it. The principle called Satyagraha came into being before that name was invented. Indeed when it was born, I myself could not say what it was. In Gujarati also we used the English phrase "passive resistance" to describe it. When in a meeting of Europeans I found that the term "passive resistance" was too narrowly construed that it was supposed to be a weapon of the weak, that it could be characterized by hatred and that it could finally manifest itself as violence; I had to demur to all these statements and explain the real nature of the Indian movement. It was clear that a new word must be coined by the Indians to designate their struggle.

But I could not for the life of me find out a new name, and therefore offered **a** nominal prize through *Indian Opinion* to the reader who made the best suggestion on the subject. As a result Maganlal Gandhi coined the word "Sadagraha" (Sat = truth, Agraha = firmness) and won the prize. But in order to make it clearer I changed the word to "Satyagraha" which has since become current in Gujarati as a designation for the struggle.

The history of this struggle is for all practical purposes a history of the remainder of my life in South Africa and especially of my experiments with truth in that subcontinent. I wrote the major portion of this history in Yeravda jail and finished it after I was released. It was published in *Navajivan* and subsequently issued in book form. Sjt. Valji Govindji Desai has been translating it into English for *Current Thought,* but I am now arranging to have the English translation[27] published in book form at an early date, so that those who will may be able to familiarize themselves with my most important experiments in South Africa. I would recommend a perusal of my history of Satyagraha in South Africa to such readers as have not seen it already. I will not repeat what I have put down there but in the next few chapters will deal only with a few personal incidents of my life in South Africa which have not been covered by that history. And when

---

[27] The English translation has since been published by S. Ganesan, Triplicane, Madras.

I have done with these, I will at once proceed to give the reader some idea of my experiments in India. Therefore, anyone who wishes to consider these experiments in their strict chronological order will now do well to keep the history of Satyagraha in South Africa before him.

Chapter 33

Calvin Coolidge

Calvin Coolidge (1872–1929) was the 30th President of the United States. He was Vice President and became President when Warren G. Harding died suddenly in 1923. Coolidge was elected President in 1924 and declined the invitation to run for President in 1928. He was a Republican lawyer from the state of Vermont, but became the governor of Massachusetts.

The more I read about Coolidge the more I like him. "The Press Under a Free Government" extract contains the famous line: "After all, the chief business of the American people is business." Taken out of context, it indicates a shallow man. Read it in context, it is part of a very insightful speech.

After the scandals of Harding's administration, it was necessary to restore public confidence in the President's office. Coolidge as a small Republican government achieved that goal. From 1923–1928, the USA prospered. He handed over the Presidency to Hoover in 1928 and the country was in excellent shape. Of course, there are those that are critical of his laissez-faire philosophy for the central government. He was an early supporter of women's suffrage.

In 1919, the police of Boston went on strike. Coolidge, the Governor of the state of Massachusetts, sent a telegram to Samuel Gompers, the union organizer, that stated: "There is no right to strike against the public safety by anyone, anywhere, any time." (September 14, 1919.) This telegram made Coolidge famous throughout the country.

In the 1928 election, Coolidge refused to run for a second full term. The result was Herbert Hoover ran and was elected. The 1929 stock market crash and 1931–1939 depression resulted. Would history have been different with Coolidge as President? Maybe.

Coolidge could write a striking thought. In the supports of civilization, we have: "There is no force so democratic as the force of an idea." And "This glory we owe in no small part to the all-embracing influence of our colleges and universities."

In "Thought, the Master of Things," we have "It is not enough to teach men science; the great thing is to teach them how to use science." Of course, we now know that it should be "to teach men and women science..."

In "The Press Under a Free Government," we have the famous quotation: "After all, the chief business of the American people is business." He goes on to state: "Wealth is the product of industry, ambition, character and untiring effort." He then describes the good things that wealth enables "multiplication of schools, the increase of knowledge, the dissemination of intelligence, the encouragement of science, the broadening of outlook, the expansion of liberties..."

Coolidge was a fine President and an eloquent spokesperson for the USA.

Coolidge, Calvin, *The Price of Freedom, Speeches and Addresses*, New York, Charles Scribner's Sons, 1924, pp. 3–10, 57–67.

Coolidge, Calvin, *Foundations of the Republic, Speeches and Addresses*, New York, Charles Scribner's Sons, 1926, pp. 183–190, pp. 317–332.

1. The Supports of Civilization

At the Amherst College Alumni Dinner, New York City, November 27, 1920.

The process of civilization consists of the discovery by men of the laws of the universe, and of living in harmony with those laws. The most important of them to men are the laws of their own nature.

This is education, the method whereby man is revealed to himself. It is the instruction of his understanding, the training of his sentiments, the direction of his action. It discloses the physical and the spiritual, the unseen and the seen. It includes every human relationship and shows forth every duty. It is alike the source of the intellectual and moral force of all mankind.

I shall assume that civilization is desirable. I do not think that is questioned in any respectable quarter, though I recall that a wise old Massachusetts magistrate once observed to me that perhaps we should all be better off if our entire efforts were directed to a hoe and a potato. There is honest difference of opinion whether the results of civilization are equitably distributed. That I shall not now discuss. It seems obvious that the present population of the globe could not subsist by that ancient method of the tillage of the soil represented by the hoe-and-potato era. But, even if it could, it is enough to say that existence in such a state is totally inadequate to employ all the powers of man, and it cannot be, either, that man ought to be satisfied to be anything but his best, or that being his best can be inconsistent with the highest welfare of society. The question I propose to consider is what it is necessary to do to sustain modern civilization and provide for its advancement and further development.

It is not necessary to suppose that our civilization is perfect. We Amherst men have heard that "there is first the blade, then the ear, after that the full corn in the ear," and we have further heard that "it doth not yet appear what *man* shall be." It is necessary to be assured that civilization is on a sound foundation, that it is in such a state that it can grow and develop for the general welfare.

Both the answer to this main question and this necessary assurance are found in part in history. Great light is always shed on the question of what ought to be done by finding out what has been done. Progress has lain in the cultivation and maintenance of a state of mind. It has been in general a strong adherence to ideals. The ideal around which the ancient tribes of Israel developed was monotheism. The ideal of Greece was beauty. That of Rome was glory. The strength of the British Empire has been in a sense of obligation. Well might Admiral Nelson appeal to that sense by flying at his masthead as he swung his fleet into battle: "England expects every man to do his duty." To the French it has been a personification of their country. To one of her generals, on trial for surrendering his army, who plead that with many of her cities in the hands of the enemy, with her forces disintegrated, her government in flight, there was no longer anything for him to fight for, went the reply: "There is always France." The strongest sentiment of America has been for that independence which is the basis of self-government. These are but main features. There clustered about them many other ideals which in all instances lent strength to the character of the people of each nation. It was only when the people fell away from their adherence to their ideals that the disintegration began which ended in the final downfall of the nations of antiquity. It has but lately been demonstrated to the fullest extent that the self-governing peoples of the modern world are strong and vigorous, still true to their traditions, still loyal to their ideals. Such a condition has always indicated a sound foundation in the past, and must be the best index of it in the present.

Our modern life is very complex. Its conduct is dependent on technical skill. Strike out what is known of physics and substantially every mechanical device, all transportation by power-driven motors, all manufacturing, heating, and lighting plants, water-supply, and drainage would fail to operate; strike out chemistry and pestilence would overwhelm the earth in a few days. These are results which affect the entire human race. There is nothing of such broad application as the practical results of learning. There is no force so democratic as the force of an ideal.

But it is not only by technical skill that modem civilization is sustained. It depends to a large degree on accumulated and invested capital, and for its advance will depend more and more on accumulation and investment of capital. Civilization and profits go hand in hand. It is out of the surplus of our efforts that progress is made. It is only necessary to remember the method of conducting all industry, transportation, banking, mining, and commerce and to observe that they not only need constant renewal but ever-increasing facilities with which to meet enlarged demands, to determine that what we call capital is the chief material minister to the general welfare of all mankind.

Invested capital is the result of brains. All the elements that are assembled in a Corliss engine, a modern printing-press, or an aeroplane have lain in the earth throughout all the ages. For countless generations there has been sufficient human labor to assemble them, yet they did not appear. They came into being only when called by the skill and brains of men. The same is true of the plant whereby is carried on all modern business. It is also by organizations, by management, that labor is so directed as to produce a surplus for present and future investment. Truly capital, surplus, profits, and progress are the result of brains. In fact, that which we call labor is intelligent effort directed toward some desired end. Otherwise such result could well be secured from a machine. In its last analysis, what the workman sells is his intelligence. But it is still true that the management and direction, of which surplus and profits are born, is a rarer skill, a yet more acute intelligence, which we in general designate as brains. It is on the continued existence of this power in man, which is the result of effort and training, that not only the advance but the maintenance of our present standards depends.

But there is need not only of patriotic ideals and a trained intelligence in our economic life, there is need of a deep understanding of man and his relationship to the physical universe and to his fellow man. There has always been evil in the world. John Fiske has demonstrated very clearly that of necessity evil and good are coexistent possibilities. What virtue would there be in choosing the good unless thereby the evil was rejected? There are evil forces at work now. They are apparently organized and seek the disintegration of society. They can always be recognized by a direct appeal to selfishness and nothing else. They deny that the present relationship of men to each other, which exists by reason of organized society, has any sound basis for its existence. They point out to men with untrained minds that it takes effort to maintain themselves and support government, and claim that they ought to exist without effort on the accumulation of others, and they deny that men have any obligations toward each other.

The answer to this lies in a knowledge of past human experience and a realization of what man is. These claims are very old. They have had trial times without number, and always with disastrous results. Men are not so constituted that selfishness satisfies them, and the only result of attempting to evade their obligations to others has been to destroy themselves. Man has been so created, his environment is such, his nature is such, that he cannot succeed in that way.

Surely the wonderful experience of man shows he is a being that can only be satisfied with higher things than these. After contemplating his advance from the beginnings of evolution up to the scientist and the philosopher, of him well might the ancient prophet Isaiah have inquired: "Who hath measured the waters in the hollow of his hand, and meted out Heaven with the span, and comprehended the dust of the earth in a measure, and weighed the mountains in scales, and the hills in a balance?"

"Who hath directed the spirit of *man* or being his counsellor hath taught him?"

"With whom took he counsel, and who instructed him, and taught him in the path of judgment, and taught him knowledge, and showed to him the way of understanding?"

They little understand what men have done, or what they are, who expect they can long be content with the husks of existence. Surely men will not long follow false prophets or long serve their betrayers.

What are the sources, then, of that state of mind which supports civilization? There are but two sources, education and religion. From them are derived the teachings of science necessary to give the requisite technical skill and moral ideals sufficient to support and advance civilization. But when we ask what education, the answer must be the higher education; for in the first place primary schools have been a development of higher education and would not long survive without it, and in the second place we have seen that modern society cannot exist save by the ministrations of the highest scientific skill. We could not survive, then, with only primary education. But what about religion? In so far as that is dependent upon the teachings of the clergy, we come at once to the inquiry, who teach the clergy? And we learn that the higher education was anciently instituted solely for their instruction. Not only the higher sciences, but philosophy, morals, and religion all center in our colleges and universities. It is not too much to say that in them is the foundation of all civilization, and that their influence is all-embracing.

That is not saying that everybody ought to have a university education. It is saying that in these days everybody must and does come under the influence of a university education. Neither Washington nor Lincoln had the advantage of a college education, but had it not been for colleges neither Washington nor Lincoln would ever have been heard of.

Is not the conclusion of all this perfectly plain? We hold by the modern standards of society. We believe in maintaining modern civilization for the protection and support of free governments, and the development of our economic welfare. We claim they are sound and minister in the best way to human welfare. The great test of an institution is its ability to perpetuate itself. It seems fairly plain that whether or not these institutions can survive with the aid of higher education, without it they have not the slightest chance. We justify the greater and greater accumulations of capital because we believe that therefrom flows the support of all science, art, learning, and the charities which minister to the humanities of life, all carrying their beneficent effects to the people as a whole. Unless this is measurably true our system of civilization ought to stand condemned. It is to be condemned, anyway, unless it possesses the ability to perpetuate itself. This can only be true by supporting higher education to such a degree that its good influence may more than match the rising tide of the influence of evil. Those who want a continuation of stability and confidence must seek it by supporting the efforts of our colleges and universities. It is not too much to say that all that we mean when we say America is dependent on the adequacy of this support.

This appeal has not failed. From earliest times Americans have lavished the most solicitous care on advanced education. As our settlements have swept westward they have set up the most efficient State universities. There is no contemporary effort of greater promise or more propitious than the increasing endowment that has been sought and secured by our institutions of higher learning. It shows a recognition of the need both by those intrusted with their management and by those who have the means to respond.

There is satisfaction too in the greatly increased college attendance. With these manifestations all about, what wonder that while the rest of the world is in a turmoil America is serene. This glory we owe in no small part to the all-embracing influence of our colleges and universities. They have wrought mightily in the making of America. While they can command adequate support America cannot fail. They stand like mighty fortresses within whose protection the truth is secure. Against them no enemy shall prevail.

2. Thought, The Master of Things

At the Annual Meeting of the American Classical League, the University of Pennsylvania, July 7, 1921.

We come here today in defense of some of the great realities of life. We come to continue the guarantee of progress in the future by continuing a knowledge of progress in the past. We come to proclaim our allegiance to those ideals which have made the predominant civilization of the earth. We come because we believe that thought is the master of things. We come because we realize that the only road to freedom lies through a knowledge of the truth.

Mankind have always had classics. They always will. That is only another way of saying they have always set up ideals and always will. Always the question has been, always the question will be, what are those ideals to be, what are to be the classics? For many centuries, in education, the classics have meant Greek and Latin literature. It does not need much argument to demonstrate that in the Western world society can have little liberal culture which is not based on these. Without them there could be no interpretation of language and literature, no adequate comprehension of history, no understanding of the foundations of philosophy and law. In fact, the natural sciences are so much the product of those trained in the classics that, without such training, their very terminology cannot be fully understood.

Education is undertaken to give a larger comprehension of life. In the last fifty years its scope has been very much broadened. It is scarcely possible to consider it in the light of the individual. It is easy to see that it must be discussed in the light of society. The question for consideration is not what shall be taught to a few individuals. Nor can it be determined by the example of the accomplishments of a few individuals. There have been great men with little of what we call education. There have been small men with a great deal of learning. There has never been a great people who did not possess great learning. The whole question at issue is, what does the public welfare require for the purpose of education? What are the fundamental things that young Americans should be taught? What is necessary for society to come to a larger comprehension of life?

The present age has been marked by science and commercialism. In its primary purpose it reveals mankind undertaking to overcome their physical limitations. This is being accomplished by wonderful discoveries which have given the race dominion over new powers. The chief demand of all the world has seemed to be for new increases in these directions. There has been a great impatience with everything which did not appear to minister to this requirement.

This has resulted in the establishment of technical schools and in general provisions for vocational education. There has been a theory that all learning ought to be at once translated into scientific and commercial activities. Of course the world today is absolutely dependent on science and on commerce. Without them great areas would be depopulated by famine and pestilence almost in a day. With them there is a general diffusion of comfort and prosperity, not only unexcelled, but continually increasing. These advantages, these very necessities, are not only not to be denied, but acknowledged and given the highest commendation. All this is not absolute but relative. It is neither self-sufficient nor self-existing. It represents the physical side of life. It is the product of centuries of an earlier culture, a culture which was none the less real because it supposed the earth was flat, a culture which was preeminent in the development of the moral and spiritual forces of life.

The age of science and commercialism is here. There is no sound reason for wishing it otherwise. The wise desire is not to destroy it, but to use it and direct it rather than to be used and directed by it, that it may be, as it should be, not the master but the servant, that the physical forces may not prevail over the moral forces, and that the rule of life may not be expediency but righteousness.

No question can be adequately comprehended without knowing its historical background. Modern civilization dates from Greece and Rome. The world was not new in their day. They were the inheritors of a civilization which had gone before, but what they had inherited they recast, enlarged, and intensified and made their own, so that their culture took on a distinctive form, embracing all that the past held best in the Roman world of the Caesars. That great empire fell a prey, first to itself and then to the barbarians. After this seeming catastrophe scholarship and culture almost disappeared for nearly a thousand years, finally to emerge again in the revival of learning.

It is impossible for society to break with its past. It is the product of all which has gone before. We could not cut ourselves off from all influence which existed prior to the Declaration of Independence and expect any success by undertaking to ignore all that happened before that date. The development of society is a gradual accomplishment. Culture is the product of a continuing effort. The education of the race is never accomplished. It must be gone over with each individual and it must continue from the beginning to the ending of life. Society cannot say it has attained culture and can therefore rest from its labors. All that it can say is that it has learned the method and process by which culture is secured, and go on applying such method and process.

Biology teaches us that the individual goes through the various stages of evolution which have brought him to his present state of perfection. All theories of education teach us that the mind develops in the same way, rising through the various stages that have marked the ascent of mankind from the lowest savagery to the highest civilization. This principle is a compelling reason for the continuance of the classics as the foundation of our educational system. It was by the use of this method that we reached our present state of development.

This does not mean that every person must be a classical scholar. It is not necessary for every one who crosses the ocean to be an experienced mariner, nor for every one who works on a building to be a learned architect, but if the foreign shore is to be reached in safety, if the building is to take on a form of utility and beauty, it will be because of direction and instruction given according to established principles and ideals. The principles and ideals on which we must depend not only for a continuance of modern culture but, I believe, for a continuance of the development of science itself, come to us from the classics. All this is the reason that the sciences and the professions reach their highest development as the supplement of a classical education.

Perhaps the chief criticism of education and its resulting effect upon the community today is superficiality. A generation ago the business man who had made a success without the advantages of a liberal education, sent his son to the university, where he took a course in Greek and Latin. On his return home, because he could not immediately take his father's place in the conduct of business, the conclusion was drawn that his education had been a failure. In order to judge the correctness of this conclusion it would be necessary to know whether the young man had really been educated or whether he had gone through certain prescribed courses, in the first place, and, in the second place, whether he finally developed executive ability. It cannot be denied that a superficial knowledge of the classics is only a superficial knowledge. There cannot be expected to be derived from it the ability to think correctly, which is the characteristic of a disciplined mind. Without doubt a superficial study of the classics is of less value than a superficial acquaintance with some of the sciences or a superficial business course. One of the advantages of the classics as a course of training is that in modern institutions there is little chance of going through them in a superficial way. Another of their advantages is that the master of them lives in something more than the present and thinks of something more than the external problems of the hour, and after all it was the study of the classics that produced the glories of the Elizabethan age with its poets, its philosophers, its artists, its explorers, its soldiers, its statesmen, and its churchmen.

The most pressing requirement of the present hour is not how we are to solve our economic problems, but: Where are we to find the sustaining influences for the realities of life? How are we to justify the existing form of government in our republic? Where shall we resort for teachings in patriotism? On what can we rely for a continuation of that service of sacrifice which has made modern civilization possible? The progress of the present era gives no new answers to these problems. There are no examples of heroism which outrival Leonidas at Thermopyhe, or Horatius at the bridge. The literature of Greece and Rome is through and through an inspiring plea for patriotism — from the meditations of their philosophers to the orations of their statesmen and the despatches of their soldiers.

The world has recently awakened to the value and the righteousness of democracy. This ideal is not new. It has been the vision which the people of many nations have followed through centuries. Because men knew that ideal had been partially realized in Greece and Rome, they have had faith that it would be fully realized in Europe and America. The beginnings of modern democracy were in Athens and Sparta. That form of human relationship can neither be explained nor defended, except by reference to these examples, and a restatement of the principles on which their government rested. Both of these nations speak to us eloquently of the progress they made so long as their citizens held to these ideals, and they admonish us with an eloquence even more convincing of the decay and ruin which comes to any people when it falls away from these ideals. There is no surer road to destruction than prosperity without character.

There is little need to mention the debt which modern literature owes to the great examples of Greece and

Rome. Even the New Testament was written in Greek. It is unthinkable that any institution founded for the purpose of teaching literature should neglect the classics. Nowhere have the niceties of thought been better expressed than in their prose. Nowhere have music and reason been more harmoniously combined than in their poetry, and nowhere is there greater eloquence than in their orations. We look to them not merely as the writers and speakers of great thoughts, but as the doers of greater deeds. There is a glory in the achievements of the Greeks under Themistocles, there is an admiration for the heroics of Salamis, there is even a pride in the successful retreat of the Ten Thousand which the humiliating days of Philip and Alexander cannot take away.

But when we turn to Rome we are overwhelmed by its greatness. When we recall the difficulties of the transportation of that day, which made the defense easy and attack difficult, her achievement not only in conquering all that there was of the then civilized Western world, but of holding it in subjection with a reign of law so absolute that the world has never known a peace so secure as that of the Pax Romana, strikes us with wonder. They gave to the world the first great example of order and a tolerable state of liberty under the law. As we study their history there is revealed to us one of the greatest peoples, under the guidance of great leaders, exhausting themselves in their efforts that the civilized world might be unified and the stage set for the entrance of Christianity. In their conquests we see one of the most stupendous services, and in their disintegration one of the most gigantic tragedies which ever befell a great people.

Every one knows that the culture of Greece and Rome is gone. It could not be restored; it could not be successfully imitated. What those who advocate their continued study desire to bring about is the endurance of that modern culture which has been the result of a familiarity with the classics of these two great peoples. We do not wish to be Greek, we do not wish to be Roman. We have a great desire to be supremely American. That purpose we know we can accomplish by continuing the process which has made us Americans. We must search out and think the thoughts of those who established our institutions. The education which made them must not be divorced from the education which is to make us. In our efforts to minister to man's material welfare we must not forget to minister to his spiritual welfare. It is not enough to teach men science; the great thing is to teach them how to use science.

We believe in our republic. We believe in the principles of democracy. We believe in liberty. We believe in order under the established provisions of law. We believe in the promotion of literature and the arts. We believe in the righteous authority of organized government. We believe in patriotism. These beliefs must be supported and strengthened. They are not to be inquired of for gain or profit, though without them all gain and all profit would pass away. They will not be found in the teachings devoted exclusively to commercialism, though without them commerce would not exist. These are the higher things of life. Their teaching has come to us from the classics. If they are to be maintained they will find their support in the institutions of the liberal arts. When we are drawing away from them, we are drawing away from the path of security and progress. It is not yet possible that instruction in the classics could be the portion of every American. That opportunity ought to be not diminished but increased. But while every American has not had and may not have the privilege, America has had it. Our leadership has been directed in accordance with these ideals. Our faith is in them still.

We have seen many periods which tried the soul of our republic. We shall see many more. There will be times when efforts will be great and profits will vanish. There have been and will be times when the people will be called upon to make great sacrifices for their country. Unless Americans shall continue to live in something more than the present, to be moved by something more than material gains, they will not be able to respond to these requirements and they will go down as other peoples have gone down before some nation possessed of a greater moral force. The will to endure is not the creation of the moment; it is the result of long training. That will has been our possession up to the present hour. By its exercise we have prospered and brought forth many wonderful works. The object of our education is to continue us in this great power. That power depends upon our ideals. The great and unfailing source of that power and these ideals has been the influence of the classics of Greece and Rome. Those who believe in America, in her language, her arts, her literature, and in her science, will seek to perpetuate them by perpetuating the education which has produced them.

3. The Press Under a Free Government

Address before the American Society of Newspaper Editors in Washington, January 11, 1925.

The relationship between governments and the press has always been recognized as a matter of large importance. Wherever despotism abounds, the sources of public information are the first to be brought under its control. Wherever the cause of liberty is making its way, one of its highest accomplishments is the guarantee of the freedom of the press. It has always been realized, sometimes instinctively, oftentimes expressly, that truth and freedom are inseparable. An absolutism could never rest upon anything save a perverted and distorted view of human relationships and upon false standards set up and maintained by force. It has always found it necessary to attempt to dominate the entire field of education and instruction. It has thrived on ignorance. While it has sought to train the minds of a few, it has been largely with the purpose of attempting to give them a superior facility for misleading the many. Men have been educated under absolutism, not that they might bear witness to the truth, but that they might be the more ingenious advocates and defenders of false standards and hollow pretenses. This has always been the method of privilege, the method of class and caste, the method of master and slave.

When a community has sufficiently advanced so that its government begins to take on that of the nature of a republic, the processes of education become even more important, but the method is necessarily reversed. It is all the more necessary under a system of free government that the people should be enlightened, *that* they should be correctly informed, than it is under an absolute government that they should be ignorant. Under a republic the institutions of learning, while bound by the constitution and laws, are in no way subservient to the government.

The principles which they enunciate do not depend for their authority upon whether they square with the wish of the ruling dynasty, but whether they square with the everlasting truth. Under these conditions the press, which had before been made an instrument for concealing or perverting the facts, must be made an instrument for their true representation and their sound and logical interpretation. From the position of a mere organ, constantly bound to servitude, public prints rise to a dignity, not only of independence, but of a great educational and enlightening factor. They attain new powers, which it is almost impossible to measure, and become charged with commensurate responsibilities.

The public press under an autocracy is necessarily a true agency of propaganda. Under a free government it must be the very reverse. Propaganda seeks to present a part of the facts, to distort their relations, and to force conclusions which could not be drawn from a complete and candid survey of all the facts. It has been observed that propaganda seeks to close the mind, while education seeks to open it. This has become one of the dangers of the present day.

The great difficulty in combating unfair propaganda, or even in recognizing it, arises from the fact that at the present time we confront so many new and technical problems that it is an enormous task to keep ourselves accurately informed concerning them. In this respect, you gentlemen of the press face the same perplexities that are encountered by legislators and government administrators. Whoever deals with current public questions is compelled to rely greatly upon the information and judgments of experts and specialists. Unfortunately, not all experts are to be trusted as entirely disinterested. Not all specialists are completely without guile. In our increasing dependence on specialized authority, we tend to become easier victims for the propagandists, and need to cultivate sedulously the habit of the open mind. No doubt every generation feels that its problems are the most intricate and baffling that have ever been presented for solution. But with all recognition of the disposition to exaggerate in this respect, I think we can fairly say that our times in all their social and economic aspects are more complex than any past period. We need to keep our minds free from prejudice and bias. Of education, and of real information we cannot get too much. But of propaganda, which is tainted or perverted information, we cannot have too little.

Newspaper men, therefore, endlessly discuss the question of what is news. I judge that they will go on discussing it as long as there are newspapers. It has seemed to me that quite obviously the news-giving function of a newspaper cannot possibly require that it give a photographic presentation of everything that happens in the community. That is an obvious impossibility. It seems fair to say that the proper presentation of the news bears about the same relation to the whole field of happenings that a painting does to a photograph. The photograph might give the more accurate presentation of details, but in doing so it might sacrifice the opportunity the more clearly to delineate character. My college professor was wont to tell us a good many years ago that if a painting of a tree was only the exact representation of the original, so that it looked just like the tree, there would be no reason for making it; we might as well look at the tree itself. But the painting, if it is of the right sort, gives something that neither a photograph nor a view of the tree conveys.

It emphasizes something of character, quality, individuality. We are not lost in looking at thorns and defects; we catch a vision of the grandeur and beauty of a king of the forest.

And so I have conceived that the news, properly presented, should be a sort of cross-section of the character of current human experience. It should delineate character, quality, tendencies and implications. In this way the reporter exercises his genius. Out of the current events he does not make a drab and sordid story, but rather an informing and enlightened epic. His work becomes no longer imitative, but rises to an original art.

Our American newspapers serve a double purpose. They bring knowledge and information to their readers, and at the same time they play a most important part in connection with the business interests of the community, both through their news and advertising departments. Probably there is no rule of your profession to which you gentlemen are more devoted than that which prescribes that the editorial and the business policies of the paper are to be conducted by strictly separate departments. Editorial policy and news policy must not be influenced by business consideration; business policies must not be affected by editorial programs. Such a dictum strikes the outsider as involving a good deal of difficulty in the practical adjustments of everyday management. Yet, in fact, I doubt if those adjustments are any more difficult than have to be made in every other department of human effort. Life is a long succession of compromises and adjustments, and it may be doubted whether the press is compelled to make them more frequently than others do.

When I have contemplated these adjustments of business and editorial policy, it has always seemed to me that

American newspapers are peculiarly representative of the practical idealism of our country. Quite recently the construction of a revenue statute resulted in giving publicity to some highly interesting facts about incomes. It must have been observed that nearly all the newspapers published these interesting facts in their news columns, while very many of them protested in their editorial columns that such publicity was a bad policy. Yet this was not inconsistent. I am referring to the incident by way of illustrating what I just said about the newspapers representing the practical idealism of America. As practical newsmen they printed the facts. As editorial idealists they protested that there ought to be no such facts available.

Some people feel concerned about the commercialism of the press. They note that great newspapers are great business enterprises earning large profits and controlled by men of wealth. So they fear that in such control the press may tend to support the private interests of those who own the papers, rather than the general interest of the whole people. It seems to me, however, that the real test is not whether the newspapers are controlled by men of wealth, but whether they are sincerely trying to serve the public interests. There will be little occasion for worry about who owns a newspaper, so long as its attitudes on public questions are such as to promote the general welfare. A press which is actuated by the purpose of genuine usefulness to the public interest can never be too strong financially, so long as its strength is used for the support of popular government.

There does not seem to be cause for alarm in the dual relationship of the press to the public, whereby it is on one side a purveyor of information and opinion and on the other side a purely business enterprise. Rather, it is probable that a press which maintains an intimate touch with the business currents of the nation, is likely to be more reliable than it would be if it were a stranger to these influences. After all, the chief business of the American people is business. They are profoundly concerned with producing, buying, selling, investing and prospering in the world. I am strongly of opinion that the great majority of people will always find these are moving impulses of our life. The opposite view was oracularly and poetically set forth in those lines of Goldsmith which everybody repeats, but few really believe:

> Ill fares the land, to hastening ills a prey,
> Where wealth accumulates, and men decay.

Excellent poetry, but not a good working philosophy. Goldsmith would have been right, if, in fact, the accumulation of wealth meant the decay of men. It is rare indeed that the men who are accumulating wealth decay. It is only when they cease production, when accumulation stops, that an irreparable decay begins. Wealth is the product of industry, ambition, character and untiring effort. In all experience, the accumulation of wealth means the multiplication of schools, the increase of knowledge, the dissemination of intelligence, the encouragement of science, the broadening of outlook, the expansion of liberties, the widening of culture. Of course, the accumulation of wealth cannot be justified as the chief end of existence. But we are compelled to recognize it as a means to well-nigh every desirable achievement. So long as wealth is made the means and not the end, we need not greatly fear it. And there never was a time when wealth was so generally regarded as a means, or so little regarded as an end, as today.

Just a little time ago we read in your newspapers that two leaders of American business, whose efforts at accumulation had been most astonishingly successful, had given fifty or sixty million dollars as endowments to educational works. That was real news. It was characteristic of our American experience with men of large resources. They use their power to serve, not themselves and their own families, but the public. I feel sure that the coming generations, which will benefit by those endowments, will not be easily convinced that they have suffered greatly because of these particular accumulations of wealth.

So there is little cause for the fear that our journalism, merely because it is prosperous, is likely to betray us. But it calls for additional effort to avoid even the appearance of the evil of selfishness. In every worthy profession, of course, there will always be a minority who will appeal to the baser instinct. There always have been, and probably always will be some who will feel that their own temporary interest may be furthered by betraying the interest of others. But these are becoming constantly a less numerous and less potential element in the community. Their influence, whatever it may seem at a particular moment, is always ephemeral. They will not long interfere with the progress of the race which is determined to go its own forward and upward way. They may at times somewhat retard and delay its progress, but in the end their opposition will be overcome. They have no permanent effect. They accomplish no permanent result. The race is not traveling in that direction. The power of the spirit always prevails over the power of the flesh. These furnish us no justification for interfering with the freedom of the press, because all freedom, though it may sometime tend toward excesses, bears within it those remedies which will finally effect a cure for its own disorders.

American newspapers have seemed to me to be particularly representative of this practical idealism of our people. Therefore, I feel secure in saying that they are the best newspapers in the world. I believe that they print more real news and more reliable and characteristic news than any other newspaper. I believe their editorial opinions are less colored in influence by mere partisanship or selfish interest, than are those of any other country. Moreover, I believe that our American press is more independent, more reliable and less partisan today than at any other time in its history. I believe this of our press, precisely as I believe it of those who manage our public affairs. Both are cleaner, finer, less influenced by improper considerations, than ever before. Whoever disagrees with this judgment must take the chance of marking himself as ignorant of conditions which notoriously affected our public life, thoughts and methods, even within the memory of many men who are still among us.

It can safely be assumed that self-interest will always place sufficient emphasis on the business side of newspapers, so that they do not need any outside encouragement for that part of their activities. Important, however, as this factor is, it is not the main element which appeals to the American people. It is only those who do not understand our people, who believe that our national life is entirely absorbed by material motives. We make no concealment of the fact that we want wealth, but there are many other things that we want very much more. We want peace and honor, and that charity which is so strong an element of all civilization. The chief ideal of the American people is idealism. I cannot repeat too often that America is a nation of idealists. That is the only motive to which they ever give any strong and lasting reaction. No newspaper can be a success which fails to appeal to that element of our national life. It is in this direction that the public press can lend its strongest support to our Government. I could not truly criticize the vast importance of the counting room, but my ultimate faith I would place in the high idealism of the editorial room of the American newspaper.

4. Government and Business

Address before the Chamber of Commerce of the State of New York, New York City, November 19, 1925.

This time and place naturally suggest some consideration of commerce in its relation to Government and society. We are finishing a year which can justly be said to surpass all others in the overwhelming success of general business. We are met not only in the greatest American metropolis, but in the greatest center of population and business that the world has ever known. If any one wishes to gauge the power which is represented by the genius of the American spirit, let him contemplate the wonders which have been wrought in this region in the short space of 200 years. Not only does it stand unequaled by any other place on earth, but it is impossible to conceive of any other place where it could be equaled.

The foundation of this enormous development rests upon commerce. New York is an imperial city, but it is not a seat of government. The empire over which it rules is not political, but commercial. The great cities of the ancient world were the seats of both government and industrial power. The Middle Ages furnished a few exceptions. The great capitals of former times were not only seats of government but they actually governed. In the modern world government is inclined to be merely a tenant of the city. Political life and industrial life flow on side by side, but practically separated from each other. When we contemplate the enormous power, autocratic and uncontrolled, which would have been created by joining the authority of government with the influence of business, we can better appreciate the wisdom of the fathers in their wise dispensation which made Washington the political center of the country and left New York to develop into its business center. They wrought mightily for freedom.

The great advantages of this arrangement seem to me to be obvious. The only disadvantages which appear lie in the possibility that otherwise business and government might have had a better understanding of each other and been less likely to develop mutual misapprehensions and suspicions. If a contest could be held to determine how much those who are really prominent in our government life know about business, and how much those who are really prominent in our business life know about government, it is my firm conviction that the prize would be awarded to those who are in government life. This is as it ought to be, for those who have the greater authority ought to have the greater knowledge. But it is my even firmer conviction that the general welfare of our country could be very much advanced through a better knowledge by both of those parties of the multifold problems with which each has to deal. While our system gives an opportunity for great benefit by encouraging detachment and breadth of vision which ought not to be sacrificed, it does not have the advantages which could be secured if each had a better conception of their mutual requirements.

While I have spoken of what I believed would be the advantages of a more sympathetic understanding, I should put an even stronger emphasis on the desirability of the largest possible independence between government and business. Each ought to be sovereign in its own sphere. When government comes unduly under the influence of business, the tendency is to develop an administration which closes the door of opportunity; becomes narrow and selfish in its outlook, and results in an oligarchy. When government enters the field of business with its great resources, it has a tendency to extravagance and inefficiency, but, having the power to crush all competitors, likewise closes the door of opportunity and results in monopoly. It is always a problem in a republic to maintain on the one side that efficiency which comes only from trained and skillful management without running into fossilization and autocracy, and to maintain on the other that equality of opportunity which is the result of political and economic liberty without running into dissolution and anarchy. The general results in our country, our freedom and prosperity, warrant the assertion that our system of institutions has been advancing in the right direction in the attempt to solve these problems. We have order, opportunity, wealth, and progress.

While there has been in the past and will be in the future a considerable effort in this country of different business interests to attempt to run the Government in such a way as to set up a system of privilege, and while there have been and will be those who are constantly seeking to commit the Government to a policy of infringing upon the domain of private business, both of these efforts have been very largely discredited, and with reasonable vigilance on the part of the people to preserve their freedom do not now appear to be dangerous.

When I have been referring to business, I have used the word in its all-inclusive sense to denote alike the employer and employee, the production of agriculture and industry, the distribution of transportation and commerce, and the service of finance and banking. It is the work of the world. In modern life, with all its intricacies, business has come to hold a very dominant position in the thoughts of all enlightened peoples. Rightly understood, this is not a criticism, but a compliment. In its great economic organization it does not represent, as some have hastily concluded, a mere desire to minister to selfishness. The New York Chamber of Commerce is not made up of men merely animated with a purpose to get the better of each other. It is something far more important than a sordid desire for gain. It could not successively succeed on that basis. It is dominated by a more worthy impulse; its rests on a higher law. True business represents the mutual organized effort of society to minister to the economic requirements of civilization. It is an effort by which men provide for the material needs of each other. While it is not an end in itself, it is the important means for the attainment of a supreme end. It rests squarely on the law of service. It has for its main reliance truth and faith and justice. In its larger sense it is one of the greatest contributing forces to the moral and spiritual advancement of the race.

It is the important and righteous position that business holds in relation to life which gives warrant to the great interest which the National Government constantly exercises for the promotion of its success. This is not exercised as has been the autocratic practice abroad of directly supporting and financing different business projects, except in case of great emergency; but we have rather held to a democratic policy of cherishing the general structure of business while holding its avenues open to the widest competition, in order that its opportunities and its benefits might be given the broadest possible participation. While it is true that the Government ought not to be and is not committed to certain methods of acquisition which, while partaking of the nature of unfair practices, try to masquerade under the guise of business, the Government is and ought to be thoroughly committed to every endeavor of production and distribution which is entitled to be designated as true business. Those who are so engaged, instead of regarding the Government as their opponent and enemy, ought to regard it as their vigilant supporter and friend.

It is only in exceptional instances that this means a change on the part of the national administration so much as it means a change on the part of trade. Except for the requirements of safety, health and taxation, the law enters very little into the work of production. It is mostly when we come to the problems of distribution that we meet the more rigid exactions of legislation. The main reason why certain practices in this direction have been denounced is because they are a species of unfair competition on the one hand or tend to monopoly and restraint of trade on the other. The whole policy of the Government in its system of opposition to monopoly, and its public regulation of transportation and trade, has been animated by a desire to have business remain business. We are politically free people and must be an economically free people.

It is my belief that the whole material development of our country has been enormously stimulated by reason of the general insistence on the part of the public authorities that economic effort ought not to partake of privilege, and that business should be unhampered and free. This could never have been done under a system of freight-rate discriminations or monopolistic trade associations. These might have enriched a few for a limited period, but they never would have enriched the country, while on the firmer foundation of justice we have achieved even more ample individual fortunes and a perfectly unprecedented era of general prosperity. This has resulted in no small part from the general acceptance on the part of those who own and control the wealth of the Nation, that it is to be used not to oppress but to serve. It is that policy, sometimes perhaps imperfectly expressed and clumsily administered, that has animated the National Government. In its observance there is unlimited opportunity for progress and prosperity.

It would be difficult, if not impossible, to estimate the contribution which government makes to business. It is notorious that where the government is bad, business is bad. The mere fundamental precepts of the administration of justice, the providing of order and security, are priceless. The prime element in the value of all property is the knowledge that its peaceful enjoyment will be publicly defended. If disorder should break out in your city, if there should be a conviction extending over any length of time that the rights of persons and property could no longer be protected by law, the value of your tall buildings would shrink to about the price of what are now water fronts of old Carthage or what are now corner lots in ancient Babylon. It is really the extension of these fundamental rights that the Government is constantly attempting to apply to modern business. It wants its rightful possessors to rest in security, it wants any wrongs that they may suffer to have a legal remedy, and it is all the time striving through administrative machinery to prevent in advance the infliction of injustice.

These undoubtedly represent policies which are wise and sound and necessary. That they have often been misapplied and many times run into excesses, nobody can deny. Regulation has often become restriction, and inspection has too frequently been little less than obstruction. This was the natural result of those times in the past when there were practices in business which warranted severe disapprobation. It was only natural that when these abuses were reformed by an aroused public opinion a great deal of prejudice which ought to have been discriminating and directed only at certain evil practices came to include almost the whole domain of business, especially where it had been gathered into large units. After the abuses had been discontinued the prejudice remained to produce a large amount of legislation, which, however well meant in its application to trade, undoubtedly hampered but did not improve. It is this misconception and misapplication, disturbing and wasteful in their results, which the National Government is attempting to avoid. Proper regulation and control are disagreeable and expensive. They represent the suffering that the just must endure because of the unjust. They are a part of the price which must be paid to promote the cause of economic justice.

Undoubtedly if public vigilance were relaxed, the generation to come might suffer a relapse. But the present generation of business almost universally throughout its responsible organization and management has shown every disposition to correct its own abuses with as little intervention of the Government as possible. This position is recognized by the public, and due to the appreciation of the needs which the country has for great units of production in time of war, and to the better understanding of the service which they perform in time of peace, resulting very largely from the discussion of our tax problems, a new attitude of the public mind is distinctly discernible toward great aggregations of capital. Their prosperity goes very far to insure the prosperity of all the country. The contending elements have each learned a most profitable lesson.

This development has left the Government free to advance from the problems of reform and repression to those of economy and construction. A very large progress is being made in these directions. Our country is in a state of unexampled and apparently sound and well distributed prosperity. It did not gain wealth, as some might hastily conclude, as a result of the war. Here and there individuals may have profited greatly, but the country as a whole was a heavy loser. Forty billions of the wealth of the Nation was directly exhausted, while the indirect expenditure and depreciation can not be estimated. The Government appreciated that the only method of regeneration lay in economy and production. It has followed a policy of economy in national expenditures. By an enormous reduction in taxation it has released great amounts of capital for use in productive effort. It has sought to stimulate domestic production by a moderate application of the system of protective tariff duties. The results of these efforts are known to all the world.

Another phase of this progress is not so well understood, but upon its continuance depends our future ability to meet the competition of the lower standards of living in foreign countries. During the past five years the Department of Commerce has unceasingly directed attention to the necessity for the elimination of waste. This effort has been directed toward better cooperation to improve efficiency in the use of labor and materials in all branches of business. This has been sought by the necessary cooperative action among individual concerns within industrial groups, and between producers and consumers. This does not imply any diminution of fair competition or any violation of the laws against restraint of trade. In fact, these proposals have been a protection to the smaller units of business and a most valuable asset alike to the producer, wage earner and consumer.

The result of the realization of these wastes and the large cooperative effort that has been instituted in the community to cure them, whether with the assistance of the Government departments or by independent action of the groups, has been the most profound factor in this recovery made in the past five years. There can be no question that great wastes have been eliminated by these activities in the business community through such actions as the abolition of car shortages; by improved equipment and methods of management of our railways; the cooperation with shippers to save delays; the remarkable advance in electrification of the country with all of its economies in labor and coal; the provision of better economic and statistical information as to production, stocks, and consumption of all commodities in order that producers and consumers may better adjust supply to demand, thereby eliminating speculation and loss; the great progress made in the technology of standardizing quality and dimensions in heavy manufactured products like building materials and commodities generally which do not involve problems of style or individuality; the reduction of seasonal employment in the construction and other industries and of losses through fire and through traffic accidents; advancement of commercial arbitration; development of farmers' cooperatives for the more economical and stable marketing of farm produce; and in general the elimination of waste due to lost motion and material throughout our whole economic fabric.

All this represents a movement as important as that of twenty years ago for the regulation of corporations and conservation of our natural resources. This effort for conservation of use of materials and conservation of energy in which our whole country has engaged during these five years has been in no small part responsible for the rich reward in the increasing comfort and living standards of the people. But in addition to bringing about a condition in which the Government debt is being rapidly liquidated while at the same time taxes are greatly reduced, capital has become abundant and prosperity reigns. The most remarkable results of economy and the elimination of waste are shown in the wage and commodity indexes. In 1920 wages were about 100 per cent above the pre-war rates and the average wholesale price of commodities was about 120 per cent above the pre-war rates. A steady increase in the wage index took place, so that during the last year it was 120 per cent above the pre-war rate. As the cost of our production is so largely a matter of wages, and as tax returns show that for the last year profits were ample; it would naturally have been expected that the prices of commodities would have increased. Yet during this period the average wholesale price level of commodities declined from 120% above the pre-war level that it was in 1920, to only 57% above the pre-war level in 1925. Thus, as a result of greater economy and efficiency, and the elimination of waste in the conduct of the National Government and of the business of the country, prices went down while wages went up. The wage earner receives more, while the dollar of the consumer will purchase more. The significance and importance of this result can not be overestimated.

This is real and solid progress. No one can deny that it represents an increase in national efficiency. It must be maintained. Great as the accomplishments have been, they are yet but partly completed. We need further improvement in transportation facilities by development of inland waterways; we need railroad consolidations; we need further improvement of our railway terminals for more economical distribution of commodities in the great congested centers; we need reorganization of Government departments; we need still larger extension of electrification; in general, we need still further effort against all the various categories of waste which the Department of Commerce has enumerated and so actively attacked, for in this direction lies not only increased economic progress but the maintenance of that progress against foreign competition. There is still plenty of work for business to do.

By these wise policies, pursued with tremendous economic effort, our country has reached its present prosperous condition. The people have been willing to work because they have had something to work for. The per capita production has greatly increased. Out of our surplus savings we have been able to advance great sums for refinancing the Old World and developing the New. While Europe has attracted more public attention, Latin America, Japan, and even Australia, have been very large participators in these loans. If rightly directed, they ought to be of benefit to both lender and borrower. If used to establish industry and support commerce abroad, through adding to the wealth and productive capacity of those countries, they create their own security and increase consuming power to the probable advantage of our trade. But when used in ways that are not productive, like the maintenance of great military establishments or to meet municipal expenditures which should either be eliminated by government economy or supplied by taxation, they do not appear to serve a useful purpose and ought to be discouraged. Our bankers have a great deal of responsibility in relation to the soundness of these loans when they undertake to invest the savings of our country abroad. I should regret very much to see our possession of resources which are available to meet needs in other countries be the cause of any sentiment of envy or unfriendliness toward us. It ought everywhere to be welcomed with rejoicing and considered as a part of the good fortune of the entire world that such an economic reservoir exists here which can be made available in case of need.

Everyone knows that it was our resources that saved Europe from a complete collapse immediately following the armistice. Without the benefit of our credit an appalling famine would have prevailed over great areas. In accordance with the light of all past history, disorder and revolution, with the utter breaking down of all legal restraints and the loosing of all the passions which had been aroused by four years of conflict, would have rapidly followed. Others did what they could, and no doubt made larger proportionate sacrifices, but it was the credits and food which we supplied that saved the situation.

When the work of restoring the fiscal condition of Europe began, it was accomplished again with our assistance. When Austria determined to put her financial house in order, we furnished a part of the capital. When Germany sought to establish a sound fiscal condition, we again contributed a large proportion of the necessary gold loan. Without this, the reparations plan would have utterly failed. Germany could not otherwise have paid. The armies of occupation would have gone on increasing international irritation and ill will. It was our large guarantee of credit that assisted Great Britain to return to a gold basis. What we have done for France, Italy, Belgium, Czechoslovakia, Poland, and other countries, is all a piece of the same endeavor. These efforts and accomplishments, whether they be appreciated at home or received with gratitude abroad, which have been brought about by the business interests of our country, constitute an enormous world service. Others have made plans and adopted agreements for future action which hold a rank of great importance. But when we come to the consideration of what has been done, when we turn aside from what has been promised, to examine what has been performed, no positive and constructive accomplishment of the past five years compares with the support which America has contributed to the financial stability of the world. It clearly marks a new epoch.

This holds a distinctly higher rank than a mere barter and sale. It reaches above the ordinary business transaction into a broader realm. America has disbanded her huge armies and reduced her powerful fleet, but in attempting to deal justly through the sharing of our financial resources we have done more for peace than we could have done with all our military power. Peace, we know, rests to a great extent upon justice, but it is very difficult for the public mind to divorce justice from economic opportunity. The problem for which we have been attempting a solution is in the first instance to place the people of the earth back into avenues of profitable employment. It was necessary to restore hope, to renew courage. A great contribution to this end has been made with American money. The work is not all done yet. No doubt it will develop that this has not been accomplished without some mistakes, but the important fact remains that when the world needed to be revived we did respond. As nations see their way to a safer economic existence, they will see their way to a more peaceful existence. Possessed of the means to meet personal and public obligations, people are reestablishing their self-respect. The financial strength of America has contributed to the spiritual restoration of the world. It has risen into the domain of true business.

Accompanying these efforts to assist in rehabilitation have lately come the negotiations for the settlement of our foreign debts. Ten nations have already made settlements for $6,383,411,669 of these debts, exclusive of accrued interest. The principal sums and interest which have been funded and are to be paid to the United States aggregate $15,056,486,000. There remain nine nations, with debts in the principal amount of $3,673,342,362, which have not yet been settled. Of the nine nations, France represents $3,340,000,000, Greece $15,000,000, and Yugoslavia $51,000,000. Of the remaining six, Rumania is now negotiating a settlement, Nicaragua is paying currently, and a moratorium for twenty years has been granted Austria by act of Congress. Armenia has ceased to exist as a nation, the Government of Russia has not been recognized, and Liberia owes but $26,000.

It has been the belief of the Government that no permanent stabilization of European finances and European currency can be accomplished without a definite adjustment of these obligations. While we realize that it is for our advantage to have these debts paid, it is also realized that it is greatly for the advantage of our debtors to have them finally liquidated. We created these values and sent them abroad in a period of about two years. We are extending the time for their return over a term of sixty-two years. While settlements already made and ratified by Congress, and those which will be presented for ratification, are very generous, I believe they will be alike beneficial to ourselves and the countries concerned. They maintain the principle of the integrity of international obligations. They help foreign governments to reestablish their fiscal operations and will contribute to the economic recovery of their people. They will assist both in the continuance of friendly relations, which are always jeopardized by unsettled differences, and the mutual improvement of trade opportunities by increasing the prosperity of the countries involved.

The working out of these problems of regulation, Government economy, the elimination of waste in the use of human effort and of materials, conservation and the proper investment of our savings both at home and abroad, is all a part of the mighty task which was imposed upon mankind of subduing the earth. America must either perform her full share in the accomplishment of this great world destiny or fail. For almost three centuries we were intent upon our domestic development. We sought the help of the people and the wealth of other lands by which to increase our numerical strength and augment our national fortune. We have grown exceedingly great in population and in riches. This power and this prosperity we can continue for ourselves if we will but proceed with moderation. If our people will but use those resources which have been intrusted to them, whether of command over large numbers of men or of command over large investments of capital, not selfishly but generously, not to exploit others but to serve others, there will be no doubt of an increasing production and distribution of wealth.

All of these efforts represent the processes of reducing our domestic and foreign relations to a system of law. They consist of a determination of clear and definite rules of action. It is a civilizing and humanizing method adopted by means of conference, discussion, deliberation, and determination. If it is to have any continuing success, or any permanent value, it will be because it has not been brought about by one will compelling another by force, but has resulted from men reasoning together. It has sought to remove compulsion from the business life of the country and from our relationship with other nations. It has sought to bestow a greater freedom upon our own people and upon the people of the world. We have worshiped the ideals of force long enough. We have turned to worship at the true shrine of understanding and reason.

In our domestic affairs we have adopted practical methods for the accomplishment of our ideals. We have translated our aspirations into appropriate actions. We have followed the declaration that we believe in justice, by establishing tribunals that would insure the administration of justice. What we have been able to do in this respect in relation to the different States of our Union, we ought to encourage and support in its proper application in relation to the different nations of the world. With our already enormous and constantly increasing interests abroad, there are constantly accumulating reasons why we should signify our adherence to the Permanent Court of International Justice. Mindful of our determination to avoid all interference in the political affairs, which do not concern us, of other nations, I can think of no more reassuring action than the declaration of America that it will whole-heartedly join with others in the support of the tribunal for the administration of international justice which they have created. I can conceive of nothing that we could do, which involves assuming so few obligations on our part, that would be likely to prove of so much value to the world. Beyond its practical effect, which might be somewhat small, it would have a sentimental effect which would be tremendous. It would be public notice that the enormous influences of our country were to be cast upon the side of the enlightening processes of civilization. It would be the beginning of a new world spirit.

This is the land of George Washington. We can do no less than work toward the realization of his hope. It ought to be our ambition to see the institutions which he founded grow in the blessings which they bestow upon our own citizens and increase in the good which their influence casts upon all the world. He did not hesitate to meet peril or encounter danger or make sacrifices. There is no cause which can be supported by any other methods. We can not listen to the counsels of perfection; we can not pursue a timorous policy; we can not avoid the obligations of a common humanity. We must meet our perils; we must encounter our dangers; we must make our sacrifices; or history will recount that the works of Washington have failed. I do not believe the future is to be dismayed by that record. The truth and faith and justice of the ancient days have not departed from us.

Chapter 34

Alfred E. Smith

Alfred E. Smith was born on New York's lower East Side in 1873 and died in 1944. Smith was elected Governor of New York State four times and was the Democratic party U.S. presidential candidate in 1928. He lost the election to Herbert Hoover, the Republican candidate.

After losing the presidential election, he became president of the for profit corporation Empire State, Inc., which then built the Empire State Building.

He had a long political career that was untarnished by corruption. He was consistently a liberal in the best sense of the word. In 1928, based on the book containing his speeches, I conclude that he ran an excellent campaign.

At the 1924 Democratic National Convention, Franklin Roosevelt made the nominating speech giving Smith the title of "the happy warrior of the political battlefield." Smith lost the nomination in 1924 but won it in 1928. In the 1928 election, Smith's New York accent cost him some votes. Franklin Roosevelt replaced Smith as Governor.

In 1936 and 1940, Smith supported the Republican presidential candidates having split with Roosevelt on his treatment of American business.

Smith, Alfred E., *Campaign Addresses of Governor Alfred E. Smith, Democratic Candidate for President 1928*, The Democratic National Committee, Washington, D.C., 1929.

1. Post-Election Radio Address

New York City, November 13, 1928

Now that the dust and smoke of battle have cleared away, I am grateful for the privilege extended to me by the Democratic National Committee of speaking to millions of my fellow citizens and of presenting to them some reflections on the campaign just ended.

The Democratic Party is the oldest political organization in the United States. So well defined are the doctrines and the principles upon which it is founded that it has survived defeat after defeat. In the sixty-five years that have passed since the Civil War only two Presidents were elected on the Democratic ticket. No political organization otherwise founded would have been able, during all these years, to maintain an appeal to the people that brought to the polls on last election day 14,500,000 voters, subscribing once more to its platform and renewing their allegiance to the principles which it has upheld throughout its long history.

The verdict of the American people last Tuesday was not the crushing defeat of the Democratic Party that some of the headlines in the public press would have us believe. On the contrary, let us see what the facts are: Take the popular vote — a change of 10 per cent of the total number of votes cast would have changed the popular result. Considering it from the viewpoint of our Electoral College system, a change of less than 500,000 votes, spread around the country, would have altered the result.

We have, therefore, the assurance from the election returns that the Democratic Party is a live, a vigorous and a forceful major minority party.

The existence of such a party is necessary under our system of government. The people rule negatively as well as affirmatively, and a vigorous and intelligent minority is a necessary check upon the tyranny of the majority.

Experience has always shown, even in our smaller political subdivisions, that when the minority party is weak and helpless, grave abuses creep into the structure of government and the administration of its affairs. When the majority party believes that it has everything its own way, it loses its fear of reprisal at the polls for mismanagement or misconduct of the government.

A political party is organized to help the country, and not merely to achieve victory. It survives, not on the basis of the rewards it secures for its followers, but on the strength and on the soundness of the principles for which it stands. A political party can only justify its existence in so far as it operates for the purpose of promoting the welfare, the well-being and the best interests of the people.

The principles for which the Democratic Party stands are as sacred in defeat as they would have been in victory. If the cause of democracy was right before the election, it is still right, and it is our duty to carry on and vindicate the principles for which we fought. The Democratic Party today is the great liberal party of the nation. It leads the progressive, forward-looking thought of the country. It holds out the only hope of return to the fundamental principles upon which this country was built and as a result of which it has grown and prospered.

To the young men and women of the country the Democratic Party, with its fine traditions, its high idealism and its breadth of vision, offers the only inspiration.

The Democratic Party certainly would not be in a position four years from now to solicit the confidence and support of the American people if during that period it neglected to build up a constructive program and relied entirely upon the failure of the opposition party. That cannot be done by the minority party permitting itself to become a party of obstruction and opposition for political purposes only. We have seen too much of that in this country and in many of its civil divisions.

It has been particularly noticeable in the State of New York, where great forward-looking, constructive measures were delayed for years by partisan opposition seeking to withhold from the Democratic Party credit for their accomplishment. The party responsible for such obstructive tactics has been rebuked by the people at the polls no later than last Tuesday. Too often a minority has attempted to ride into power by taking advantage of the failure of the majority to translate into an actuality the campaign promises and pledges upon which it sought the suffrage of the people.

While it is true that every party must adhere to its fundamental principles, obstruction and blockade for the sole purpose of embarrassing the party in power are not calculated to promote the best interests of the country. It would be regarded as a constructive achievement if the Democratic Party at Washington were to formulate a program, adopt it, offer it to the Congress of the United States and there defend it. A refusal on the part of the party in power to accept it, or their inability to bring about party unity for the solution of these problems, would then fix the responsibility and make a record upon which a successful campaign can be waged four years from now.

In other words, the Democratic Party would not be acting in good faith with the people of the country nor in good faith with the millions of those who rallied to its support if it were to sit by and adopt a policy of inaction with the hope of profiting solely by the mistakes or failures of the opposition. What this country demands is constructive and not destructive criticism. A constructive program, embodying the declarations of the Democratic platform, should be promptly developed.

Above all things, the function of a minority party is educational in character. It will not do for the great rank and file of the American people to be intensely interested in the issues and party programs for a couple of months before election and then permit that interest to die out when the result is announced. Political platforms and political promises are not self-enacting. The political history of the United States clearly indicates that every progressive step, every great governmental reform has been won only after a period of persistent effort and by the slow process of educating the electorate.

The first and indispensable element of education is information. A full and complete presentation of the facts. That is easier to do today than it was years ago, with the use of the radio and the increasing interest of our young people in public affairs. It must be remembered that while political parties may seriously divide public opinion throughout the country during the progress of a campaign, after the American people have made their decision the man selected is not the President of the Republican Party, but is the President of the United States. He is the President of all the people and as such he is entitled to the cooperation of every citizen in the development of a program calculated to promote the welfare and best interests of this country. He is entitled to a fair opportunity to develop such a program.

Only when he fails to accomplish it does the administration become the subject of proper criticism by the opposition party.

Premature criticism not only fails of its purpose, but often results to the disadvantage of the critic himself. Party responsibility is not confined to its handling of governmental affairs. A political party must also be accountable to the people of the United States for the management of its internal affairs, and no political party can afford to accept the support of forces for which it refuses to accept responsibility. It will not do to let bitterness, rancor or indignation over the result blind us to the one outstanding fact, that above everything else we are Americans.

No matter with what party we align ourselves on election day, our concern should be for the future welfare, happiness, content and prosperity of the American people.

At this point I desire to express my gratitude from the bottom of my heart to the millions who voted for me, to the millions who worked for me, to the party leaders throughout the United States who rendered loyal and devoted service to the Democratic Party and to our country.

I want this to include also the men and women throughout the country, not members of the Democratic Party, who took inspiration from the progressive platform adopted at the Democratic Convention and supported my declarations of purpose with respect to those principles. Thousands of letters and telegrams have come to me since election day, asking that I not lose interest in the future welfare of the Democratic Party. Let me take this modern means of making reply to them by making the definite statement that I do not regard the defeat of the

Democratic Party at this election as impairing in the slightest degree the soundness of the principles for which it stands. I am just as anxious to see them succeed as I was when the party honored me with the nomination, and with all the vigor that I can command I will not only stand for them, but I will battle for them.

It would be unnatural for me not to be disappointed at the result. Tonight, however, as I address these few remarks to my friends all over the country, I look back on my twenty-five years of public service. I recall them from the first time the Democratic Party selected me, a struggling youth, for elective office as member of the Legislature. I recall my first official visit to the Capitol at Albany, and never shall I forget the thoughts that ran through my mind at that time.

Many years later I felt that I had achieved my greatest ambition when the Democratic Party made me its standard bearer in the State. To that party and to the people of this State, who have four times elected me as their Chief Executive, I shall always be profoundly grateful. I have in a measure attempted to express that gratitude in the form of devotion to public service. In return for the confidence reposed in me by the people of my State, I endeavored to administer the affairs of the State with an eye single to the welfare and the happiness of her people.

The Democratic Party this year conferred upon me the greatest honor that it can offer to any of its members, the nomination for the presidency of the United States. Regardless of the outcome, in a spirit of the deepest appreciation of the opportunities afforded me and of the loyal support given to me by upward of 15,000,000 of my fellow citizens, I pledge my unceasing interest and concern with public affairs and the well-being of the American people.

CHAPTER 35

Owen D. Young

Owen D. Young (1879–1962) was a great American industrialist becoming GE's president in 1922 and was president until 1939. In 1929, he was named "Time Magazine's Man of the Year."

He extensively advised five U.S. presidents from 1920 to 1939. In 1932, he was a leading candidate for the Democratic Presidential nomination (awarded to Franklin Roosevelt). From 1924 to 1929, he served on several international committees with his agenda being to reduce the amount of German reparations. He was only partially successful, but he tried.

The following extracts from his biography *Owen D. Young: A New Type of Industrial Leader* by Ida M. Targell gives us a window into the mind of Owen D. Young regarding the status of labor and large corporations. The author was one of the leading "muckrakers" of her period (1857–1944). She wrote a glowing biography of Owen D. Young. She preferred to be described as an historian rather than muckraker.

Tarbell, Ida M., *Owen D. Young, A New Type of Industrial Leader*, New York, MacMillan Company, 1932, pp. 150–158.

1. General Electric Develops a Labor Policy

A pension plan was worked out and adopted by the council. The council estimates that at the end of thirty-five years' service in the company a man who has invested in and held his security bonds will, with the aid of his pension, be able to retire with an income equal to about three fourths of the average earned in the last ten years of his working life.

While this was going on Mr. Young and Mr. Swope were engrossed in developing a plan for taking care of wage earners in periods of depression, that is, putting into practice what Mr. Young's report on business cycles had preached. It was a plan which required a small weekly contribution from everybody on salary or wage from the top down, as well as a contribution from the business itself. It was put up to the work's council in 1924, but prosperity was back to stay forever — why talk about unemployment insurance? And they turned it down. But the work's council is a sensible body and when prosperity retired in 1930 — the schedule time if you agree to the theory of a business cycle — they, asked to reconsider the unemployment plan, adopted it. And with what result? Early in 1931 the chairman of the mayor's committee on unemployment in Schenectady, home of the General Electric, reported that not a single employee of the great concern who had been with the company a year — a provision of the plan — had asked relief for himself or family; that all who had been laid off or put on half time were taken care of by the fund which each of them had helped to create along with Mr. Young and Mr. Swope and every scientist, clerk, salesman, factory worker in the great aggregation. Mr. Swope has estimated that if in 1924 when the plan was first submitted to the men they had agreed to it they would have had five million dollars available for the emergency. What a blessing this would have been in 1932!

Owen Young was not satisfied. His thinking was running far ahead of these excellent practical achievements. A way must be found, on that he and Gerard Swope were agreed, to stabilize not only General Electric but the whole electrical industry. How could it be done? They must keep thinking about it.

But his mind ran farther. He was not willing to agree that industry should give the working man only enough to keep himself and family in physical comfort, even if it was enough to take care of them through periods of depression and through declining years. What was simmering in his mind came to the top first publicly in 1926 when he was talking to a group of New England power men.

"We must aim," he told them, "to make human beings directors instead of generators of power. We must aim to make the earning power of human beings so large as to supply them not only with a living wage, but a cultural wage. No man is free until want is removed from his door and until his intellect may be developed to take advantage of all the opportunities which may be available and are guaranteed to him in a free country. Let no man think that power supply is remote in its reactions on human welfare."

The phrase, "cultural wage," caught. It stirred hope in the worker. This was more than he had dreamed. It brought sharp reproof from the substantial group who looked on "these things that Young and Swope are doing up in Schenectady" as upsetting, impractical. It brought from smart and irresponsible phrase-makers priding themselves on their realism the charge of "idealistic inefficiency," the title of "Super-Babbitt." Mr. Young, if the comments came to his ears, weighed them undisturbed, seeking a kernel of soundness in them to help in the correction he continually gives his notions. It was enough for him to know that in this case a few men in responsible places were asking themselves if, how, when, a "cultural wage" could be made a reality. He had set a lodestar in the industrial sky.

But the discussion only stimulated Owen Young. He put into order the dreaming and pondering and experimenting he had been doing since back in 1918 he had first set his mind to the problems of industrial unrest, industrial cooperation, industrial stabilization, put them in order and incorporated them in a remarkable address made in June of 1927 at the dedication of a new group of buildings at the Harvard School of Business Administration, buildings made possible by the generosity of the late George F. Baker. The paragraphs are so important in any study of Owen D. Young as an industrial leader that they are quoted in full:

> Into these, the modern corporation, we have brought together larger amounts of capital and larger numbers of workers than existed in cities once thought great. We have been put to it, however, to discover the true principles which should govern their relations. From one point of view, they were partners in a common enterprise. From another, they were enemies fighting for the spoils of their common achievement. In dealing with this problem, there has been much misunderstanding and frequently want of sympathy. The organization has not always functioned well, and even today in that field we have great problems yet unsolved.
>
> Gradually we are reducing the area of conflict between the two. Slowly we are learning that low wages for labor do not necessarily mean high profits for

capital. We are learning that an increasing wage level is wholly consistent with a diminishing commodity price level. We are learning that productivity of labor is not measured alone by the hours of work, nor even by the test of physical fatigue in a particular job. What we need to deal with are not the limits to which men may go without physical exhaustion, but the limits within which they may work with zest and spirit and pride of accomplishment. When zest departs, labor becomes drudgery. When exhaustion enters, labor becomes slavery. Zest is partly a matter of physical condition, but it is also largely influenced by mental reactions. These are common to all of us in every position. Are we doing well with our lives? Are we providing for our families — not merely clothes and food and shelter while we are working, but an insurance of them when our working time is ended either by age, disability, or death? Are we providing more cultural opportunities for ourselves and our children? In a word, are we free men? Here in America, we have raised the standard of political equality. Shall we be able to add to that, full equality in economic opportunity? No man is wholly free until he is both politically and economically free. No man with an uneconomic and failing business is free. He is unable to meet his obligations to his family, to society, and to himself. No man with an inadequate wage is free. He is unable to meet his obligations to his family, to society, and to himself. No man is free who can provide only for physical needs. He must also be in a position to take advantage of cultural opportunities. Business, as the process of co-ordinating men's capital and effort in all fields of activity, will not have accomplished its full service until it shall have provided the opportunity for all men to be economically free. I have referred elsewhere to the cultural wage. I repeat it here as an appropriate term with which to measure the right earnings of every member of a sound society competent and willing to work.

Zest in labor is influenced by another mental reaction well known to us all but too frequently neglected. Is a man working for himself or is he a hired man? It has been assumed that with the evolution of business into large organizations, it was necessary to increase the percentage of hired men. That feeling was encouraged by our old habit of thinking. Capital was the employer, buying labor as a commodity in the cheapest market and entitled to all the profits of the undertaking. Managers were considered the paid attorneys of capital to devise ways and means to squeeze out of labor its last ounce of effort and last penny of compensation. Is it any wonder that in this land of political freedom men resented the notion of being servant to a master? Capital justified its action on the plea that it took all the risk. Many men, however, knew from their own experience that they also took a risk in this common business undertaking. With the greater division of labor, it was essential that a man be trained for a highly specialized job. In order to obtain the benefit of his training, he had to take employment in a plant which could use it. He accordingly moved into that community. He bought his home, he made his friends, he established his family and social connections. All of his relationships in life were there. If that business failed and the plant were closed, it was not alone the invested capital which suffered. That man, if no other job in a highly specialized field existed in the community, must move. His home must be sold, his ties broken, and perhaps too late in life he must attempt to take up again the forming of new friends elsewhere. Is it any wonder that he resented the notion that capital takes all the risks?

Fortunately, we are making great progress in America in these difficult relationships. We are trying to think in terms of human beings — one group of human beings who put their capital in, and another group who put their lives and labor in a common enterprise for mutual advantage. We are learning as one result of our widespread prosperity that the human being who puts his capital in is no longer the gentleman of the cartoonist in need of fat-reducing exercises. It is rather the lean school teacher, the small merchant, the carpenter, the blacksmith, who are trying to conserve and increase their surplus earnings as a guaranty fund against disaster. Or if it be not they directly, then it is most likely to be the insurance company and the savings bank which is investing the savings of millions of our people of all classes in the capital of widely diversified concerns. We think of managers no longer as the partisan attorneys of either group against the other. Rather we have come to consider them trustees of the whole undertaking, whose responsibility is to see to it on the one side that the invested capital is safe and that its return is adequate and continuous; and on the other side that competent and conscientious men are found to do the work and that their job is safe and their earnings are adequate and continuous. Managers may not be able to realize that ideal either for capital or labor. It is a great advance, however, for us to have formulated that objective and to be striving toward that goal.

Perhaps some day we may be able to organize the human beings engaged in a particular undertaking so that they truly will be the employer buying capital as a commodity in the market at the lowest price. It will be necessary for them to provide an adequate guaranty fund in order to buy their capital at all. If that is realized, the human beings will then be entitled to all the profits over the cost of capital. I hope the day may come when these great business organizations will truly belong to the men who are giving their lives and their efforts to them, I care not in what capacity. Then they will use capital truly as a tool, and they will be all interested in working it to the highest economic advantage. Then an idle machine will mean to every man in the plant who sees it an unproductive charge against himself. Then every piece of material not in motion will mean to the man who sees it an unproductive charge against himself. Then we shall have zest in labor, provided the leadership is competent and the division fair. Then we shall dispose, once and for all, of the charge that in industry organizations are autocratic and not democratic. Then we shall have all the opportunities for a cultural wage which the business can provide. Then, in a word, men will be as free in co-operative undertakings and subject only to the same limitations and chances as men in individual businesses. Then we shall have no hired men. That objective may be a long way off, but it is worthy to engage the research and efforts of the Harvard School of Business.

The fact that such a condition is not here today is not chargeable, as so often alleged, to the selfishness or dominance of capital. It is not due to the fact that the workers together have not adequate resources to margin the capital which they seek. It is due, in my judgment, solely to the unwillingness of men to assume responsibility and take a risk in such a co-operative undertaking. Most men yet prefer a fixed income without risk to a share in the profits of the enterprise with the responsibility which that involves. Gradually, however, we are making our advance. Men are becoming both wage earners and investors. As workers, they seek the most for their labor. As investors, they seek the largest returns from their capital. The ownership of great concerns, under the impetus of our present prosperity, is being widely spread, and in some instances is largely held by the workers.

Then, too, we must deal with this question of unemployment, which I regard as the greatest economic blot on our capitalistic system. There is no answer except that the managers of business have not yet learned how to make their system function so that men willing and able to work may do so. There is no limit to the consumption of the world. It is limited only in its individual compartments. We cannot eat more than so much bread or meat. We cannot wear more than so many clothes, and so we may have over-production in individual lines. But there are innumerable wants of men yet unserved, and as long as culture grows, these wants will out run our capacity to produce the things to satisfy them. The world does not owe men a living, but business, if it is to fulfill its ideal, owes men an opportunity to earn a living.

As the report on business cycles received greater attention because the name of the chairman of the General Electric headed the committee that had framed it, so now this address reverberated farther — much farther than it would have done if Owen Young had not been by this time an international figure, a man who had won regard and admiration in both Europe and America for the help he had been in the first attempt to settle by business instead of political methods the world-wide economic war growing out of the Great War. Mr. Young had made a distinguished name for himself by his contribution to what is known as the Dawes Plan.

Chapter 36

William O. Douglas

William O. Douglas (1892–1980) was a civil libertarian who also sat on the U.S. Supreme Court. It is said that he was a more committed civil libertarian than Louis Brandeis but the current author suspects that Brandeis is more than competitive on that dimension. Douglas actually replaced Brandeis on the court.

Douglas was the third Chairman of the Securities and Exchange Commission (1937–1939).

There were two attempts to remove Douglas from the Supreme Court. Both attempts were not successful. They were both based on differences with Douglas' intellectual positions, and political considerations not because of unethical acts by him. Douglas attracted controversy.

The first paragraph of "Corporation Management" (and the subsequent paragraphs) was written before 1940 but it applies with no changes to 2010 and subsequent years. Consider "Responsible management has always recognized its position as the servant of the stockholders." Check out the conversions of public corporations (e.g., Quintiles, B-Way, etc.) into private equity in recent years and see if in these cases management was a servant of the stockholders.

A statement written many years ago but that applies today is contained in "The Forces of Disorder" lecture. Consider:

> "The financial and industrial world has been afflicted with termites as insidious and destructive as the insect termites. Instead of feeding on wood they feed and thrive on other people's money. Enterprises ostensibly secure collapse as a consequence of their subtle operations. Their mysterious and destructive work has ruined many fine businesses. And at times the first warning which security holders have had that these termites were at work was the disastrous collapse of the company."

This paragraph applies equally to 2008 and 1938.

Douglas granted a stay of execution to Ethel and Julius Rosenberg, who had been convicted of giving the plans for the atomic bomb to the Russians, because they had been sentenced to die by a judge rather than by the jury consistent with the Atomic Secrets Act of 1946. The Supreme Court met and set aside Douglas' stay. Douglas faced impeachment proceedings in Congress but the proceedings did not receive extensive support.

Douglas relied less on past precedent in deciding cases and more on philosophical insights and logic consistent with his observations of the world.

Douglas, William O., *Democracy and Finance, The Addresses and Statements of William O. Douglas*, edited with an introduction and notes by James Allen. New Haven, Yale University Press, 1940, pp. 5–8, 12–15, 56–59.

1. Chapter I — The Forces of Disorder

This chapter consists almost entirely of an address delivered at the University of Chicago on October 27, 1936. A few paragraphs have been added from talks before the Economic Club of Chicago on February 1, 1938, and before the Bond Club of New York on March 24, 1937.

Investment in this country in the past twenty years has undergone a shift from a few but very rich private families and individuals to the masses. There have also been substantial changes in the complexion of institutional investments. The banks are considerably larger investors in corporate securities, particularly bonds, than they were, say, at the turn of the century. Life insurance companies are still the largest single factor in the bond market and have become more so in the last few years. The advent of the investment trust and investment company and the spread of stock ownership among life insurance companies have made the institutional buyer of stock a greater factor than it was twenty years ago. The most pronounced change, however, has been in the spread of ownership of corporate securities among people of small income. A list of some thirty large companies on the New York Stock Exchange shows that the total number of stockholders from 1900 to the present time has increased tenfold. It was not so long ago when dividend and interest income was an unknown quantity to the great majority of American families. The spread of ownership of bonds and stocks among the masses has had the result that more than one third of the dividend and interest income of the country is now being received by individuals or families making tax returns of $5,000 or less, while 50% of the total dividend and interest income is being received by our large middle class, people whose total income is $ 10,000 or less.

1.1. *Destructive forces in finance*

Of the many forces which breed insecurity, perhaps the most dangerous are the exploitation and dissipation of capital at the hands of what is known as "high finance." The reality of such waste and leakage comes forcibly home when one sees the tottering ruins of industry in bankruptcy or receivership. During two years in Washington we had occasion to examine into those ruins with some care. Under a mandate of Congress we made a study and investigation of dozens of protective and reorganization committees. Our examination of the files of companies, trustees, committees, and lawyers ranged from Los Angeles to Boston.

Through the window of reorganization most of the many varieties of capital exploitation and dissipation can be seen — certainly if a reorganization is studied, as it should be, in its financial and economic setting. Reorganization is frequently but the aftermath of such practices, for the result of the operations of high finance is to weaken the vitality of companies and to cause or to contribute to their failure.

In a competitive, capitalistic system business failures are inevitable. In any system of free enterprise investors will always be forced to pay the price of progress and competition. This is unavoidable. In a sense, capital is a thing to be lost, not saved, anomalous as that may seem. The silent and rotted water wheels of New England bear mute evidence to this. The onward rush of technology, the displacement of old devices by the new and more efficient, makes certain that this phenomenon will be constantly repeated. But dissipation and exploitation of capital are other matters. They relate not to progress but to tribute at the hands of those who may be accurately termed financial "termites."

The financial and industrial world has been afflicted with termites as insidious and destructive as the insect termites. Instead of feeding on wood they feed and thrive on other people's money. Enterprises ostensibly secure collapse as a consequence of their subtle operations. Their mysterious and destructive work has ruined many fine businesses. And at times the first warning which security holders have had that these termites were at work was the disastrous collapse of the company.

These financial termites are those who practice the art of predatory or high finance. They destroy the legitimate function of finance and become a common enemy of investors and business. While they are not seen in the antecedents of every business failure, they have been present with such frequency that the importance of dealing with them directly and forthrightly cannot be denied.

In the eyes of high finance, business becomes pieces of paper — mere conglomerations of stocks, bonds, notes, debentures. Transportation, manufacture, distribution, investment become not vital processes in economic society but channels of money which can be diverted and appropriated by those in control. The farmer with his raw materials, the laborer whose blood and sweat have gone into the steel and the cement, the investor and the consumer who are dependent on the enterprise, become either secondary or inconsequential rather than primary or paramount. Business becomes not service at a profit but a preserve for exploitation. The basic social and economic values in free enterprise disappear. For such reasons one of the chief characteristics of such finance has been its inhumanity, its disregard of social and human values.

The transactions themselves are often involved, intricate, and mysterious. Their legal garb is often baffling. Frequently, only the analyst or the lawyer is able to fathom them. Actually, however, the fundamental problem is neither intricate nor involved. It is not one reserved for analysts, financiers, or lawyers. It is so simple that he who runs may read and understand. It is basically nothing more nor less than a man attempting to serve at least two masters — security holders on the one hand, himself on the other. I say it is nothing more nor less than a man serving at *least* two masters, because more often than not high finance has a plurality rather than a mere duality of interest. When a man has a plurality or duality of interest, history has it that one of his several self-interests will be served first.

It is not simply a question of policing and curtailing the activities of dishonest men. If the system is provided so that honest men may have their two or more masters, the dishonest will rush to take advantage of the opportunities afforded. Furthermore, it is not solely and simply a question of honesty on the one hand and dishonesty on the other. No man's judgment can be trusted to act in a sound and disinterested way in those situations where the issue is whether he shall make a turn in the market, or some other profit, if he can use only other people's money to finance it.

This duality or plurality of interest permeates the whole fabric of our financial system. One sees it wherever one turns. The whole mechanism has become so complicated and intricate that frequently it is hidden and concealed even from the deep probings of investigation. But it exists in a multitude of subtle and indirect ways. It has been accepted in practice. It has gone so far that frequently the very cornerstones of certain institutions seem bottomed on it. In fact, it is commonly said that one who seeks to tinker with that part of our financial mechanism is retarding prosperity, interfering with the American way, and stifling freedom and initiative. As one banker recently put it, if steps are made in that direction "you are going to crab the initiative of lots of financial concerns." Hence, when protest is made against practices which violate ancient standards for trustees and there is insistence that they be discontinued, wails and objections go up, even from responsible and socially minded individuals, who protest that business cannot be conducted without these practices. More often than not these are but the protestations of spokesmen for the predatory elements in finance, though they appear in the guise of the profound judgment of practical men of affair.

1.2. *The "curse of bigness"*

Complexity in corporate structures is usually an incidence of bigness. But bigness has other consequences which justify the expression, "the curse of bigness," uttered by Mr. Justice Brandeis years ago.

In the first place, bigness taxes the ability to manage intelligently. The energies and abilities of man are limited. No single man or group of men can intelligently conceive, promulgate, supervise, and execute from day to day intimate business details necessary for intelligent operation of big business. They cannot give management policies that painstaking and careful personal consideration necessary for responsible management. Those details must be assigned to others. So-called responsible management officials become removed from the active arena of their business affairs; they cannot give their businesses the personal care which they demand. They build themselves an elaborate bureaucracy to run the business. At the top they become so-called formulators of policy. But they are so removed from the actualities of their business — the laborers in their mills, their production problems, their intimate financial affairs — that they lose perspective and judgment. Opportunity for intelligent management decreases with the growth of business. The needs of a small Middle Western community are apt to be better served by a banker at the head of a small local bank than by the same banker at the head of the nation's biggest bank. It is not a question of ability but of capacity.

In the second place, bigness concentrates tremendous economic and financial power in the hands of a few. This may be used dishonestly; but an even greater risk is its unwise use from the national viewpoint. Enterprises or institutions which command tremendous resources, which hold the fate of whole communities of workers in their hands, which have a virtual or actual monopoly, which dominate markets and control vast resources tip the scales on the side of prosperity or on the side of depression, depending on the decisions of the men at the top. This is tremendous power, tremendous responsibility. Such men become virtual governments in the power at their disposal. In fact, if not in law, they become affected with a public interest. The impact between their stockholders' interest and the public interest at times becomes acute. Incompatibility is often in evidence. This does not necessarily mean that they are enemies of the democratic system. But it does increase the duties of government to police them, at times to break them up, to deter their further growth. And it also means that if their growth continues at the rate of the last few decades capitalism will be eclipsed. For the inherent characteristic of capitalism is competition, individual initiative, freedom of opportunity. If present tendencies continue, the only hope of economic order within the architecture of the present system will be government by cartels. That raises no hope in the breasts of those who love democracy.

In the third place, the growth of bigness has resulted in ruthless sacrifices of human values, The disappearance of free enterprise has submerged the individual in the impersonal corporation. And when a nation of shopkeepers is transformed into a nation of clerks enormous spiritual sacrifices are made. Communities everywhere lose men of stature and independence. Man loses opportunities to develop his personality and his capacities. He is denied a chance to stand on his own before man and God. He is subservient to others and his thinking is done for him from afar. His opportunities to become a leader, to grow in stature, to be independent in mind and spirit, are greatly reduced. Widespread submergence of the individual in a corporation has as insidious an effect on democracy as has his submergence in the state in other lands.

America, including American finance, needs reeducation on these simple and obvious principles. Whatever the world of high finance may think, he who has not much meditated upon ethics, the human mind, and the summum bonum may possibly make a thriving termite, but he will most indubitably make a sorry fiduciary and a sorry economic statesman.

2. Chapter V — Corporation Managements

This address was given in Washington, D.C., before the meeting of the International Management Congress on September 27, 1938.

Responsible management has always recognized its position as the servant of the stockholders. Yet the blight of capitalism has been a specious brand of morality for corporations, a morality which drew a distinction between the allegiance which the management demanded of its staff and the allegiance which management owed to its stockholders. There can be no such distinction. Once capitalism forsakes the standards of trusteeship, it bids fair to destroy itself. It is the job of such agencies as the Securities and Exchange Commission to eradicate that specious brand of morality and to restore old-fashioned standards which place business above suspicion or reproach for questionable financial practices.

The efforts of the S.E.C. to buttress our corporate standards of trusteeship obviously serve the interest of all responsible management. For misrepresentation is unfair competition, whether it is used to attract capital or to solicit new business. But misrepresentation in bidding for capital, or in any dealings with security holders, is more than unfair competition. It is a direct undermining of that free economic system which is necessary for the preservation and perpetuation of capitalism under a democratic form of government. That is why, when a company enters the capital market for funds with which to carry on or expand its business, it is important that it has told the truth about its affairs. And when a company solicits proxies for its annual meeting of stockholders, or for some special project, it is important that investors feel that they have a solid basis of facts for an informed judgment. When your securities are listed on stock exchanges, it is important that no one make a football out of them. The country has learned that a manipulated security is a poor rather than a good advertisement for a company seeking additional capital, as well as a curse to investors. Business at last knows that it does not pay to become a stooge for market traders, since it knows that no conscientious management can divide its loyalty between its bankers and its stockholders. When finance becomes the master rather than the servant of business, a process of disintegration sets in.

There are those who would have it appear that the cost of living up to the requirements of our new securities regulation constitutes a restrictive burden on financing. That charge I feel perfectly confident in denying. The S.E.C. itself has been careful to guard against costs which might be burdensome or restrictive. Whatever costs there are, they represent only the pains which conscientious management has always taken in all of its activities.[28] Obviously, they are a restrictive influence on irresponsible management. For that, we may all well be grateful.

In its aims and ideals the Securities and Exchange Commission has much in common with responsible and conservative business management. Both seek, above all

---

[28] The Research and Statistics Section of the S.E.C. studied the registration costs, as supplied by the issuers, of all security issues registered under the Securities Act between 1936 and 1938. The study showed that the cost reasonably attributable to the S.E.C. (i.e., registration fee plus that share of legal, accounting, printing, and other expenses fairly allocable to registration) in no case exceeded 1% of the proceeds of the issue. *Statistical Release No. 418, May 4, 1940*, Securities and Exchange Commission.

else, a careful conservative stewardship of the interests of investors. The responsibility of corporate management is to its own stockholders and bondholders. The duty of the S.E.C., as a public servant, is to American investors as a group.

The contact which the S.E.C. has with management comes from the financial aspects of business. The managers of companies which have brought out securities issues in recent years have come into contact with the S.E.C. through the Securities Act of 1933. This statute, probably the simplest administered by the Commission, requires that those who seek to sell their securities to the public must make a full and fair disclosure of their business history, their financial condition, the purposes for which the funds are to be used, and the rights of the various classes of security holders. The theory of the Act is not to control the raising of capital through the sale of securities but simply that capital cannot be raised without full disclosure of all the facts when you are asking for other people's money. The S.E.C. does not pass on the merits of securities to be offered; that is left to the investor. All it asks for the investor is the facts. Managements of companies which have securities listed on stock exchanges have come to know the S.E.C. through the Securities Exchange Act of 1934. That law calls for a similar statement as to the company, its business, and its financial condition for all so-called listed companies; it also calls for annual reports keeping that information up to date. In addition, the Securities Exchange Act operates to prevent pools and manipulations in the securities of your companies. It sets up standards for providing certain minimum information in the solicitation of proxies. Equally important, it recognizes that officers, directors, and dominant stockholders are fiduciaries and should not trade on inside information; and accordingly it penalizes certain purchases and sales. Public utility managers, if their companies are members of holding-company systems, may have done business with the S.E.C. through the Public Utility Holding Company Act of 1935 in the issuance of securities, in the purchase or sale of securities or properties, in the solicitation of proxies, or in making adjustments in accounting methods or financial structure. Under this law, the S.E.C. is required to give approval or disapproval to many holding-company activities. Here there is an element of supervision over the acts of management which does not characterize the other laws. For example, there is a limitation by the Act of the geographical area embraced by any one holding-company system; there is protection of investors against payment of dividends out of capital; there are limitations on the presence of bankers on the boards of directors, and the like. Finally, under Chapter X of the new Federal Bankruptcy Act, the managements of companies which have the misfortune to go into bankruptcy for the purpose of being reorganized will find the S.E.C. serving in an advisory capacity to the courts and rendering them technical assistance in the analysis of plans of reorganization.

These tasks are varied. But whatever they are — whether they be insistence on disclosure of the truth, prosecution of manipulators, simplification of holding-company structures — they constitute various types of patrol of finance for the purpose of preventing malpractices. They are in tune with the standards of conservative management, for they reflect the simple fundamentals which should govern the relationship of a manager to an owner.

Service to stockholders cannot be a passive thing. It is not something to be rendered with the lips. It calls for constant diligence and tireless devotion to the standards of fiduciary responsibility upon which our capitalistic system is based. It is not enough to make an honest and revealing annual report. Management must, in every act, inspire the confidence of investors whose funds are its lifeblood. For, if the American public has a large stake in the country's corporate business, so American corporations have their stake in the public confidence. It is in that respect that this part of the President's program has its greatest significance to those who believe in capitalism and democracy.

CHAPTER 37

Arthur E. Nilsson

Arthur E. Nilsson (1900–1985) earned a Ph.D. in Economics from Yale University in 1931 studying with Irving Fisher. Nilsson taught at the College of William and Mary (1924–1927), Yale University (1927–1929), Oberlin College (1929–1948). In 1948, he became a Professor of Finance at Cornell University's School of Business and Public Administration.

He was named emeritus professor at Cornell in 1970.

From 1934–1937 on leave from Oberlin College, he was Head Security Analyst for the Securities Exchange Commission. In 1937, William O. Douglas was Nilsson's boss. The paper to follow was included in a set of working papers that he gave to Cornell University on his retirement. The first three paragraphs are important investment truths that should be remembered.

Consider the first paragraph of the paper:

> "I wish I could tell you how to make securities secure and I should like to add that upwards of ten million American investors would pay handsomely for the formula whose application would achieve this happy objective. To prescribe the means whereby securities could be made secure, in full sense of the meaning of this phrase, would be tantamount to offering a plan of a

> riskless capitalistic society; needless to say, I carry not that pretentious blueprint."

Having admitted that no one can make securities secure, he then goes on:

> "Precisely, then, what should be the objective of a securities act? The answer: To provide investors with a full disclosure of the facts essential to a fair judgment of securities offered for sale."

These are two very important lessons.

Nilsson, Arthur, *Making Securities Secure*, Ithaca, New York, Unpublished.

The paper, *Making Securities Secure*, was given to Professor Bierman on Arthur E. Nilsson's retirement from Cornell University. There were no directives limiting the use of this paper (not previously printed). I like the major point of the paper and the Saint Peter story.

1. Making Securities Secure

I wish I could tell you how to make securities secure and I should like to add that upwards of ten million American investors would pay handsomely for the formula whose application would achieve this happy objective. To prescribe the means whereby securities could be made secure, in full sense of the meaning of this phrase, would be tantamount to offering a plan of a riskless capitalistic society; needless to say, I carry not that pretentious blueprint.

What then is the justification for the misleading implication in the title of this paper? None other than by borrowing a trick from the advertising bag (the "catch" headline) to emphasize a fundamental principle which is basic to any program prescribing a social control of investment finance, be it state or nationwide in its scope. That principle may be stated as follows: NO BODY OF MEN — NO GOVERNMENT — NO NATION, IS SUFFICIENTLY WISE TO DEFINE THE PERFECT INVESTMENT OR TO GUARANTEE IT OR TO ELIMINATE THE RISK OF LOSS IN INVESTMENT. Recognition of this principle is prerequisite to an intelligent understanding of the Federal Securities Act. Prospective purchasers of securities registered with the federal government are apprised of this basic limitation, (if it may be called a limitation) by the required notice on every prospectus, which states: "These securities have not been approved or disapproved by the Securities and Exchange Commission."

Precisely, then, what should be the objective of a securities act? The answer: To provide investors with a full disclosure of the facts essential to a fair judgment of securities offered for sale.

This objective has been reduced to statute by the Federal Securities Act of 1933, an act specifically designed to put an end once and for all to the buccaneering tactics and financial stratagems that mushroomed out of the free and easy ways of American investment finance during the decade of the twenties. I need not cite the bill of particulars which made imperative the enactment of this mailed-fist legislation to eliminate those abuses which rocked the very foundation of our economic society. It was Congress' response to the President's mandate to protect the public investor with the least possible interference with honest business. Christened by the financial world as a "truth-in-securities act," it aims to compel full and fair disclosure to investors of material facts regarding securities publicly offered and sold in interstate commerce or through the mails, and to prevent fraud in the sale of securities. Compulsory publicity is its essence. To put it tersely the government's edict to issuers and merchants of securities now reads: State the facts, state all the facts, and don't dare twist them.

In brief, the Securities Act provides that except in the case of certain exempt securities and transactions, securities may not be offered or sold to the public unless an effective registration statement is in force. This document is the public record which sets forth the pertinent facts relating to a security, the academic record in the Government Dean's Office, so to speak. The information required in a registration statement aims particularly to the disclosure of the existence of interests of directors, officers, and other "insiders" which might be adverse to the security holder.

Under the Act, the Commission is given certain preventative authority. This authority includes (1) the power to investigate the facts relating to the issue of securities and (2) the power to issue a stop-order suspending the effectiveness of a registration statement in the event that the Commission finds misstatement of material facts or omission to state material facts therein. Immediate penalty for such misstatement or omission is expulsion from registration; and the Commission's night stick is the Stop-Order.

The problem continually facing the Commission in the administration of the Act is one of reconciling the policy of enforcing adequate disclosure with the need of making finance operations free from unnecessary burdens and restrictions. On the one hand the public investor must be given an irreducible minimum of information upon which to weigh the chance of success or failure of his investment. In as much as securities are extremely complicated pieces of merchandise, this requirement cannot be satisfied by simple rule. On the other hand honest business must not be penalized and subjected to onerous burdens through unreasonable requirements. The Commission's responsibility clearly is that of giving all the aid of which government is capable to the better organization of the investment business and at the same time of stamping out fraud in the sales of securities. In terms of social consequences, it is generally conceded, this dual assignment makes for one of the most delicate tasks ever given to a government agency.

The administration of the Act may be considered from two distinct aspects; one, from the viewpoint of the honest business man seeking additional funds for his enterprise; the other, from the point of view of the dishonest promoter. With respect to the former it should be apparent that the Commission does not regard itself as a coroner sitting on the corpse of business enterprise. It does not proceed on the theory that all persons connected with finance are to be regarded as guilty of some undefined crime. The Commission, consistent with the duty imposed upon it by law, has given honest investment enterprise constant reassurance of a cooperative administration. Honest business needs nothing more; the Commission promises nothing less.

With respect to activities of dishonest promoters, the Act makes deception more difficult and more perilous, detection more likely, and conviction more certain. The Commission, in enforcing the Act, has declared war without quarter on these who attempt to sell securities by fraud and misrepresentation. It is aggressively meeting the challenge of the financial pirates who still resort to the artifices and techniques of an earlier day. The shrewdness, cleverness and daring, of these parasites is amazing. With a remarkable, almost psychic sense of what the public is likely to "fall for" these racketeers constantly shift their wares and their techniques. In fashionableness and up-to-dateness they are stylists supreme. The Sunday magazines feature the electric eye, the photo-electric cell, and the security underworld, aided by the tipster sheet, speaks caressingly of the golden dawn of tomorrow's wealth. The government boasts the price of gold and mines long since abandoned are glorified in the language of fantastic promises to catch the unwary investor, the only requisite being a hole in the ground, a ladder and a feverish imagination. Remonetization of silver is discussed and a flurry of silver mines with romantic names make their entry to the market. Beer comes back and its return is heralded by fraudulent brewery and beer barrel stocks. Comes repeal and with it the intoxicating super salesmanship of the distillery promoter. All these are compelling evidence of the astonishing energy of the crook and the appalling credulity of the public.

It should not be inferred that all stock promotions in the enterprises just enumerated are fraudulent. It is fair to say, I believe, that most new companies are sponsored by honest persons. The experience of the Commission, however, bears out the fact that whenever a reputable company capitalizes something new there are rascals at all times ready to dispose of their worthless wares in the company of decent securities. Neither should it be assumed that promoters as a class are less respectable and less straightforward than other professional business groups. It should be emphasized, perhaps, that the promoter, properly conceived, performs an indispensable function in our capitalistic economy. He is the spearhead of economic enterprise. Not always is he of the type suggested by the story of the oil promoter who appeared before Saint Peter and presented his credentials for admission to Paradise. He was informed by Saint Peter that the quota for promoters was filled and no more of his profession could enter for the time being at least. Not dismayed, the promoter queried, "As I understand it then the only condition under which I can gain admission is that a vacancy be created?" "Precisely," replied Peter. A faint smile appeared on the candidate's face; it was apparent that he could meet that situation. He asked for the privilege of making an announcement to his former colleagues. Directed to the celestial microphone he delivered himself of a brief message. "Fellow promoters, oil has been discovered on Jupiter!" The words were no sooner spoken than several thousand of the tribe stormed out through the gates. Peter, somewhat surprised by the exodus, turned to the candidate, "Well, I guess you may come in now." The reply: "Saint Peter, I've changed my mind... I'm going too... There may be some truth in that report."

It is not easy to distinguish between highly speculative but straightforward and honest promotions and those fraught with fraud. The line between is indistinct and often difficult to draw. The essence of fraud is the intention to deceive, but this is subjective and not easily detected. To ferret out the fraudulent promoters calls for aggressive and searching inquiry. The recent paddling given to the Commission by the Supreme Court of the United States in the Jones case for pressing its inquiries too vigorously suggests one of the many difficulties confronting the Commission in the performance of this difficult task.

Over two thousand registration statements have been filed since the passage of the Act. In approximately seventy-five cases stop orders have been issued, that is, suspension orders. With the issuance of each stop order the Commission prepares an opinion which sets forth the basis for its action. These opinions are given wide publicity and serve to expose those who have attempted to practice fraud in the sale of securities. They should have a most salutary effect on the financial morals of the community.

Chapter 38

Fred Schwed, Jr.

Fred Schwed, Jr. (1902–1966) was an American author who wrote books and articles on financial matters with insight and humor. Unfortunately in 1960 he suffered a severe stroke.

Where Are the Customers Yachts? was first published in 1940 by Simon and Schuster. Subsequent editions came out in 1955 and 1960. While Schwed wrote other books, this is his classic. Even if you do not read the entire book, the illustrations by Peter Arno are well worth the price of admission.

The first paragraph of Chapter 8 captures well Schwed's wisdom, knowledge, and humor.

> "Investment and speculation are said to be two different things, and the prudent man is advised to engage in the one and avoid the other. This is something like explaining to the troubled adolescent that Love and Passion are two different things. He perceives that they are different, but they don't seem quite different enough to clear up his problems."

Schwed, Jr., Fred, *Where Are the Customers' Yachts?,* Simon and Schuster, New York, 1940, p. xii, pp. 171–191.

Once in the dear dead days beyond recall, an out-of-town visitor was being shown the wonders of the New York financial district. When the party arrived at the Battery, one of his guides indicated some handsome ships riding at anchor. He said,

"Look, those are the bankers' and brokers' yachts."

"Where are the customers' yachts?" asked the naïve visitor.

Ancient story

1. Chapter Eight — Investment — Many Questions and a Few Answers

Investment and speculation are said to be two different things, and the prudent man is advised to engage in the one and avoid the other. This is something like explaining to the troubled adolescent that Love and Passion are two different things. He perceives that they are different, but they don't seem quite different enough to clear up his problems.

Investment and speculation have been so often defined that a couple more faulty definitions should do no harm, the science of economics having reached a point where further confusion is impossible. Thus,

Speculation is an effort, probably unsuccessful, to turn a little money into a lot.

Investment is an effort, which should be successful, to prevent a lot of money from becoming a little.

If you take a thousand dollars down to Wall Street and attempt to run it up to $25,000 in the course of a year, you are speculating. If you take $25,000 down there and attempt to earn a thousand dollars a year with it (by buying twenty-five four per cent bonds) you are investing. The odds against your being successful in the first venture are roughly 25-1. The odds against the success of the second venture are "odds on," or something like 1–25.[29]

Thus the difference becomes one of degree, rather than of kind. Of course, a bond salesman never says, come on, mister, buy these bonds. They will yield you four per cent return and there is scarcely one chance in twenty-five that they will go bust. The salesman tries to avoid even thinking of his bonds in such ghastly terms. He prefers to base his thinking on a more orderly and conventional pattern. Thus, common stocks are speculative, preferred stocks are not nearly so speculative, debenture bonds are pretty darned safe, and mortgage bonds are safe. Unfortunately, the exceptions to this are enormous and continuous. Year after year it is demonstrated that the common stocks of some corporations are a great deal safer than the mortgage bonds of certain others.

Headaches of the Wealthy

People with money feel that they should be able to rent out their money at a modest rental to people who need it, and that there shouldn't be any real danger of the money being lost. Marxists feel that this entire procedure is perfectly disgusting. In any case, the procedure is becoming so extremely difficult that the Marxists must feel gratified.

The problems of safe investment seem particularly tough at the present moment. They were never really easy, though at times they seemed to be. Great family

---

[29] These "odds" are, of course, only vague approximations. But here is an attractively unfair wager if you care to make it and can find the necessary sucker: challenge an investment man to write down a list of the twenty-five safest corporate bonds he knows (each on a different corporation). The bet is that they won't all pay their interest for the next *five* years.

fortunes seldom last long — occasionally the heirs spend all the money; more often they lose it in the course of investing it. For instance, a century ago it must have been very easy to sell canal bonds to the most conservative type of investor. The story that went with them was cogent and reasonable. Canals were far and away the best and cheapest method of transporting goods. Commerce could not get along without them, it was difficult and costly to build competing ones, etc. We all know what happened to canal bonds then, and what seems to be happening to railroad bonds now. And what is going to happen to your own good toll-bridge bonds, madam, just as soon as someone invents a device which will enable automobiles to leap over rivers?

Trust companies and investment counselors warn us that our investments, even the most conservative ones, will not take care of themselves, but that they must be constantly watched. They never said a truer word, but in my case, at least, the use of the word "watch" is unfortunate. It calls to my mind the common promise of a customers' man to "watch" for you a certain stock in which you have just taken a speculative commitment. This promise he assiduously keeps. He watches every quotation of the stock on the tape, and if the stock gets weak he doesn't even go out for lunch. He munches a sandwich and continues to stare at it. If it breaks badly he watches even harder; his eyes begin to bug out a little. But the stock is not made self-conscious by his staring — it continues down. Watching is apparently more effective on kettles than on securities.

It is not known at the present time just how much more effective this is than the watching done by investment counselors. No box score is kept in the investment-counsel game and no batting averages. My own method of research was to ask a number of investment counselors how their clients were doing. They all replied that their clients were doing quite well, thank you, taking into consideration, of course, this, that, and the other. That marks the practical limits of research in this field. You can't ask for the books to be thrown open for your study, because you will be told, quite rightly, that their clients' business is none of your business.

(Before going further into this subject, I had better include a note as to whom I am talking about. It must be understood that when I refer to investment counselors I am only referring to investment counselors who are investment counselors, as Gertrude Stein might put it. There are less than a hundred of these firms in existence. Unfortunately, there are also several thousand burglars extant, all of whom refer to themselves these days as investment counsel. This is not the fault of the bona fide investment counsel; it is no doubt a subtle compliment to them. Some of these other gentry allocate the funds between themselves and their clients in the ancient classic manner, i.e., at the close of the day's business they take all the money and throw it up in the air. Everything that sticks to the ceiling belongs to the clients.)

The underlying principle of the genuine investment counsel seems to be sound and important. It is a mundane one, i.e., it has to do with how the counselors are paid off. They receive a stated fee for giving advice; they do not get their pay in commissions or profits on trades, as most brokers and dealers do. Nor are they tempted to sell the client some security which they own and which, by a mischance, no one else at the moment seems to care to buy. Thus a wealthy person may at least feel sure that the advice he gets from investment counsel is sincere, and unbiased by hope of gain or fear of loss. This reduces the wealthy person's problems to two:

1. Is there such a thing as consistently useful financial advice?
2. If there is, which investment counselor can supply it?

In spite of the fact that the counsel's method of compensation approaches the ideal, he has some odd troubles collecting his reasonable fees. Sometimes a number of rich men will band together and send one of their number in to get and pay for the service. Then they will all use it. If it surprises you that there are millionaires who will stoop to such petty chiseling you should get out and meet more millionaires. Sometimes the advice, though perhaps good, does not seem sufficiently spectacular. There was a man who took his large estate to the investment counsel and emerged looking a little dazed.

"What did they tell you to do?" asked his friend.

"They told me to sell everything and put all the money, except $3500, into government bonds."

"What did they tell you to do with the $3500?"

"They told me to give it to them."

A Little Wonderful Advice

For no fee at all I am prepared to offer to any wealthy person an investment program which will last a lifetime and will not only preserve the estate but greatly increase it. Like other great ideas, this one is simple:

When there is a stock-market boom, and everyone is scrambling for common stocks, take all your common stocks and sell them. Take the proceeds and buy conservative bonds. No doubt the stocks you sold will go higher. Pay no attention to this — just wait for the depression which will come sooner or later. When this depression, or panic, becomes a national catastrophe, sell out the bonds (perhaps at a loss) and buy back the stocks. No doubt the stocks will go still lower. Again pay no attention. Wait for the next boom. Continue to repeat this operation as long as you live, and you'll have the pleasure of dying rich.

A glance at financial history will show that there never was a generation for whom this advice would not have worked splendidly. But it distresses me to report that I have never enjoyed the social acquaintance of anyone who managed to do it. It looks as easy as rolling off a log, but it isn't. The chief difficulties, of course, are psychological. It requires buying bonds when bonds are generally unpopular, and buying stocks when stocks are universally detested.

I suspect that there are actually a few people who do something like this, even though I have never had the pleasure of meeting them. I suspect it because someone must buy the stocks that the suckers sell at those awful prices — a fact usually outside the consciousness of the public and of financial reporters. An experienced reporter's poetic account in the paper following a day of terrible panic reads this way:

> Large selling was in evidence at the opening bell and gained steadily in volume and violence throughout the morning session. At noon a rally, dishearteningly brief, took place as a result of short covering. But a new selling wave soon threw the market into utter chaos, and during the final hour equities were thrown overboard in huge lots, without regard for price or value.

The public reads the papers, and reading the foregoing, it gets the impression that on that catastrophic day everyone sold and nobody bought, except that little band of shorts (who most likely didn't exist). Of course, there is just no truth in that at all. If on that day the terrific "selling" amounted to seven million, three hundred and sixty-five thousand shares, the volume of the buying can also be calculated. In this case it was 7,365,000 shares.

Price and Value — Our Special Market Letter

At this point we shall take up the subject of Price and Value, because any financial writer who doesn't explain this knotty matter has his union card taken away from him. I shall not beat around the bush with generalities but I will step right in and analyze for you the Price, and Value, of the best-known stock in the world. This is the common stock of the United States Steel Corporation, familiarly called "Steel," "Big Steel," and "Bix X" by its many cronies.

First, as to Price, on which I happen to be well informed: I can state without fear of successful contradiction that Steel closed yesterday quoted 57 5/8–58, last sale *57 3/4*.[30] This Price was arrived at because at about 3 P.M. Yesterday someone, maybe one of the specialists, maybe a lady in Brooklyn, was willing to pay *57 5/8* for at least 100 shares and someone else, maybe another specialist, maybe a fat man with a wen, in Brussels, was willing to sell at 58. Goodness only knows what were the motives of these people. So you can see that the Price of U.S. Steel was determined in an extremely chancy

[30] Source material: this morning's paper.

fashion. There is only one nice thing to be said in favor of that Price — it was a very definite number and good all over the world at that time.

Now let us turn to that eternal verity, Value. We will examine the corporation's earnings which are applicable to the common stock over a period of the last ten years. My word! There are more losses than earnings! There was a period of time when not even the preferred stock earned its keep. And now they have a large bond issue out. And what will be the effects of the war? That just shows you how silly a price of *57 3/4* is — 17 3/4 would be more like it, and a man ought to have his head examined who pays more than that for it in anything except Confederate money.

But, on the other hand, and notwithstanding and not so fast, there are other elements in the picture and a broader viewpoint to be considered. The steel industry is the most basic of basic industries, and the United States Steel Corporation is, and has been for forty years, a veritable giant in the field — irreproducible and unapproachable. The total of its yearly losses during the late depression is less than its earnings in any one of several profitable years prior to 1930. And it would not require much of an increase in operations for great profits again to pour forth. And what will be the effect of the war? Look at that big bond issue. How easily and on what favorable terms that financing was done! In view of these, and many other bullish factors, it is hard to see why this, the most seasoned stock known to finance, is not selling at 157 3/4. And who shall call us visionary to suggest 257 3/4? It once did a trifle better than that and looked cheap to a great many experienced people.

It is quite unnecessary for you all to crowd around in this fashion, thanking me for the above analysis of the true Value of Steel common. It really wasn't difficult. The steel business is a comprehensible one, and all facts and figures on it are published in *Iron Age.* In many other industries, such precise figuring is not possible. The analysis of a chemical company, for instance, is more difficult. After considering everything else, the investor never knows just when one of the company's scientists, working in a green eyeshade in the research laboratories, will discover how to distill vitamin V[31] out of discarded cellophane wrappers.

I will conclude this discussion of Price and Value with the following unimportant occurrence, circa 1928. There was at that time engaged in the bank stock business, along with an awful lot of others, a large red-necked Texan. He had brought to his profession a booming Texas voice and a calcified conscience. On this occasion he had just sold a customer twenty shares of Guarantee Trust Company stock at $760 a share at a moment when it could have been purchased anywhere else at $730. The customer, the big sorehead, had just found this out, and had called back with a view toward remonstrance. The Texan cut him short. "Suh," he boomed, "you-all don't appreciate what the policy of this firm is. This-heah firm selects investments foh its clients not on a basis of Price, but of Value!"

Cash as a Long-Term Investment

For those wealthy people who have not yet found in these pages an investment program which appeals to them,

[31] The vitamin which must be included in the diet in order to grow a healthy goatee.

here is another plan which at least has a certain originality. It was outlined to me by a bond trader one afternoon. We had been discussing the broad history of investment bonds — a depressing subject. This man had spent the last thirty years trading bonds with other people's money. His own money he had always carefully spent.

I finally said, "What a hopeless game! Tell me, Mac, what would you do if you had, today, two hundred and fifty thousand dollars of your own?"

He answered with such promptness that I could see he had given a good deal of thought to this improbability.

"I would put it into twenty-five envelopes, in cash, of ten thousand dollars each. I would put the envelopes into a safe-deposit box. I have been told you can get a small one, such as I would need, for only six dollars a year. At the beginning of each year I would take out an envelope and I would risk not living more than twenty-five years longer. That would give me two hundred dollars a week. But since a man has to be doing something and I like gambling, I would live on a hundred a week and with the other hundred I would play the horse races. That would give me a real interest in life. Most weeks I'd live at the rate of a hundred, but occasionally at the rate of a thousand. And for an added pleasure, I could laugh at the income-tax collector."

"But the percentage against you on the horses is certainly as bad as in the market," I reminded him.

"Worse," he said cheerfully, "but playing the horses is at least fun."

Your Way of Life and the Basis Book

The "basis book," usually bound in limp black and religious in appearance, is a collection of tables by which bond men can quickly calculate precise income yields on various bond investments. A good investment adviser is supposed to run his finger across the tables to as high a yield as is "commensurate with the amount of safety required by the particular investor," and his experienced finger should stop right there, like a divining rod.

Just how far his finger should venture toward the right-hand side of the page is a matter of tremendous importance for the investor. The problem is not limited to mathematics — it invades the borders of philosophy. The investor's life, liberty, and pursuit of happiness are all at stake.

"Take care of the pennies and the dollars will take care of themselves" is better than a half-truth — about a five-eighths-truth, I should say. At least as accurate is, "Take care of the million dollars and the pennies will take care of themselves."

The British, as a race, have been engaged with the problems of capital investment for a longer period than we have, and accordingly have reached a greater maturity regarding it. Have you ever noticed that when you ask a Britisher about a man's wealth you get an answer quite different from that an American gives you? The American says, "I wouldn't be surprised if he's worth close to a million dollars." The Englishman says, "I fancy he has five thousand pounds a year." The Englishman's habitual way of speaking and thinking about wealth is of course much closer to the nub of the matter. A man's true wealth is his income, not his bank balance. There are times and places when it is better to have a hundred thousand dollars than it was to have had two hundred thousand at another time and place. (And there have been other occasions when it was better to have a cargo of potatoes, or a supply of axes and glass beads, than either sum.)

The emphasis in the investment problem is usually placed on the proper selection of securities. I suggest that the emphasis would be better placed on how the investor intends to spend his income. The initial mistakes are made in this latter department; the wrong securities are chosen largely as a result of this initial philosophic error. The peculiar investment plan of my horse-betting gentleman lacked nobility, but it did have the virtue of being modest, and hence workable, just so long as the "investor" would abide by his promises to himself.

Consider the case of a family which has, besides a modest earned income, $100,000 to invest. Just now it seems that they ought to be able to glean from this an average yield of something better than three thousand dollars a year, with reasonable safety. (No, I don't quite know what "reasonable safety" means, but all we investment men use the expression.)

Suppose the family invests the money at this rate. Their chief problem now, I suggest, is not so much to watch their investments as to watch themselves. So long as they can attune their material needs and their social dignity to that income they can retain that reasonable safety. But perhaps the time comes when the family feels they can no longer hold their heads up on the block unless little Paula goes to a fashionable finishing school. For that it will be necessary to jack up their income yield to $5500. Perhaps the family's feeling about Paula's education is unreal and unreasonable, but this is a problem more for discussion with their minister, or a psychologist, than with an investment broker.

Their investment man, however, can arrange the larger yield in a jiffy if the family asks for it. Let us suppose he arranges it. He simply sells out the conservative bonds and substitutes riskier securities. Little Paula goes off to the school with a cute wardrobe, and it is to be hoped that while there she gets jammed full of fascinating social graces. She may come to need them in all earnest, because by the time she is graduated, her marriage portion may indeed consist exclusively of social graces.

Sources

Confucius

Confucius, "Wit and Wisdom" (Aphorisms of Confucius) in The Wisdom of Confucius, edited and translated with notes by Lin Yutang. New York, Modern Library, 1938, pp. 179–184.

Laozi (also Lao Tse, Lao Tu, Lao-Tzu, Laotze)

Laotze, The Simple Way, [by] Laotze, a new translation of the Tao-teh-king; with introduction and commentary, by Walter Gorn Old. London, William Rider, 1913, p. 179.

Aristotle

Aristotle, "The Subject of Ethics is the Good for Man," [Nicomachean Ethics 1094a1-b11] in Aristotle Selections, edited by W. D. Ross. Charles Scribner's Sons, New York, 1938, pp. 218–220.

Murasaki Shikibu (Lady Murasaki)

Shikibu, Lady Murasaki, The Tale of Genji, translated by Arthur Waley, London, George Allen & Unwin Ltd., 1929, pp. 2–38.

Bernier

Bernier, "The Divided Horsecloth," in Aucassin and Nicolette and Other Medieval Romances and Legends, translated form the French by Eugene Mason. E.P. Dutton & Co., Inc., New York, 1937, pp. 75–83.

Niccolo Machiavelli

Machiavelli, Niccolo, The Prince, New York, National Alumni, 1907, pp. 96–97, 102–105.

Francis Bacon

Bacon, Francis. "Of Studies," and "Icarus and Scylla and Charybdis, or the Middle Way" in Essays, [by] Francis Bacon, New York, Hurst & Company Publishers, 1883, pp. 210–211, 355–356.

William Shakespeare

Shakespeare, William, "Hamlet, Prince of Denmark," in Shakespeare, A Historical and Critical Study with Annotated Texts of Twenty-one Plays, by Hardin Craig, Chicago, Scott, Foresman and Company, 1931, p. 743.

Thomas Hobbes

Hobbes, Thomas, "Of Man, Being the First Part of Leviathan," in French and English Philosophers: Descartes, Rousseau, Voltaire, Hobbes, New York, P. F. Collier & Son, 1910, p. 319, 373, pp. 374–375.

René Descartes

Descartes, René. "Discourse on the Method of Rightly conducting the Reason and Seeking of Truth in the Sciences," in French and English Philosophers: Descartes, Rousseau, Voltaire, Hobbes, New York, P. F. Collier & Son, 1910, pp. 5–11.

Jean-Jacques Rousseau

Rousseau, Jean-Jacques, "A Discourse upon the origin and the Foundation of the Inequality Among Mankind," in French and English Philosophers: Descartes, Rousseau, Voltaire, Hobbes, New York, P. F. Collier & Son, 1910, pp. 167–170.

Adam Smith

Smith, Adam, Wealth of Nations, P.F. Collier & Son, New York, 1909, pp. 9–11, 19–23.

George Washington

Washington, George, "Farewell Address, Delivered in 1797," in G.M. Whitman, American Orators and Oratory, Fairbanks, Palmer & Co., Chicago, 1884, pp.

John Adams

Adams, John. "Independence," in G.M. Whitman, American Orators and Oratory, Fairbanks, Palmer & Co., Chicago, 1884, pp. 27–28.

Patrick Henry

Henry, Patrick, "An Appeal to Arms" and "Give Me Liberty, or Give Me Death," in The Patriotic Anthology, introduced by Carl Van Doren, New York, Literary Guild of America, Inc., 1941, pp. 82–85.

Thomas Jefferson

Jefferson, Thomas, "Inaugural Address," in G.M. Whitman, American Orators and Oratory, Fairbanks, Palmer & Co., Chicago, 1884, pp. 65–67.

Thomas Paine

Paine, Thomas, "These are the Times That Try Men's Souls," in The Patriotic Anthology, introduced by Carl Van Doren, New York, Literary Guild of America, Inc., 1941, pp. 71–73.

Ralph Waldo Emerson

Emerson, Ralph Waldo. "Self-Reliance," and "Compensation," and "Power" in Essays, by Ralph Waldo Emerson, New York, P.F. Collier & Son, 1903, Vol. 7, pp. 27–29, 30–35, 58–64, Vol. 9, pp. 47–48, 50–52.

Abraham Lincoln

Lincoln, Abraham, "Lincoln at Gettysburg," in G.M. Whitman, American Orators and Oratory, Chicago, Fairbanks, Palmer & Co., 1884, p. 367.

Karl Heinrich Marx

Marx, Karl and Engels, Friedrich, Manifesto of the Communist Party, New York, International Publishers, 1937, pp. 43–44.

Andrew Carnegie

Carnegie, Andrew. Problems of To-Day, Wealth, Labor, Socialism. Garden City, New York, Doubleday, Doran & Company, 1932, pp. 43–69.

Alfred Marshall

Marshall, Alfred, "The Scope of Economics"and "Industrial Organization," in Economics of Industry, Alfred Marshall, London and New York, Macmillan and Co., 1892, pp. 33–39, 159–161.

Russell Conwell

Conwell, Russell H., Acres of Diamonds, Harper & Brothers Publishers, New York, 1915, pp. 3–59.

Elbert Hubbard

Hubbard, Elbert, A Message to Garcia and Other Essays, New York, Thomas Y. Crowell Company, 1917, pp. 5–23.

Louis Brandeis

Brandeis, Louis D. "Industrial Democracy" and "Absolutism in Industry" in The Social and Economic Views of Mr. Justice Brandeis, collected, with introductory notes by Alfred Lief. New York; Vanguard Press, 1930, pp. 369–370, 380–385.

Thorstein Veblen

Thorstein, Veblen, The Place of Science in Modern Civilization, B.W. Heubsch, New York, 1919.

Alfred North Whitehead

Whitehead, Alfred North, An Introduction to Business Adrift, by W.B. Donham, Whittlesey House, McGraw-Hill, New York, 1931. On Foresight

O. Henry

Henry, O., "The Gift of the Magi" and "The Unknown Quantity," William Lyon Phelps, The Complete Works of O. Henry, edited by William Lyon Phelps, Garden City, New York, Doubleday, Doran & Company, Inc., 1937, pp. 8–12, 1492–1495.

George Santayana

Edman, Irwin, The Philosophy of Santayana, The Modern Library, Random House, 1935, p. 596.

Irving Fisher

Fisher, Irving, The Nature of Capital and Income, London, Macmillan Company, 1906, pp. 295–300.

W.E.B. DuBois

Du Bois, W. E. Burghardt. Black Folk, Then and Now, An Essay in the History and Sociology of the Negro Race, New York, Henry Holt and Company, 1939, pp. 196–198.

Mohandas Karamchand Gandhi (Mahatma Gandhi)

Gandhi, M. K., An Autobiography or The Story of My Experiments With Truth, by M. K. Gandhi, translated by Mahadev Desai, Ahmedabad, Navajivan Publishing House, 1927, pp. 389–390.

Calvin Coolidge

Coolidge, Calvin, The Price of Freedom, Speeches and Addresses, New York, Charles Scribner's Sons, 1924, pp. 3–10, 57–67.

Coolidge, Calvin, Foundations of the Republic, Speeches and Addresses, New York, Charles Scribner's Sons, 1926, pp. 183–190, 317–332.

Alfred E. Smith

Smith, Alfred E., Campaign Addresses of Governor Alfred E. Smith, Democratic Candidate for President 1928, The Democratic National Committee, Washington, D.C., 1929.

Owen D. Young

Tarbell, Ida M., Owen D. Young, A New Type of Industrial Leader, New York, MacMillan Company, 1932, pp. 150–158.

William O. Douglas

Douglas, William O., Democracy and Finance, The Addresses and Statements of William O. Douglas, edited with an introduction and notes by James Allen, New Haven, Yale University Press, 1940, pp. 5–8, 12–15, 56–59.

Arthur E. Nilsson

Nilsson, Arthur, E., Making Securites Secure, Zthaca, New York, Unpublished.

Fred Schwed, Jr.

Schwed, Jr., Fred, Where Are the Customers' Yachts?, Simon and Schuster, New York, 1940, p. xii, pp. 171–191.